BENCHMARKING NATIONAL TOURISM ORGANISATIONS AND AGENCIES

UNDERSTANDING BEST PRACTICE

J. JOHN LENNON

Glasgow Caledonian University, Glasgow, UK

HUGH SMITH

Glasgow Caledonian University, Glasgow, UK

NANCY COCKERELL

The Travel Business Partnership, London, UK

JILL TREW

The Travel Business Partnership, London, UK

Amsterdam • Boston • Heidelberg • London • New York • Oxford
Paris • San Diego • San Francisco • Singapore • Sydney • Tokyo

ELSEVIER

Elsevier
The Boulevard, Langford Lane, Kidlington, Oxford OX5 1GB, UK
Radarweg 29, PO Box 211, 1000 AE Amsterdam, The Netherlands

First edition 2006

British Library Cataloguing in Publication Data
A catalogue record for this book is available from the British Library

Library of Congress Cataloging-in-Publication Data
A catalog record for this book is available from the Library of Congress

ISBN-10: 0-08-044657-4
ISBN-13: 978-0-08-044657-8

For information on all Elsevier publications
visit our website at books.elsevier.com

Printed and bound in The Netherlands

06 07 08 09 10 10 9 8 7 6 5 4 3 2 1

Working together to grow
libraries in developing countries

www.elsevier.com | www.bookaid.org | www.sabre.org

ELSEVIER   BOOK AID
International   Sabre Foundation

bs
9·11·06

BENCHMARKING NATIONAL TOURISM ORGANISATIONS AND AGENCIES

UNDERSTANDING BEST PRACTICE

ADVANCES IN TOURISM RESEARCH

Series Editor: Professor Stephen J. Page
University of Stirling, UK
s.j.page@stir.ac.uk

Advances in Tourism Research series publishes monographs and edited volumes that comprise state-of-the-art research findings, written and edited by leading researchers working in the wider field of tourism studies. The series has been designed to provide a cutting edge focus for researchers interested in tourism, particularly the management issues now facing decision-makers, policy analysts and the public sector. The audience is much wider than just academics and each book seeks to make a significant contribution to the literature in the field of study by not only reviewing the state of knowledge relating to each topic but also questioning some of the prevailing assumptions and research paradigms which currently exist in tourism research. The series also aims to provide a platform for further studies in each area by highlighting key research agendas, which will stimulate further debate and interest in the expanding area of tourism research. The series is always willing to consider new ideas for innovative and scholarly books, inquiries should be made directly to the series editor.

Published:

Destination Marketing Organisations
PIKE

Small Firms in Tourism: International Perspectives
THOMAS

Tourism and Transport
LUMSDON & PAGE

Tourism Public Policy and the Strategic Management of Failure
KERR

Managing Tourist Health and Safety in the New Millennium
WILKS & PAGE

Indigenous Tourism
RYAN AND AICKEN

Taking Tourism to the Limits
RYAN, PAGE & AICKEN

An International Handbook of Tourism Education
AIREY & TRIBE

Tourism in Turbulent Times
WILKS

Tourism Local Systems and Networking
LAZERETTI & PETRILLO

Extreme Tourism: Lessons from the World's Cold Water Islands
BALDACCHINO

Forthcoming titles include:

Quality Evaluation of Research Performance
ZEHRER

Related Elsevier Journals — sample copies available on request
Annals of Tourism Research
International Journal of Hospitality Management
Tourism Management
World Development

Contents

Abbreviations   vii

Measures Used in Tourist Statistics   ix

Symbols and Abbreviations Used in Tables   xi

Exchange Rates Used Throughout the Report   xiii

List of Figures   xv

List of Tables   xvii

Preface   xxi

1   Benchmarking: A Range of Approaches   1

2   Current Trends and Issues: The Rationale for States' Involvement in Tourism   5

3   Trends in Tourism Performance   11

4   Structure, Legal Status and the Role of NTOs   17

5   Australia   37

6   Canada   67

7   France   97

8   Ireland   121

9   The Netherlands   139

10   New Zealand   161

11   South Africa   185

12   Spain   207

13   Benchmark Lessons   227

References 239

Author Index 245

Subject Index 247

Abbreviations

ADS	Approved Destination Status
DMO	Destination Marketing Organisation
DMS	Destination Management System
EFRD	European Fund for Regional Development
ETC	European Travel Commission
EU	European Union
GDP	Gross Domestic Product
GSA	General Sales Agent
NTA	National Tourism Administration
NTO	National Tourism Organisation
OECD	Organisation for Economic Co-operation and Development
SME	Small and medium-sized enterprises
TSA	Tourism Satellite Account
WTO	World Tourism Organization

Measures Used in Tourist Statistics

TCE   International tourist arrivals or nights in all forms of commercial accommodation

TF   International tourist arrivals at frontiers (i.e. visitors spending at least one night in the country)

THS   International tourist arrivals or nights in hotels and similar establishments

VF   Tourist arrivals at Frontiers (including same-day visitors)

Symbols and Abbreviations Used in Tables

bn	billion
€	Euro
FY	Financial year
mn	million
na	not available
—	not applicable/appropriate
neg	negligible, not identifiable
0	zero, or less than 0.5% of the smallest unit
Rep	Republic (of Ireland)

Exchange Rates Used Throughout the Report

Units of currency to £1	2000	2001	2002	2003
Euro	1.64	1.61	1.58	1.45
Australian dollar	2.60	2.78	2.76	2.54
Canadian dollar	2.26	2.23	2.35	2.31
New Zealand dollar	3.33	3.42	3.24	2.85
South African rand	10.51	12.41	15.80	12.70
Rand: FY Apr.–Mar. (for budgets etc.)	—	11.14	13.54	14.77
US dollar	1.52	1.44	1.50	1.64

List of Figures

Figure 3.1	International receipts	12
Figure 3.2	Number of arrivals	13
Figure 3.3	Number of international nights	13
Figure 5.1	Structure of the Australian tourism support system	42
Figure 5.2	The Australian Tourist Commission's structure at HQ	52
Figure 6.1	The structure of tourism in Canada	74
Figure 6.2	CTC planning cycle	80
Figure 7.1	Structure of the French tourism support system	102
Figure 8.1	Overseas visitors to Ireland 1990–2002	123
Figure 8.2	Structure of tourism support system in Ireland (including Northern Ireland)	126
Figure 8.3	Tourism Ireland — senior management	130
Figure 9.1	Structure of Dutch tourism support system	144
Figure 10.1	New Zealand Tourism projections	163
Figure 10.2	New Zealand Ministry for Economic Development	166
Figure 10.3	New Zealand Core Tourism data set	167
Figure 10.4	TNZ Executive Structure	168
Figure 11.1	Structure of the South African tourism support system	190
Figure 11.2	Structure of South African tourism's HQ	194
Figure 12.1	Structure of the Spanish tourism support system	211
Figure 12.2	Organisational structure of Turespaña's HQ	216

List of Tables

Table 1.1   Example of typology utilised in NTO/NTA benchmarking analysis   3

Table 3.1   Key comparative data, 2002   12

Table 3.2   Main purpose of visitation (% of international arrivals)   15

Table 3.3   International tourism receipts per arrival (short-haul destinations)   15

Table 3.4   International tourism receipts per arrival (long-haul destinations)   16

Table 3.5   International tourism receipts per overnight   16

Table 4.1   NTOs' total budgets and share of state/government funding (2002)   18

Table 4.2   Percentage changes in NTO budgets (2003 and 2004)   19

Table 4.3   Share of state/government funding (2002–2004)   20

Table 4.4   Marketing and promotions vs fixed/other costs (2002)   20

Table 4.5   Details of NTO domestic marketing budgets where relevant (2003)   22

Table 4.6   Offices and representation abroad of the NTOs under survey (2004)   26

Table 4.7   Summary of representation abroad   28

Table 4.8   Staff of the NTOs under survey (2003)   30

Table 4.9   Budgeted spending by NTOs per office (abroad) and per member of staff (2002)   31

Table 5.1   Australia — key facts (2002)   38

Table 5.2   International visitor arrivals and receipts, 2000–2003   38

Table 5.3   Australia's leading international markets, 2000–2002 ('000)   39

Table 5.4   International tourist arrivals in Australia by purpose of visit, 2000–2002 ('000)   40

Table 5.5   Direct tourism-related spending by the Australian Government, 2002/2003   43

Table 5.6   The ATC's annual budget, 2001/2002 to 2003/2004 (£000)   55

Table 6.1   Canada: key facts — 2002   68

Table 6.2   Inbound trips to Canada 1999–2002   69

Table 6.3   Canada's Top international markets in 2002   70

Table 6.4   International tourist trips to Canada   70

Table 6.5   Purpose of international visit analysis by arrivals (%): 2000–2002   71

Table 6.6   Marketing investment to overnight receipts   73

Table 6.7   Budget allocation 2002–2004   78

Table 6.8   CTC strategy for 2002–2003   81

Table 6.9   Industry partners per programme   82

Table 6.10   Performance indicators   87

Table 6.11   The UK market 1995–2002   88

Table 6.12   Purpose of travel to Canada from UK   88

Table 6.13   Targeted ratio for CTC partners   89

Table 6.14   London office primary markets   90

Table 6.15   Trends in UK consumer holiday preferences   91

Table 7.1   France: key facts — 2002   98

Table 7.2   International tourist arrivals and overnights in France, 1982, 1992,
              and 1996–2002   99

Table 7.3   Breakdown of foreign arrivals in France by length of stay, 2002   99

Table 7.4   Breakdown of arrivals, overnights and tourism receipts by key
              source regions and individual markets, 2002   100

Table 7.5   France's share of European international trips by selected
              holiday sectors, 2000   101

Table 7.6   Staff responsibilities in Paris headquarters   108

Table 7.7   Maison de la France's budget, 2002–2004   109

Table 8.1   Ireland: key facts — 2002   122

Table 8.2   Overseas visitors to the Republic of Ireland by source
              1990–2002 (000's)   122

Table 8.3   Overseas visitors by purpose of visit (percentage of total
              visitation), 2002   123

Table 8.4   Tourists' expenditure in Ireland (£ bn)   123

Table 8.5   Northern Ireland and domestic tourism in Ireland (1997–2002)   125

Table 8.6   NTO budget   132

Table 8.7   NTO marketing budget   133

Table 9.1   The Netherlands: key facts — 2002   140

Table 9.2   Growth trends in tourism to and in the Netherlands, 2002–2003   141

Table 9.3   The Netherlands' leading international markets, 2000–2002 ('000)   141

Table 9.4   The value of international MICE business for the Netherlands, 2002   142

Table 9.5   Netherlands tourist board staff responsibilities   147

Table 9.6   NBT/TRN's budget, 2002–2004   148

Table 9.7   Economic significance of small regional events in the Netherlands, 1990–2002   153

Table 9.8   Increase in visitors to events and other attractions in the Netherlands, 1995–2001   153

Table 9.9   Selected major international exhibitions/events in the Netherlands, 1990–2002   154

Table 9.10   Visitors at international exhibitions/events in the Netherlands, 1990–1992   154

Table 9.11   Importance of international exhibitions/events in foreign visitor motivation, 1990–1992   155

Table 10.1   New Zealand: key facts (2002)   162

Table 10.2   Comparative tourism indicators, New Zealand (2000–2002)   162

Table 10.3   Type of visitor   163

Table 10.4   Main visitor markets for New Zealand (1999–2002)   164

Table 10.5   Average length of stay (nights) for international visitors (2000–2002)   164

Table 10.6   Expenditure of major international visitors, 2001–2002 (£ mn)   165

Table 10.7   TNZ staff responsibilities   170

Table 10.8   Major attraction visitation (1999–2001)   176

Table 10.9   New Zealand thematic brands   178

Table 10.10   New Zealand image positioning   179

Table 11.1   South Africa key facts — 2002   186

Table 11.2   South Africa's international arrivals and receipts, 2000–2003   186

Table 11.3   South Africa's leading international tourism markets, 2000–2002 ('000)   187

Table 11.4   Purpose of trip   189

Table 11.5   DEAT's annual budget, 2003/2004 to 2004/2005 (£mn)   192

Table 11.6   South African Tourism's budget, 2001/2002 to 2003/2004   195

Table 12.1   Spain key facts — 2002   207

Table 12.2   Spain's international tourist arrivals and tourism receipts, 2000–2003   208

Table 12.3   Spain's leading international markets, 2000–2002 ('000)   209

Table 12.4   Inbound tourist arrivals in Spain by main destination region, 2003   210

Table 12.5   Budget of the Secretary General of Tourism, 2002–2003 (£ mn)   212

Table 12.6   Turespaña's budget, 2002–2004   217

Preface

Changing Competitive Environments

The benchmarking analysis in this book has been based on desk research and interviews conducted with representatives of the National Tourism Organisations (NTOs) of Australia, Canada, France, Ireland, the Netherlands, New Zealand, South Africa and Spain. We wish to thank the various NTOs for their contributions and support with our research. We also would like to express our gratitude to VisitBritain for allowing us to use as the basis for this book the information gathered while conducting a study on their behalf.

The information and analysis contained in this book was produced during late 2003 and early 2004, at which time the best available information was used. However, as clearly indicated, there have been numerous changes in the structure, roles and even names of the respective NTOs since the study was completed. As an example, our reference to Australia's NTO as the Australian Tourist Commission (ATC) was accurate at the time of undertaking the research, but the ATC has now, of course, been replaced by Tourism Australia.

We hope that our work will, however, be appreciated as a 'snapshot in time' and that it can provide a valuable insight into the workings of NTOs within the dynamic tourism environment of the early 21st century. Statistics become quickly outdated and methods of calculation change. What we are attempting to do here is look behind purely numerical indicators to provide a coherent but holistic perspective on how National Tourism Administrations (NTAs) and NTOs can, and should, develop.

We would draw attention to the following comment that should be borne in mind when using the information and analysis in the statistical tables and text of the book.

Absolute Statistical Comparison and use of Accounting Ratio Comparison

In reality, the evaluation of NTO activities and structures presented problems and it was only by being aware of the imprecise nature of comparative data that realistic recommendations could be drawn. Baum (1999) acknowledged the potential problems and issues involved in comparative research. Key difficulties in the research undertaken in this study existed in:

- disaggregating the impact of NTOs on tourism visitation;
- disaggregating the real impact of elements such as positive public relations, brand awareness, brand buy-in, etc;
- isolating the impact of the NTO in marketing and other areas of operation, such as quality assurance from the private sector or other public sector agency activities;
- isolating the impact of shocks or other uncontrollable variables from the impact of NTO activities.

This study, like many that have preceded it, has drawn attention to the problems of absolute comparison. There is such a wide variation of measurement of a whole range of indices in the different countries discussed, that strict comparison is both dangerous and erroneous. It is interesting that one of the reasons for the widespread promotion of tourism satellite accounts by international agencies such as World Tourism Organization (WTO) and Organisation for Economic Co-operation and Development (OECD) is that they allow such comparisons to be made. Furthermore, accounting formula and ratio analysis frequently used in such benchmarking is predominantly derived from the UK management accounting. This is predicated on reporting of data and definitions that are detailed in UK legislation, and to simply apply such measures in an international context gives cause for concern. The numerical indices provide a comparison and a basis for consideration of quantitative data, but should not be treated in absolute terms.

While the overall numerical currency data in this report is given in sterling to facilitate comparison, the trends analyses have been retained in the original currency of the country under discussion.

Definitions

For the purposes of this report, the following definitions as developed by WTO (1996) are used. NTA is defined as:

- the central government body with administrative responsibility for tourism at the highest level; or
- the central government body with powers of direct intervention in the tourism sector; or
- all administrative bodies within national government with powers to intervene in the tourism sector.

The Department for Culture Media and Sport in the UK, for example, is responsible for government policy on tourism. Other governmental or official bodies of lower rank — either incorporated within a higher body or autonomous — may be regarded as NTA executive bodies. These may also include central organisations legally or financially linked to the NTA. One prime example is the NTO — also known as the national tourist office — such as VisitBritain, defined as:

- an autonomous body of public, semi-public or private status, established or recognised by the state as the body with competence at national level for the promotion — and, in some cases, marketing and research — of inbound international tourism.

The term 'local authority' implies a public or public–private sector authority at either provincial/regional or municipal/city level.

Use of Data from Earlier Studies

It should be noted that part of the comparative analysis in Chapter 3 has been taken from the findings of a separate study, carried out on behalf of the Swedish Tourist

Authority by The Travel Business Partnership in September/October 2003. *A Study of National Tourism Organisations in Selected European Countries*, this earlier study had two prime objectives, to:

- determine — through objective analysis and interviews with key tourism players from public and private sector stakeholders in the different countries — the real and/or perceived success of the respective NTOs; and
- draw some lessons from the different countries' experiences in tourism management and promotion, highlighting those NTOs or NTAs that have successfully adapted their structure, roles and responsibilities to changing economic and political circumstances.

Furthermore, the research for VisitBritain and this book has also drawn significantly on earlier research conducted for OECD and WTO — carried out between 1995 and 2000 by one of the authors of this book — and which resulted in three separate reports published by WTO and cited in the References. Ongoing benchmark analysis conducted for VisitScotland, and selective analysis conducted for the Canadian Tourism Commission (CTC) on future trends, has also helped inform general analysis and understanding. The team of authors' direct involvement with NTAs, NTOs and with industry itself — through practical research projects — has allowed an industry perspective to evolve that is informed by 'real time' commercial input, and by an understanding of the rapidly changing competitive environment.

Chapter 1

Benchmarking: A Range of Approaches

Benchmarking has been used extensively by the public and private sectors as a tool to develop competitive advantage (Dorsch & Yasin, 1998). The process is defined as:

> ... a continuous, systematic process for evaluating the products, services, and work processes of organisations that are recognised as representing best practices for the purposes of organisational improvement. (Spendolini, 1992a, p. 9)

For many organisations, whether from the public or private sector, this process is fused with the analysis of competition and competitor benchmarking. Xerox, IT & T and Texas Instrument were early proponents of this approach (see Bemowski, 1991, 1994; Shetty, 1993; King, 1993, respectively), which has now become extremely common in a range of private sector companies. This process involves identification of products, services and operations of an organisation's or business's direct competitors (Spendolini, 1992b, p. 18).

Two main approaches to benchmarking have been identified (see Cook, 1995; Wöber, 2002) namely, internal benchmarking (analysis of exemplary practice within an organisation/destination) and external benchmarking, where practices adopted by other organisations/destinations are considered. The external benchmarking approach can be further categorised as:

- best practice benchmarking (considering an exemplar in a different sector);
- competitive benchmarking (considering a competitor in the same sector as an exemplar);
- sector benchmarking (considering an exemplar within a specific or similar sector, but not necessarily a competitor) (Wöber, 2002).

Benchmarking involving National Tourism Administrations (NTAs) and National Tourism Organisations (NTOs) was first covered by Organization for Economic Co-operation and Development's (OECD's) Tourism Committee in the early 1990s, but was addressed in greater depth by World Tourism Organization (WTO) from the mid-1990s (WTO, 1994, 1996a,b, 2000, 2003). The process involves a range of data gathering that enables the NTO/NTA and the destination to compare their practices and achievements with those of others (Pizam, 1999). In the case of exemplar destinations, they can be identified as short- and long-haul competitors to aid analysis (Ooi, 2002). Benchmarking can be applied from a basic to an advanced level. In more sophisticated cases, comparative analogous destination analysis can involve much more than basic information gathering. Rather, the analysis may probe and compare practices and outcomes with those of other NTOs and destinations and can assist in measuring competitiveness (Dwyer & Kim, 2003). Key performance indicators measured over a period of time could include:

- tourism revenue;
- arrivals;

- principal existing markets;
- emerging markets;
- seasonality.

In addition to major benchmarking analysis, monthly or sporadic benchmarking may be undertaken to provide 'real' time indicators on performance levels, etc. An alternative is the tracking of business confidence levels carried out either in partnership with the NTO or via the public sector (see for example Wales Tourist Board, 2002–2003).

In tourism terms, benchmarking is increasingly being used by NTOs and NTAs as a means of situational analysis. However, longer appraisal of country NTO/NTA analysis is also favoured and, more recently, some national tourist boards have chosen to employ a full time team of staff to carry out regular benchmarking of major long-haul and short-haul competitors.

Crucial in practical application of the process in the tourism sector is the measurement of the key areas:

- situational analysis;
- competitive destinations review;
- improvement planning;
- adoption of best practice;
- identification of critical success factors.

At the start of any analysis, goals and objectives must be clearly identified and then the scope of the analysis should be highlighted. For example, the analysis may be based on analysis of key competitors' marketing strategies, but the scope could be confined to analysis of short-haul competitors. Other areas of consideration may be outlined in the scope/dimensions of the study, including the use of electronic marketing, the efforts undertaken to reduce seasonality, etc. Of key importance is the identification of appropriate competitor organisations or destinations. There is a clear logic in comparing performance with analogous destinations in terms of location, economy, significance of tourism to the economy and socio-economic profile. However, value to studies can also be added by comparison with non-analogous destinations in order to learn and gain insights from international exemplars, or 'world class' cases (Cook, 1995), which might make a simple scale or profile comparison meaningless.

In the example below, an outline of the kind of quantitative and qualitative measures used in many studies is provided in order to help construct an outline matrix for basic evaluation. The categories and dimensions identified are not intended to be exhaustive or definitive. Rather, they are typical of the areas examined (Table 1.1).

Benchmarking, which had its origins in manufacturing (see Balm, 1992; Breiter & Kline, 1995; CBI and DTI, 1994; Coopers and Lybrand, 1995), has now become a mainstream tool in the tourism industry and can be considered 'a catalyst for fast learning' (Fuchs & Weiermair, 2004, p. 213). From the early work undertaken predominantly in the context of the hotel sector (see Barsky, 1996; CBI and DTI, 1994; Coopers and Lybrand, 1995), scope and coverage has now grown to encompass NTOs/NTAs, destinations, tour operators and other travel intermediaries (see Bordas, 1994; Kozak & Rimmington, 1997, 1998; WTO, 1996b, 2000, 2003). Consequently, the later chapters of this text will attempt to examine some of the major learning derived from this valuable management information tool, which has gained such popularity and application in the last decade.

Table 1.1: Example of typology utilised in NTO/NTA benchmarking analysis.

Measure	Host nation	Competitor A	Competitor B
International arrivals (nos)			
International expenditure ($/€)			
International arrivals trends (5 and 10 years)			
International expenditure (5 and 10 years)			
Domestic arrivals (nos)			
Domestic expenditure ($/€)			
Domestic arrivals trends (5 and 10 years)			
Domestic expenditure (5 and 10 years)			
Changes in tourism account (inbound:outbound)			
Occupancy trends at sectoral levels (5 and 10 years)			
Tourism as proportion of GDP/GNP			
Significance of tourism as an employer			
Trends in jobs created in tourism (5 and 10 years)			
Seasonal performance trends (5 and 10 years)			
Market share of international tourism (trend over 5 and 10 years)			
Tourism balance of payment account trends (5 and 10 years)			
Total cost of operation of NTO/NTA per annum			
Total NTO/NTA expenditure on marketing (domestic and international)			

(Continued)

Table 1.1: (*Continued*)

Measure	Host nation	Competitor A	Competitor B
Total NTO/NTA expenditure on electronic marketing			
No. of persons employed in NTO/NTA			
No. of overseas offices in NTO/NTA			
Comments			

Chapter 2

Current Trends and Issues: The Rationale for States' Involvement in Tourism

Although, tourism is an activity sustained mainly by private initiative, governments have traditionally played a key role in its development and in the promotion of their countries as tourism destinations. Examples used in the reasoning of government involvement in tourism include: improvements in the balance of payments, regional development and regeneration, diversification of the national economy, co-ordination of a fragmented industry, employment opportunities and increased revenue (Hall, 1994; Baum, 1994; Harrison, 1992; Hall & Jenkins, 1995; World Tourism Organisation, 1996a, 1996b, 2000). The state's role is clearly more important in developing countries, or countries in which tourism is in a transition stage — where government support can be crucial to kick-starting growth or indeed avoiding market failure (WTO, 1996, 2000; Edgell, 1999; Jeffries, 2001). Arguably, there is less need for public sector support of the tourism industry in countries at a high level of economic development.

Nevertheless, it is generally recognised that for tourism to develop in a sustainable manner, an appropriate physical, regulatory, fiscal and social framework is required. And this can only be provided by governments. The multi-faceted nature of tourism means that co-ordination is necessary within and between different levels of government to avoid duplication of resources in the various government bodies and the private sector (Johnson and Thomas, 1992; Hall, 1994). They also usually provide the basic physical infrastructure necessary for tourism — such as roads, airports and communications — as well as creating the legal framework within which the industry operates.

Increasing Signs of Disengagement

Over the past 15 years there have been increasing signs of a disengagement from tourism by the public sector — notably, at national, or central government level. This has resulted in the relinquishing of a number of governments' traditional responsibilities and activities in the field of tourism in favour of both local authorities and the private sector.

The trend is even causing concern for international, inter-governmental organisations such as WTO, whose membership is declining in some parts of the world as National Tourism Administrations effectively cease to exist. Under the current WTO Statutes, neither an autonomous region, such as Flanders, nor a National Tourism Organisation, can replace its government's NTA as a full WTO member, or even become an associate member — unless the NTA is a full member.

Some believe this may all lead to a review of WTO's statutes and an eventual restructuring of the organisation. The application of Bermuda, a British colony, to become a WTO member in 2003 — which had to be turned down for the same reason — caused widespread publicity and dissent among members.

Continued Constraints on Public Sector Budgets

In many ways, it might seem paradoxical that at a time when governments' recognition of tourism's importance to national economies is at an all-time high, they are increasingly questioning the rationale for their continued involvement in tourism.

This has been particularly marked in Europe and North America. But, motivated by the lending rules of international aid agencies like the International Monetary Fund and World Bank, the divesting of government-owned tourism assets has also become increasingly common in other parts of the world. And this has been followed by efforts to involve local authorities and the private sector more closely in tourism management and promotion. This trend towards such a partnership is fuelled by "…budget constraints — a major concern with which most NTAs are familiar" (WTO, 2000, p. 12).

To some extent, the trend would seem to be a natural consequence of decentralisation, which in many countries, has resulted in increasing powers of decision-making being shifted to provincial and local authorities. Spain is perhaps the best case in point but the trend is also very marked in Australia, France and South Africa. The structure of NTAs is clearly very influenced by a country's particular historical, political and cultural circumstances.

A Changing Political and Socio-Economic Climate

The traditional role of government in tourism has however changed from that of a public administration model to a model where recognition is given to "the role of the market and relations with stakeholders, usually defined as industry" (Hall, 1994, p. 43). The role of the NTO does however continue to evolve (Morrison et al, 1995). Although the importance of the NTO marketing function is recognised there is increasing involvement of the private sector in promotion and marketing functions (WTO, 1996b, 2000; Prideaux & Cooper, 2002). It is recognised that "a public sector led by marketing organisation is often less entrepreneurial and effective than one managed by the industry itself or in collaboration with the industry" (WTO, 2000, p. 12). Most NTAs that have partnerships with the private sector rely on industry contributions mainly for marketing, advertising and the funding of special promotional campaigns — or even 'contributions in kind' (e.g. complimentary hotel accommodation and air fares for journalists and the trade on familiarisation trips). But others also count on private sector funding for their core budgets. This generally results in private enterprise having a greater say in the development of tourism policy and NTA operational strategies, as well as in how the overall budgets are spent.

Interviews with private sector stakeholders in a number of countries have highlighted the fact that the industry is generally happy to contribute financially to NTO promotions as long as it feels it really contributes pro-actively to decisions regarding NTO marketing and promotional strategy and campaigns. However, the development of such a relationship is long term. It is built on trust stability and continued co-operation and is "considered critical to enhancing competitiveness" (WTO, 2000, p. 57).

Trend also Apparent at Regional and Local Levels

The trend towards public–private sector partnerships in tourism marketing and promotion is not only apparent at national level (Fayos-Solá, 1996; Lavery, 1996; Bramwell and Lane, 2000; Prideaux & Cooper, 2002), but is increasingly spreading to provincial/regional and municipal/city levels — especially in states with federal, or decentralised political systems (WTO, 1996b, 2000; Mazanec, 1997). In some countries, in fact, the central government strategy regarding public–private sector partnerships has actually been influenced by what is happening at local level (The Travel Business Partnership, 2004).

It is also interesting to note that many cities have far more sophisticated public–private partnership operating environments than those that exist at national level, and several generate up to two-thirds of their budgets through commercial activities involving the private sector. There are clearly some lessons to be learned by NTOs from these examples.

There are numerous examples worldwide of destinations whose capitals outshine the rest of the country in terms of tourism appeal. Prague is an obvious example. Similarly, Amsterdam represents a far stronger brand and more easily marketable destination than the Netherlands overall. Furthermore, the USA has long benefited from strong city marketing. Cities constitute easily packaged products rather than the more complex reality that is a nation (Mazanec, 1999). However, the work of the US Chamber of Commerce and Convention Bureaux in many cities provide exemplars in co-operative city marketing that involves better co-ordination and joint buying to maximise the use of scarce financial resources.

The NTA as a Co-ordinator and Catalyst

Government support of tourism is still widely seen as critical to the sustainable growth of the industry. However, government's role has changed and is continuing to change (WTO, 1996b, 2000; Hall, 1994; Jeffries, 2001).

With the possible exceptions of Spain and South Africa, where — for different reasons explained in the country chapters — the state plays a much more dominant role in tourism, the role of the state in the other countries surveyed is very much that of co-ordinator, or catalyst for tourism development. And even in Spain and South Africa, the respective governments are fully conscious of the need to provide the basic infrastructure for tourism development, but to allow the private sector to drive tourism growth.

With the exception again of Spain — where the government owns and operates the Paradores de España (a situation that may, reportedly, be about to change following the recent national election and switch to a new Socialist government) — the state has already divested itself of its interests in tourism plant and services. In Europe, in fact, there are very few countries (Greece is one of these) where either the NTA or NTO is still involved in real estate development and management. Indeed, even in Greece, there are clear signs of a move towards privatisation of these assets.

Increasingly, in many developed countries, the degree of regulation and legislation in evidence has increased the bureaucracy surrounding business operation and development of facilities.

A Unifying Force for a Fragmented Industry

Few governments appear to have any real doubts as to the relevance of their involvement — however, modest — in the tourism industry. They justify this in the context of market failures, or by the need to minimise impediments to growth. These include unnecessary regulations and imposts, inefficiencies in the provision of transport services, or distortions in existing tax or regulatory systems that discriminate against the industry. Governments can also facilitate access to capital, land and skilled employees. In summary, they can ensure that tourism is developing in the best interests of the community.

NTAs are, therefore, frequently involved in matters of policy and planning, as well as in trade issues that affect the country's tourism interests and the growth of the industry. In this respect, they act as co-ordinators between different government ministries and between central government, provincial and local authorities and the private sector. A number of the country case studies show that inter-ministerial committees and consultative bodies play a fairly important role in guiding tourism policy. If there is no formal structure for consultation at ministry or department level, co-operation does seem to occur in practice — based on good common sense.

In most countries, this also gives NTAs some involvement in education and generic promotion. A country's image is seen as an integral part of its overall economic development (WTO, 1996b, 2000; Ryan & Zahra, 2004). Tourism is a major source of foreign exchange and an important generator of employment, so many governments consider image promotion a legitimate partner in the general development of export markets.

As far as education is concerned, government's role is often linked to supporting small- and medium-sized enterprises (SMEs), which make up at least 90% of the private sector of the tourism industry in most countries. Governments in Australia, Canada, France, the Netherlands and South Africa all recognise they have a role in this area.

Selling the Country Brand

However, there are two major questions still generally unanswered. In a highly developed, liberal political system, does government tourism promotion still have an important place? If so, should this simply be image promotion? Or can governments justify involvement in marketing activities as well?

The results of the case studies suggest that this is the one issue that continues to trouble governments. Some — including governments in almost all the countries surveyed — do feel they have a role and responsibility to remain involved in national tourism promotion and marketing. The Dutch government has changed its mind frequently on this issue — no doubt influenced by its Nordic neighbours. But the current trend is again towards greater involvement, albeit with reduced or static funding. There are notable exceptions within the UK, where both Scotland and Wales have received increases in marketing budgets.

The rationale for government funding of tourism promotion in countries such as Australia, New Zealand and Canada is that it provides for the generic promotion of a country or region, which benefits not only the tourism industry, but also the community as a whole. This is supported by Dore and Crouch (2002, p. 138) when they argue that NTOs

"…appear to have recognised the potential value and effectiveness of publicity in destination promotion". The authors acknowledge, however, that little is known of the extent of the emphasis on such promotion due to a lack of studies on the topic. Since tourism, unlike other markets, is not product specific, tourists must be persuaded to purchase a range of goods and services — not just particular products — and this package includes the economy, environment and culture of the country. Successful destination branding can therefore be considered "…the most powerful marketing weapon available to contemporary destination marketers…" (Morgan & Pritchard, 2004, p. 60).

NTAs can act as a unifying force, co-ordinating activities undertaken by other players involved in the industry (WTO, 2000; Ryan & Zahra, 2004) — notably, provincial and local authorities and the private sector — and stimulating joint efforts.

Australia's decision to focus on brand marketing, featuring experiences that create awareness and desire for the destination of Australia as a whole, is an important change in approach — and one that has possible lessons for other NTOs. The Australian Tourist Commission (ATC)/Tourism Australia will not be involved in promoting specific products and places. This will be left to the state and provincial tourism organisations (STOs) and tourism regions, which now have the responsibility of converting the awareness created by the ATC into visits.

Some 50% of the ATC's activity will be allocated to promoting Brand Australia. While facilitating the development of appropriate products is also seen as important, promoting individual products and destinations, and converting these to sales, are excluded from the ATC's activities. Its role is solely to co-ordinate and unify the efforts of all the different stakeholders involved.

Brand Building by other Media

New Zealand has used a film-related promotion of the nation to drive a co-ordinated overseas campaign of generic promotion linked to the Lord of the Rings trilogy. This has included airline co-operation in terms of decorating Air New Zealand Boeing 737 and 747 aircraft with images promoting both the film and the destination. Similarly, strong relationships have been developed with tour operators to promote bespoke film-related packages. Interestingly, tourism has now replaced dairy/agriculture as New Zealand's most important economic sector. This suggests that co-ordinated film-based promotions can contribute significantly to brand building and positive national marketing.

Chapter 3

Trends in Tourism Performance

Caveats

We have used 2002 data for our main comparative analysis since data for 2003 was not yet finalised for most countries at the time of conducting the research — whether regarding tourism performance or NTO budgets, etc. This, of course, results in some distortion of results, since other data — e.g. covering office and staff numbers — refers to 2003 or even 2004. It proved almost impossible to determine past staff/office numbers with accuracy.

Another area of concern is the sharp fluctuation of exchange rates over the period, which results in almost meaningless year-on-year trends based on figures in sterling. Wherever possible, we have identified year-on-year trends in local currencies, although the data on absolute volumes has been translated into sterling for the purposes of this report (as already explained in the Preface).

For a full explanation of the differences in accounting procedures from one NTO to another — including such basic differences as fiscal versus calendar years — it is necessary to refer to the detailed country case studies from Chapter 5 onwards. Information for the UK has been added where possible for additional comparison.

2002 Comparisons

Table 3.1 provides a summary of comparative data for the countries under survey, including their respective populations, GDP and key tourism performance data for 2002. The comparison highlights the vast differences in size of the different countries and in the relative importance of tourism to each. France dominates in terms of arrivals and overnights but, due to its much shorter average length of stay, comes second to Spain in terms of international tourism receipts.

It is interesting to note that the UK, which ranks third among the countries under survey by all international tourism measures, generates only 31% of France's volume of international arrivals and 34% of overnight volume, but 54% of receipts. Nevertheless, it should be stressed that available statistics are by no means fully consistent across the different countries, and some of the data provided in this table has been estimated for comparative purposes.

Highlights of the information contained in Table 3.1 are shown in the following Figures 3.1–3.3.

Table 3.1: Key comparative data, 2002.

Country	International tourism				
	Population (mn)	GDP (£ bn)	Receipts (£ bn)	Arrivals[a] (mn)	Nights[b] (mn)
France	59.7	954	21.8	77.0	586.9
Ireland (Total)	5.6	106	2.2	7.0	46.9
Ireland (Rep)	3.9	80	2.1	5.9	45.3
Netherlands	16.1	281	5.8	11.6	26.4
Spain	39.9	439	22.4	51.7	221.6
UK	59.6	937	11.7	24.2	199.3
Australia	19.5	266	4.1	4.8	127.7
Canada	31.4	477	6.5	19.9	122.1
New Zealand	3.9	39	1.9	2.0	43.6
South Africa	45.0	70	2.7	6.6	79.2

[a]Arrivals are tourists at frontiers (TF) except for the UK, Australia and South Africa (VF).
[b]Nights are those of tourists staying in commercial accommodation (TCE).

Sources: Respective NTOs and NTAs, the WTO, International Monetary Fund (IMF) and the United Nations (UN).

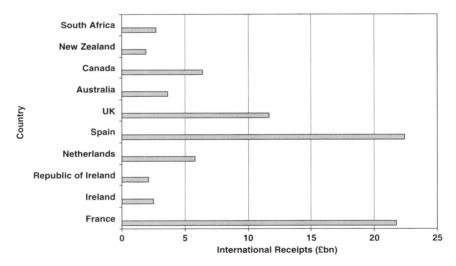

Figure 3.1: International receipts.

2003 was Generally a Difficult Year

The UK performance in terms of arrivals, nights and expenditure is at least a partial function of the shared visitor profile (see Table 3.2). It has an almost equally divided proportion of business, visiting friends and/or relations (VFR) and leisure in comparison with the other countries surveyed. This inevitably results in a shorter stay in the UK than for

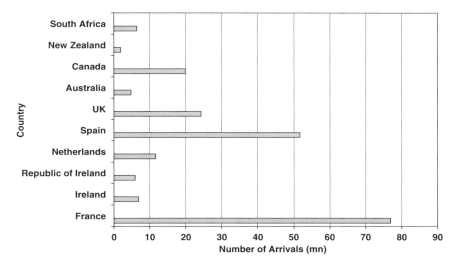

Figure 3.2: Number of arrivals.

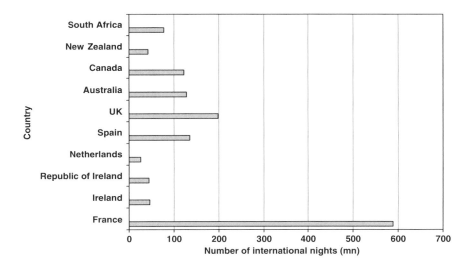

Figure 3.3: Number of international nights.

destinations attracting primarily leisure travel. It should of course be pointed out that the lower than average share of leisure tourism is largely due to the decline in leisure arrivals over the past five years or so — down from 10.8 million in 1997 (a 42% market share) to 7.7 million in 2002 (30%). Over the same five-year period, business arrivals only increased from 6.3 million a year to 7.1 million.

On a global level, following a good start to the year, demand in 2003 was severely affected by the build-up to the Iraq war — which was of greater concern in some markets than the war itself — combined with continued terrorism threats, the economic slowdown and SARS.

There are now clear signs of a recovery, reflecting the resilience of the industry and consumers' pent-up demand for travel after one of the biggest confidence crises in the history of tourism. Nevertheless, preliminary data for 2003 from the respective countries and World Tourism Organization (WTO) (based on actual results in most cases for 9–10 months of the year) highlights the lacklustre performance of most of the countries under survey.

Ireland (Republic of) achieved the best increase in international arrivals (+4.9%) in 2003, although New Zealand (+3%), South Africa and the UK also recorded positive growth. Spain's arrivals showed no change over 2002's level, and there were declines for France (−2.6%), Australia (−2.8%), the Netherlands (−5.7%) and Canada (−13.3%).

As for international tourism receipts, Canada again turned in the worst performance (−11.0%), but South Africa also registered a 7.9% decline, according to preliminary estimates. Receipts for the Netherlands and the UK stagnated, and New Zealand (+2.0%), Spain (+4.1%) and Ireland (+5.2%) achieved positive growth.

It would be very difficult to attribute the respective performances directly to efforts — or lack of efforts — on the part of the countries' NTOs. As an example, in France's case, could one possibly venture the thought that different government actions may have resulted in an improved, tourism performance? Simply put, the French response to the Iraq war clearly impacted on inbound visitation from the USA and catalysed a range of recovery programmes following the decline in inbound visitors.

Purpose of Travel

Comparisons are not yet available for 2003 but, according to 2002 data (see Table 3.2), the UK emerges as a strong business destination — or, to put it differently, a weaker leisure travel destination than the competing destinations surveyed.

The strength of business tourism and the business offer in several countries should be reinforced by investing in marketing this vital strength and, most importantly — after the example of Australia — by setting up a high-level body dedicated to the meetings, incentives, conferences and events (MICE) sector. This body can take on responsibility for branding and promoting the country as a business and events destination, as well as acting as a co-ordination unit to ensure minimum duplication of effort on the part of regional and city event agencies.

One important trend among competing NTOs is the recruitment of business travel/MICE specialists in hub overseas offices. As these specialists have an ear to the ground and know their local markets well, they can respond quickly on behalf of the NTOs as and when opportunities arise.

Business travel is also a strong market for South Africa, which is a regional business hub for Southern Africa. It should be noted that, as far as France, Ireland, the Netherlands and the UK are concerned, a considerable volume of business travel is same-day travel, and therefore does not show up in international tourism statistics.

Table 3.2: Main purpose of visitation (% of international arrivals).

Destination	Business	VFR	Holiday	Other
France	14	18	52	17
Ireland (Republic)	25	24	37	14
Netherlands	18	28	44	10
Spain	8	4	82	6
UK	30	26	32	2
Australia	15	19	55	11
Canada	16	28	48	8
New Zealand	11	26	53	10
South Africa	35	15	40	10

Source: Respective country data, WTO.

Table 3.3: International tourism receipts per arrival (short-haul destinations).

Country	Receipts per arrival (£)	Receipts (£ bn)	Arrivals (mn)
Netherlands	500	5.8	11.6
UK	483	11.7	24.2
Spain	433	22.4	51.7
Ireland (Rep)	356	2.1	5.9
Ireland	314	2.2	7.0
France	283	21.8	77.0

Source: Extrapolations by the authors.

Spain's dominance in the holiday market is clearly evident, but given the country's strong economic performance, business tourism is like to grow in the coming years.

In terms of receipts per international arrival (see Tables 3.3 and 3.4), New Zealand and Australia rank in first and second positions — well ahead of the rest of the field. This can be easily explained by the much longer average length of stay in those countries, due in no small part to the fact that a number of their key source markets are long haul. The tables have been divided between short haul and long haul from a European perspective.

The relative distance from tourism generating markets is a major factor influencing length of stay. The UK comparison is not really a fair one since the purpose of visit is much more evenly spread between business, VFR and leisure. Furthermore, the proximity to one of the main generating markets, Europe, and the quality and extent of transport links inevitably encourages a shorter stay.

It is important to note that Australia, at least, does not conform to the WTO standard of measuring arrivals of up to 12 months only — hence Australia's longer length of stay.

As explained in detail in the respective country chapter, France attracts a high share of short breaks and tourists in transit, which largely explains its much lower spend per arrival.

Table 3.4: International tourism receipts per arrival (long-haul destinations).

Country	Receipts per arrival (£)	Receipts (£ bn)	Arrivals (mn)
New Zealand	950	1.9	2.0
Australia	854	4.1	4.8
South Africa	409	2.7	6.6
Canada	327	6.5	19.9

Source: Extrapolations by the authors.

Table 3.5: International tourism receipts per overnight.

Country	Receipts per night (£)	Receipts (£ bn)	Overnights (mn)
Netherlands	220	5.8	26.4
Spain	101	22.4	221.6
UK	59	11.7	199.3
Canada	53	6.5	122.1
Ireland	47	2.2	46.9
Ireland (Rep)	46	2.1	45.3
New Zealand	43	1.9	43.6
France	37	21.8	586.9
South Africa	34	2.7	79.2
Australia	32	4.1	127.7

Source: Extrapolations by the authors.

The UK ranks slightly behind the Netherlands, in fourth position, reflecting a good balance of short- and longer-stay visitors, as well as the importance of the business sector. The UK's position appears much weaker in terms of receipts per overnight (see Table 3.5) due to a longer average length of stay compared with some of the other countries under survey. However, it still ranks third — behind the Netherlands and Spain.

As already indicated, care must be taken in interpreting these tables as measurements are not often consistent. In a number of cases arrivals are measured at frontiers — and can be visitors (e.g. including same-day travellers) rather than tourists — while nights usually only refer to overnight volume registered by commercial accommodation. So the total of receipts per arrival or night is not strictly accurate.

Chapter 4

Structure, Legal Status and the Role of NTOs

Legal Status

Among the countries surveyed, most of the National Tourism Organisations (NTOs) are either government agencies or statutory authorities/boards (a Crown Corporation in the case of Canada) — even if a share of their budgets comes from the private sector. The Netherlands Board of Tourism & Conventions (NBTC) is a private foundation.

Statutory authorities/boards have traditionally tended to have greater power and influence in the tourism decision-making process than government departments — even in cases where they are funded totally by government. But in countries like Australia and Canada, marketing and promotion strategies are elaborated in close collaboration with the industry, as well as with the state and territorial governments.

Ownership and Links with the Regions

The majority of the NTOs surveyed are 100% publicly owned. Only Maison de la France is formally known as a public–private body — because of its mixed membership — although most of the other NTOs do receive a significant share of their revenues from the private sector, primarily through contributions to joint marketing and promotional campaigns.

Four of the NTOs surveyed — in Australia, Canada, France and Spain — have formalised links/relations with the responsible regional tourism authorities. Yet, interestingly, there are signs that these do not necessarily work any better in practice than NTOs in countries where there is no formal, institutionalised link — such as the Netherlands.

The trend towards semi-public NTOs, involving a partnership with both the private sector and provincial/regional authorities, can be expected to grow, even if the links are not totally formalised. Two of the NTOs rated among the most successful in the world — the Australian Tourist Commission (ATC) and the Canadian Tourism Commission (CTC) — have operated on this basis for some time. Like Maison de la France, the CTC also counts on membership dues from its partners in the CTC product clubs, as well as contributions to marketing campaigns.

What makes some of these NTOs more successful than others is that their partners do not represent only the travel industry. In the case of Maison de la France, its partners come from a wide range of other industries and sectors — such as automobile manufacturing, department store chains, high fashion goods and French perfumes. And some of these have even contributed to the opening and operation of offices abroad.

NTO Budgets

Total Budgets

The fairly lengthy notes to the following Table 4.1 — which would have been even longer if all the points needing qualification had been included — reflect the unreliability of statistical comparisons between NTO budgets of different countries. The data was obtained directly from the NTOs concerned but, as indicated in the country case studies, has had to be qualified in some instances and supplemented as far as possible by data from annual reports and one-on-one interviews.

When compiling the information contained in Table 4.1, extrapolation of data was necessary in some cases — where details regarding data made this possible — in order to align responses into consistent categories. This was not an easy task because of the major differences in accounting convention and classification between different NTOs.

Nevertheless, despite the computational issues, a number of interesting findings have emerged from the overall analysis. Budgets are rarely set in concrete, and mid-year modifications are common. State allocations depend on the availability of funds from the Ministry of Finance which, in turn, depends on national economic performance during the course of the year. The percentage changes in the levels of budget of each NTO are provided in Table 4.2 on the following page.

The budget information contained in Table 4.1 is listed according to the volume of the total budget. However, any ranking should be treated as a statistical exercise rather than a meaningful comparative analysis — the lack of strict comparability makes this impossible.

Table 4.1: NTOs' total budgets and share of state/government funding (2002).

Country	Total budget (£ mn)	State funding (£ mn)	State share (%)
Spain	55.5	48.3	87
Canada	54.1	47.0	87
Australia	44.3	35.5	80
France	36.2	16.3	45
Ireland	31.6	30.3	96
South Africa	26.1	14.4	65
Netherlands	22.5	14.2	63
New Zealand	17.0	17.0	100

Note: Full Years for Australia and New Zealand (1 July–30 June) and South Africa (1 April–31 March). Otherwise, calendar years.

State refers only to the central government. In the case of Spain, for example, the balance of funding comes from the EU Structural Funds (EFRD).

Tourism Ireland only (Fáilte Ireland and NITB not included).

New Zealand has acknowledged in its strategy document that the private sector must be involved in funding in the medium term.

The Budgets for Canada and Netherlands include an element of funding for domestic tourism amounting to around £4 million and £1.4 million, respectively.

Source: Extrapolations by the authors.

Table 4.2: Percentage changes in NTO Budgets (2003 and 2004).

Country	Percentage change 2002–2003	Percentage change 2003–2004[a]
Australia	−0.3	NA
Canada	−7.0	−21.0
France	−5.1	+7.2
Ireland	+20.0	0.0
Netherlands	−4.5	−7.1
New Zealand	0.0	0.0
South Africa	−14.3	+37.5
Spain	+20.2	+7.7

[a]Projected changes — budgets are not definite until the end of the years in question.
Source: Extrapolations by the authors.

Maison de la France's and the CTC's budgets (see country case studies for more details) exclude contributions from members/partners for marketing campaigns, and the stated government contribution refers only to the funds from central government. For example, in Canada an additional £40 million was received from joint marketing and research partnerships taking the total budget to £94 million with the state contribution being 50%. In the case of Turespaña, the balance of funding (i.e. the 13% from non-government sources) is actually from European Union (EU) Structural Funds, although obviously still categorised as public funding. Ireland's budget refers only to Tourism Ireland, the relatively new NTO, ignoring government funding provided to the Northern Ireland Tourist Board (NITB) and Fáilte Ireland, the Republic of Ireland's national tourism development agency, which is also responsible for some marketing and promotion.

State Funding Still Dominates

There is no doubt that public sector — and, in most cases, central government — funding accounts for the biggest share of revenues of the NTOs analysed, ranging from a low of 45% in France (see above qualification) to 100%.

As already indicated, budgets for 2003 are still provisional — they will only be confirmed with the publication of the respective annual reports. However, with the data currently available, no clear trend is evident across all the countries studied. Most receive annual increases — in total budgets and state funding — but this is not always guaranteed. The NBTC, for example, will lose 25% of its grant in aid/state funding over the next five years.

Details of year-on-year trends in NTO budgets are included in the country case studies. There is little point in showing comparative trends in sterling because of the huge distortions created by the fluctuations in exchange rates. For ease of comparison a summary of the findings is shown in Table 4.3.

The Importance of Marketing and Promotion

The largest single item of expenditure in an NTO's budget is marketing and promotion, although this generally includes market research as well. However, this of course depends

Table 4.3: Share of state/government funding (2002–2004).

Country	2002 (%)	2003 (%)	2004 (%)
New Zealand	100	100	100
Ireland	96	96	96
Canada	87	91	88
Spain	87	88	88
Australia	80	80	80
South Africa	62	73	71
Netherlands	62.9	65	63.9
France	45	46	NA

Source: Extrapolations by the authors.

Table 4.4: Marketing and promotions vs fixed/other costs (2002).

Country	Marketing (£ mn)	Percentage share	Fixed/other (£ mn)	Percentage share
Canada	44.9	83	9.2	17
Australia	35.4	80	8.9	20
Spain	33.3	60	22.2	40
UK	26.9	76	8.6	24
France	26.4	73	9.8	27
South Africa	20.5	83	4.1	17
Ireland	19.7	62.4	11.9	37.6
New Zealand	13.6	80	3.4	20
Netherlands	10.9	48.5	11.6	51.5

Note: See text — particularly country case studies — for further details and explanations as to inconsistencies.
Source: Extrapolations by the authors.

on the role and activities of the NTO. Some are involved in a number of different activities in addition to marketing and promotion.

The Netherlands is a case in point, since the NBTC (under its former name, Toerisme Recreatie Nederland) was — until 2004, at least — responsible for a number of management tasks formerly carried out by the ministry to which it reported. So it is hardly surprising that the share of marketing and promotion in its overall budget is lower than for other NTOs (Table 4.4).

Although private sector funding is growing as a portion of marketing and promotional budgets, it still represents a fairly modest share in some countries. Moreover, for the majority of NTOs, the private sector's contribution does not come as easily as one might imagine. The bulk of partner funding — whether from local authorities or the private sector — has to be earned and, in some cases, bid for on a programme-by-programme, or campaign-by-campaign basis.

Particular care needs to be taken in analysing marketing and promotional budgets because of the differences in accounting methods from one country to another. There is also hidden collateral — or contributions which do not appear on any balance sheet — since private sector funding of advertising campaigns often goes direct to advertising companies or the media, rather than through the respective NTOs.

It is therefore difficult to ascertain the true amount of private sector leverage that is obtained. In the case of France and Canada, for example, the marketing budgets quoted do not include industry joint marketing and research partnership funds outside the NTOs' financial records. For Canada, the funds referred to totalled as much as £40 million in 2002.

Building Private Sector Buy-in

Governments are increasingly looking to boost private sector buy-in to tourism marketing and promotion (WTO, 1996b, 2000). This represents a long-term ambition for many NTOs, which must first establish credibility with the private sector as far as their ability to handle marketing and promotion is concerned. The development of a strong brand, which enjoys high levels of buy-in from tourism and non-tourism sectors (such as the 100% Pure New Zealand brand), will make such a task easier.

Some caution is, however, necessary when looking at the extent of industrial leverage that is claimed by many NTOs, and close scrutiny of the nature and extent of leverage is suggested. In the case of CTC in Canada, the funding from state-operated airlines artificially inflates the level of 'private' sector income.

Domestic Tourism Marketing and Promotion

Only one of the NTOs under survey, Canada, has domestic marketing and promotion as part of its overall mandate. [The situation has since changed with Australia, France and South Africa — see below — now quite heavily involved in domestic tourism marketing and promotional activities.] However, this statement needs to be qualified, as only New Zealand and Spain have absolutely no involvement in the sector at all. Even so, much of the brand/image promotion carried out by their respective NTOs has always been in part designed to raise awareness among consumer of tourism's importance to their national economies and, therefore, to ensure buy-in from the public.

Domestic tourism in Australia has until now been the responsibility of a separate body (see Chapter 5). However, following the implementation of the government's *White Paper* — which will result in becoming part of the new NTO (see Chapter 5), Tourism Australia — domestic marketing will become a key responsibility of the new NTO, but at a top level only. This means that Tourism Australia will not be responsible for promoting specific products, as this is the responsibility of the state and territorial organisations and local tourism authorities. Domestic tourism will receive an allocation of £7.5 million from Tourism Australia's budget in 2004.

The domestic tourism sector has been given little attention to date in South Africa, but this is set to change, with South African Tourism (SAT) pledged to play a more pro-active role in boosting domestic tourism demand. This follows the decision by the Department of Environmental Affairs & Tourism to include domestic tourism as part of SAT's mandate. It is currently inviting tenders to conduct research on the domestic market (Table 4.5).

Although Maison de la France has no official responsibility for domestic tourism promotion, it does carry out ad hoc campaigns on behalf of the Direction du Tourisme and the Secretary of State to stimulate tourism demand in the French market, particularly at times of crisis. In addition, Maison de la France carries out marketing and promotions in France on behalf of the country's overseas dominions and territories (DOM-TOM). The cost of the domestic tourism campaigns is not included in Maison de la France's budget. Funds are provided, as and when required, by the Secretary of State.

An estimated 6% of the NBTC's total budget in 2003, or 14% of its marketing budget — down from 17% in 2002 — was allocated to domestic tourism promotion, almost exclusively for national campaigns. Most thematic/product promotions in the domestic market are carried out at regional/local level. National campaigns are conducted at trade and consumer fairs and exhibitions and on TV. The NBTC's efforts in domestic tourism promotion will decline further over the next few years, and will be limited to general promotions. Marketing of products and regions will be the responsibility of the industry and provincial boards of tourism.

The situation in Ireland is rather confusing. Tourism Ireland is supposed to be the only body involved in international marketing, with responsibility for domestic marketing and promotion now in the hands of Fáilte Ireland and the NITB. Yet Fáilte Ireland has funding for niche marketing abroad and Tourism Ireland spent some £8.4 million of its budget in 2002 on domestic tourism marketing and promotions on behalf of Fáilte Ireland and the NITB. Fundamentally, much of this research is related to marketing and the development of host destinations.

Table 4.5: Details of NTO domestic marketing budgets where relevant (2003).

	Domestic marketing's share of total marketing budgets	
Country	**(% of total)**	**(£ mn)**
France	Negligible	Negligible
Ireland	33	9.2
Netherlands	14	1.4
Spain[a]	—	—
UK[b]	22	10.4
Australia[a]	—	—
Canada	8	3.8
New Zealand[a]	—	—
South Africa[a]	—	—

[a]NTOs have no responsibility (or did not have any in 2003) for domestic marketing and promotion. NTOs in both Australia and South Africa will now start to have responsibilities from 2004.
[b]2003/2004 budget to co-ordinate domestic marketing in England.
Source: The Moffat Centre and The Travel Business Partnership.

Business and MICE Tourism

The new approach of the ATC to business/MICE tourism is an interesting one. In the newly named Tourism Australia, a high-level Tourism Events division has been set up, together with the Tourism Events Australia-steering committee including representatives from the ATC, Australian Association of Convention & Visitor Bureaux (AACB), other industry organisations and the events industry.

The ATC co-ordinated a number of forums across Australia where the business tourism and MICE industry was invited to discuss and debate the contents of a discussion paper on the role of the new Tourism Events division.

The decision to set up Tourism Events Australia was based on a need to co-ordinate and expand the activities of this high-yield sector, which encompasses a diverse range of players, including industry associations, state and territorial governments, convention bureaux, major events corporations, Australian Government bodies and a wide range of industry operators.

On the event delivery side, the ATC maintains that co-operation and co-ordination are fundamental and generally work well. On the demand generation side, however, many parties currently act independently, although they are loosely co-ordinated by various events corporations and convention and visitors bureaux. In recent years, there has been increased business event marketing activity by the ATC and some joint initiatives such as Team Australia — an alliance between the convention and visitors bureaux and the ATC. The ATC has also signed an operating agreement with government agencies such as Austrade resulting in co-ordinated international marketing efforts, e.g. the Rugby Business Club Australia. However, as the Australian experience clearly shows, improved funding and a whole new government approach are required to ensure significant economic benefits.

The drivers of the business and major events industry are different from leisure tourism in a number of key aspects, including:

* Decision-making on timing and location is made by the organising units rather than by the individual participants;
* There is generally a long planning and lead time (although in the case of corporate business this lead time is decreasing);
* Event management is an essential capability;
* Clear business purpose/outcome is the primary reason for participants attending a business event.

There are natural synergies between business events and major events in terms of bidding expertise, Australian Government support, unified tourism industry support for bids, and logistical support (such as venues, service suppliers and hospitality) for event delivery. There are also some significant differences between business events and major events. These include:

* Major events are generally for public consumption and are not confined to a common interest group;
* Attendees pay for themselves or are hosted;
* Although major events attract significant overseas visitors, the majority of attendees are Australian residents;
* Business events are principally vocational and normally have a conference/meeting component.

The different ways of organising are seen as a first step towards better co-ordination of big events — and primarily business events — which will help avoid duplication and over-lapping of marketing efforts across the country. They will also provide the opportunity for a co-ordinated events branding strategy to be drawn up in consultation with all stakeholders.

Other Activities

A multitude of tasks   Although this would almost certainly not be typical of a larger cross-section of NTOs, most of those studied in the context of this survey are fortunate enough to be able to concentrate their activities on marketing and promotion. Maison de la France is one example, although its remit also encompasses research, co-operation in brand-ing development and all areas of new media (from development to e-marketing). Tourism Ireland also has a remit that is enviable because of its simplicity — on paper, at least. Apart from marketing and promotion, it owns and manages the Tourism Brand Ireland and its associated communications materials. In addition, the CTC's two main areas of business are marketing and sales and information provision, including research (Smith, 1999).

The Netherlands is more typical of NTOs in northern Europe — and especially the Nordic countries. There, the governments' progressive withdrawal from direct intervention in tourism matters (to a greater or lesser degree) has resulted in the respective NTOs assuming management tasks that, in other more traditional tourism support systems, are the responsibility of ministries/departments. But there are signs that the Dutch government has had a change of thinking, and the NBTC will in future be able to focus its efforts on international marketing and promotion, relinquishing its responsibilities in other tourism areas and notably product development.

Outsourcing tasks that are better handled by the private sector   The challenges for NTOs in responding to their evolving role is widely acknowledged by governments, the industry and academics (WTO, 2000; Henderson, 2004). In some countries, many tasks — notably quality control, product development, classification and labelling of hotels and ttractions, etc. — are now outsourced to independent bodies. In Ireland, for example, several functions previously carried out by Bord Fáilte, the former NTO of the Republic of Ireland — such as hotel classification and publications — were contracted out to the private sector in the late 1990s, and a 'Tidy Towns' scheme was transferred to the Department of Environment.

In addition, Bord Fáilte's role as administering agency for the Irish Government and the EU in the implementation of the EU Structural Funds' programmes and other European grant schemes was drastically reduced. Although Fáilte Ireland and the NITB have remained the first point of contact for applicants, the decisions on funding were devolved to independent bodies with private sector representatives.

The NBTC says that its effectiveness in terms of marketing has been impeded in recent years by its enforced focus on product development — a task that has now been taken away from the Dutch NTO.

The majority of NTOs interviewed on this subject claim that, to do their job effectively — i.e. to promote and market their countries as tourism destinations — they need to be spared the additional tasks, such as quality assurance, which are better handled by independent bodies. However, Tourism Ireland did point out, when interviewed on the subject of quality control, that it still has a responsibility to ensure its marketing messages stress the importance of quality — even if it is no longer its responsibility.

Stimulating tourism investment and supporting local (non-tourism) businesses   Time constraints have not permitted us to study the different responsibilities and activities of the NTOs in detail. However, one important trend in recent years — in fact, it emerged many years ago with NTOs such as Maison de la France and the Singapore Tourism Board — is the support and promotion of local businesses by NTOs. This is also increasingly linked to stimulating business development for the local industry and more generalised private sector support. All the NTOs surveyed are involved to a greater or lesser extent in promoting the business interests of local companies, even if the process is not formalised.

The objective is not to compete with the private sector, but rather to undertake pre-feasibility studies in new markets — studies which small, local firms could not undertake on their own — in order to provide guidance as to where new business opportunities exist.

Offices and Staff Counts

Correlation between number of offices and total budgets   Although Spain's NTO has the largest annual budget and the second-highest number of offices abroad, the correlation between office numbers and budgets is not as obvious as one might expect. Australia, for example, has the third-biggest budget of all the NTOs in the countries under survey. Yet it has adopted a policy of closing offices where they have not produced returns over the last few years. So it now only has 12 offices abroad — less than 40% of France's or Spain's count. And the situation is similar in Canada (Table 4.6).

Here again the definition and measurement of 'returns' becomes an issue. What is easier to understand is the increasing evidence of dynamic movement of overseas representation. Simply put, overseas representation is reduced in established or declining markets and grown in developing markets.

The following Table 4.7 provides a summary of the overseas offices of the eight NTOs under discussion, plus the UK. As a result of more stringent cost control, there has been a general trend for NTO representative offices abroad to share premises with other operations (for instance VisitBritain is taking space in British Council premises in some overseas locations) and to appoint General Sales Agents (GSAs) rather than establish and operate their own dedicated offices. Cost-cutting, shifting market potential and the trend towards shared premises has inevitably resulted in a number of NTO overseas office closures, with more planned. Recent closures include:

Canada: Offices in New Zealand, Singapore and Netherlands

Australia: Offices in Japan (Osaka), Denmark, Sweden, Philippines, Indonesia, South Africa and Latin America

France: Offices in the USA

Netherlands: Offices in Taiwan, Israel and Indonesia.

Ten years ago, the declared policy of many European NTOs was to cut back on numbers of home-based staff and expenditure in favour of a strengthened presence in the field. This is where they felt their activities were most effective. However, with the continued

Table 4.6: Offices and representation abroad of the NTOs under survey (2004).[a]

Country	Total (no.)	Outside own region (no.)	Outside own region[b] (% of total)
France[c]	32	17	53
Ireland[c]	13	3	23
Netherlands	15	6	40
Spain	31	11	35
UK	25	14	56
Australia	12	3	25
Canada	12	11	92
New Zealand	12	3	25
South Africa	9	9	100

Note: Includes general sales agents in some cases. Details as to the exact kind of representation are provided in the report under the country case studies.
[a]As at 1 January 2004.
[b]Own region = Europe for European countries, Asia Pacific for Australia, Americas for Canada and Africa/Middle East for South Africa.
[c]France is closing its Miami office end-March 2004.

Source: Respective NTAs and NTOs.

squeeze on budgets over the past few years, NTOs have increasingly been looking for ways of reducing numbers of offices abroad. In some cases — e.g. Netherlands — the trend has been to reduce the numbers of expatriate staff in favour of locally hired employees, in order to cut costs and improve communications with the local marketplace.

Finding the resources to tap traditional and emerging markets   The exact location of offices abroad is in principle a good indicator of which markets are priorities for the NTO, in terms of marketing and promotional efforts. However, it is important to note that some NTOs have cut back on offices in their key traditional markets so as to leave enough of their valuable resources for marketing and promotion in new, emerging markets.

Offices outside the NTOs' own regions account for between 23% (Ireland) and 100% (South Africa) of total foreign offices. Of the different European countries, France has by far the highest number of offices in long haul markets, followed by Spain, but they only represent 53% of their total office count.

There is an argument that countries with a lower share of long-haul arrivals and nights should actually be putting more effort — and investment — in long-haul markets to increase those shares.

As far as the non-European NTOs are concerned, the relatively low share of long-haul offices for Australia and New Zealand is perhaps surprising, given the importance of inter-regional tourism for the two destinations. But, in Australia's case, this relates to the poten-tial of intra-regional markets, which the ATC believes are a much more likely source of growth in the future. In addition, it is important to stress that the ATC's London office, for example, looks after several European source markets. In effect, it acts like several offices combined with a higher than average share of staff, including specialist staff. The ATC has increasingly opted for big hub operations which, it says, have better control of their respective markets and are more efficient in terms of ROI.

Tourism Australia (Europe) — A Case Study of an Overseas Representative Office

Tourism Australia (Europe) is a joint initiative between the ATC and the Australian State and Territory Tourist Organisations (STOs) that seeks to better align marketing activities and operations, improve effectiveness in marketing Australia overseas, and reduce duplication and overlap within the UK and European market.

The initiative, which was previously known under the working title of One Australia, is initially being implemented in the Europe market only. The regional office will be located in the ATC office in London. There will also be resources based in Frankfurt, Paris, Italy and Munich. As part of the agreement the ATC and STOs have agreed to a set of defined operating processes and guidelines, ensuring resources work to increase interest in Australia and provide core servicing and training to trade and retail partners.

They have also agreed to an aligned strategic approach to activities in market. The overall marketing strategy for Australia will be agreed by the ATC and STOs. States will continue to undertake marketing activities in the region, adding value to the overall strategy by being destination specialists. Each organisation will maintain control over its strategic marketing activities.

Tourism Australia (Europe) is expected to provide a number of benefits for the ATC, STOs and the tourism industry in Europe including:

- agreed strategy and direction for each market;
- increased operational synergies and scale benefits;
- increased penetration of distribution system which will reach more partners, more often;
- improved service to partners from a co-ordinated approach;
- increased ability to focus on new markets and niches;
- individuality and flexibility within the framework;
- increased market growth, product dispersal and development targeted to agreed segments.

The implementation phase for Tourism Australia (Europe) began in March 2004 and the new model was scheduled for operation by 1 July 2004.

Offices in Emerging Markets

Interviews with NTOs in the countries under survey and other countries — although by no means exhaustive — suggest that some of them will definitely go ahead and reduce numbers of offices in key markets, as they have been thinking of doing for some time, so as to have sufficient funds to open new offices in emerging markets.

Table 4.7: Summary of representation abroad.

Country	Australia	Canada	France	Ireland	Netherlands	NewZealand	South Africa	Spain	UK	Total
Argentina			x					x	x	3
Australia		x	x	x		x	x		x	6
Austria			x	xa				x	xc	4
Belgium/Luxembourg			x	x	x			x	x	5
Brazil			x					x	x	3
Canada	x		x	x	xa			x	x	5
China		x	xa		xb	x	x	x	xc	8
Czech Rep.					xa					1
Denmark			x	x				x	x	4
Dubai									x	1
Finland				x				x	xc	3
France		x		x	x		x	x	x	6
Germany	x	x		x	x		x	x	x	8
Hong Kong	x	x	xa				x	x	x	4
Hungary			xa							1
India			x			x			x	3
Ireland			x					x	x	2
Italy		x	x	x	x		x	x	x	7
Japan	x	x		xa	x	x	x	x	x	8

										Total
Korea									xc	1
Malaysia	x									1
Mexico	x		xa						x	3
Netherlands		x	x		x			x	x	5
New Zealand	x		xa					x		3
Norway								x	x	2
Poland		x				xa		x	xc	4
Portugal		xa						x	xc	3
Russia		x						x	xc	3
Singapore	x	x		x				x	x	5
South Africa		xa		xa				x	x	4
South Korea	x	xa		xa				x		4
Spain	x			x				x	x	4
Sweden	x	x		x				x	x	5
Switzerland		x		xa				x	x	4
Taiwan	x	x		x	x			xa		5
Thailand	x							x		2
UK	x	x	x	x	x		x	x	x	8
USA	x	x	x	x	x	x	x	x	x	9

x is the International office; xa the GSA: French offices shared with Air France; xb the consultancy offices; xc the representative offices.

The growing interest in China as a tourism source has prompted a number of the NTOs to think of cutting back spending, and possibly even staff and office numbers, in one or more of its existing key markets, in favour of increased effort in China. But most recognise that this may not be a wise move. A few years ago, the Austrian National Tourist Office cut back spending in Germany, its major market, to free up funds for marketing in Asia. Yet, it ended up losing more visitors and revenues from Germany than it gained from Asia.

One fairly new trend is the sharing of offices in emerging markets between NTOs. So far, only the Nordic countries have managed to operate such an alliance successfully, but others are likely to follow suit — especially given the high costs associated with opening new offices.

It is difficult to validate staff numbers ...   Staff employed abroad account for between 34% (the Netherlands and New Zealand) and 71% (France) of the NTOs' total staff counts. Spain appears to be very top-heavy in its headquarters(HQs) but — as indicated in the country case study — its administrative staff appear to be shared with other institutes/sub-directorates of the national tourism administration. The Netherlands' relatively high HQ staff count is due to the fact that it has responsibilities (or used to have) well beyond the remit of marketing and promotions (Table 4.8).

Information on the various functions of staff is included within the country case studies, but as an example:

At the ATC's HQ, the operation is divided into five areas: Marketing Development (40 staff dealing with a visiting journalist programme, brand development, advertising and design), Hemispheres (13 staff responsible for developing and implementing marketing

Table 4.8: Staff of the NTOs under survey (2003).

Country	Staff total (no.)	Staff at home (no.)	Staff abroad (no.)	Staff abroad (% of total)
France	285	83	202	71
Ireland[a]	147	52	95	65
Netherlands[b]	214	141	73	34
Spain	650	400	250	36
UK[c]	505	261	244	48
Australia[d]	228	108	120	53
Canada	159	96	63	40
New Zealand[d]	99	65	34	34
South Africa	NA	NA	NA	NA

[a]Tourism Ireland only (Fáilte Ireland and NITB not included).
[b]The NBTC will suffer a staff cut of about one-third at its HQ in 2004.
[c]UK information from 2003/2004 Budget in Corporate Plan.
[d]Includes temporary staff in their HQ (see respective country case studies).

Source: Respective NTAs and NTOs.

strategies), Organisation Development (9 staff), Public Affairs (6 staff) and Corporate Services (12 permanent plus 28 temporary/ freelance staff working on finance administration, IT and communications).

In the CTC, the 159 staff based in the Ottawa office are distributed between: marketing and sales (120 staff), research (12 staff), e-marketing (2 staff) and other activities (25 staff). The Tourism New Zealand staff based in New Zealand are divided between: corporate communications (7 staff), corporate services (8 staff), executive (6 staff), operations (8 staff), tourism development (9 staff) and marketing (27 staff). Comparison between each NTO is therefore difficult.

... let alone measure their effectiveness   Measuring the spend of each NTO per office and member of staff must be interpreted as a statistical exercise and not a meaningful assessment of the respective NTOs' cost-effectiveness. There are simply too many inconsistencies and unknowns — as detailed in the country case studies — for the exercise to be treated more seriously. Moreover, because of a lack of relevant information, it is not possible to break down marketing spend/budgets per marketing staff.

In terms of total spend per office, Canada is ahead of the field averaging £4.5 million total spending per office, followed by Australia with £3.7 million total spending per office. Canada also spends £340,000 of its total budget per member of staff, or £282,000 of its marketing budget. Australia spends £222,000 — or £177,000, respectively (Table 4.9).

Table 4.9: Budgeted spending by NTOs per office (abroad) and per member of staff (2002).[a]

Country	Total budget per office (£ mn)	Total budget per member of staff (£ '000)	Marketing budget per member of staff (£ '000)
France	1.1	127	93
Ireland[b]	2.4	215	134
Netherlands	1.5	105	51
Spain	1.8	85	51
UK	1.4	70	53
Australia[c]	3.7	222	155
Canada	4.5	340	282
New Zealand	1.4	171	137
South Africa	2.9	NA	NA

[a]2002 spending/budgets, but 2004 staff and office counts.
[b]Tourism Ireland only (Fáilte Ireland and the NITB not included).
[c]Only permanent staff numbers taken into account.

Source: Respective NTAs and NTOs.

Evaluating NTO Performance

A report published in 2003 by the World Tourism Organization and the European Travel Commission, entitled *Evaluating NTO Marketing Activities* (WTO and ETC, 2003) assesses the use and effectiveness of different methods of monitoring tourism and NTO performance. Some 82% of respondents — 46 NTOs of the 56 that responded to the questionnaire sent out as part of the survey — said they regularly conduct some kind of monitoring of promotional activity, and these included most of the big players. Spain was an exception. Of these, 21% use research consultancies and 42% Public Relations (PR) or advertising agencies, but the majority handle the research themselves.

Controlled conversion studies are the preferred methods of evaluation of the larger NTOs, since they generate Return On Investment (ROI) estimates. But a number of other methods are favoured. These include:

- assessing the number of articles generated from PR and media familiarisation trips plus advertising equivalent value and a formal assessment against objective and favourability of content;
- coupon return on print media advertising plus equivalent statistics for response to email or telephone numbers contained within advertisements;
- occasional use of advertising tracking studies;
- questionnaire-based evaluation of consumer characteristics and satisfaction;
- questionnaire-based evaluation of trade activities covering satisfaction with events and estimates of additional tourism revenues generated through the event;
- qualitative research in pre-testing advertisement effectiveness and
- continuous monitoring of 'macro' statistical data.

Of the NTOs covered in this study, Spain — as already indicated — carries out no real evaluation of performance, except that it has occasionally pre-tested advertising campaigns, including the latest worldwide consumer ad campaign, Spain Marks.

Australia says it has only really conducted one major study in an attempt to assess ROI — or, more to the point — the amount of visitor expenditure to every one dollar spent in marketing by the NTO. The study, which was conducted some years ago (Carmody), indicated a return of 13–16:1. But neither the ATC nor the government research team was totally convinced about the reliability of the methodology. And no further evaluations have been carried out since then.

Like all public sector and part-public sector enterprises in France, Maison de la France undergoes frequent controls and audits by the Inspection Générale du Tourisme. In addition, its activities are monitored by its Board of Directors and the Secretary of State for tourism. Evaluation criteria are based on the four performance indicators identified by the new Loi des Finances. These include success of its programmes and activities, the visibility of its marketing and its share/number of partners.

There are also plans to introduce more sophisticated indicators to evaluate the performance of offices abroad, notably to try to assess return on promotional spending. However, the plans are still being tested internally and there is no formal timetable for implementation. Meanwhile, Maison de la France believes that VisitBritain is probably the NTO with the most effective and sophisticated evaluation techniques — in Europe, at least — a message reiterated by Tourism Ireland, which recently decided against investing in a controlled conversion study because of the associated costs.

Canada, meanwhile, appears to have the most sophisticated evaluation methodologies of all the NTOs surveyed for this study. The CTC uses mainly controlled conversion studies, some of which are stimulated. However, unlike VisitBritain and the ATC, the CTC does not believe that it is possible to make an assumption across its whole mix of markets since the share of spending in each market is not stable. So it needs different ratios for different markets. In addition, these studies are expensive so it can only afford to carry them out in key markets.

In Conclusion — A Matter of the Right Balance

Government Intervention in Tourism …

Government involvement in tourism still varies considerably from one country to another. Yet even in the more *dirigiste* economies of the world, there have been signs of a pendulum swing over the past decade away from strong central government intervention to a more *laissez-faire* approach. Moreover, as already indicated, this pendulum swing has gained momentum in the last decade in line, not only with the squeeze on public sector budgets, but also the growing climate of liberalisation and privatisation and the political and economic shift to market-driven economies.

Despite some regional variations, current thinking even in the less-developed countries of the world is that while governments should be responsible for the development of tourism infrastructure, they should divest themselves of any interests they might have in, for example hotels and tourism services. In fact, their role should no longer be to intervene directly in the development of their country's tourism industry, but should be more that of a catalyst — stimulating market growth and supporting the private sector with fiscal and other incentives for investment.

… and Rationalisation of Responsibilities …

At the same time as this change in thinking, there has also been a rationalisation of government responsibilities and activities in the management of tourism, with a growing preference for the separation of marketing and promotional activities from policy and planning. The NTO is increasingly gaining autonomy and assuming full responsibility for marketing and promotion in partnership with provincial and local authorities and the private sector.

In countries with a high level of decentralisation, more and more activities — notably those impacting on local tourism development and industry controls — have become the responsibility of provincial and local authorities, or have even been outsourced to independent bodies. This has enhanced central government's role as a unifying force, co-ordinating the efforts of all the different players in the fragmented industry.

... But Some Governments Have Maybe Gone Too Far

It should be said that not many governments have reduced their involvement in tourism to the extent that perhaps some of the European governments have — notably the Dutch, the Belgian and Nordics. This seems to put an additional — and unwelcome — burden on the NTOs, which then have to take over management tasks that are outside their traditional remit.

The growing recognition of tourism's contribution to national economies — whether in terms of foreign exchange, employment or capital investment — adds weight to arguments in favour of governments' continued involvement in tourism. As an example, they can foster the growth of small- and medium-sized enterprises (SMEs) and poorer regions of their countries, which offer little other potential for economic growth in the short to medium term.

However, the rationale for governments' involvement in promotion and marketing is harder to justify. Government expenditure is increasingly open to scrutiny and responsibility for the use of public funds in many countries dictates that government actions meet the criteria of visibility, accountability and control. This largely explains why performance measurement and evaluation are becoming increasingly important.

Uneven Spread of Benefits If the Private Sector is in Control

Experience at provincial and local level — France and the UK are good examples of this — has also shown that when the private sector is totally responsible for promotion and marketing, the big industry players tend to dominate, with the result that the benefits are unevenly spread. Moreover, it is not so easy to generate interest nowadays from leading industry players. Airlines and hotel groups do not have only the interests of their home countries at heart. And, as a result of the current trends towards globalisation and concentration of the travel and tourism industry, even travel agency and tour-operating groups are increasingly becoming multi-national concerns.

Some industry observers also believe that the cost of private sector funding of local, regional or national promotion and marketing is eventually passed on to the consumer in the form of higher prices at hotels and restaurants or higher car rental rates, etc.

Another strong argument expressed by governments interviewed for the purposes of this survey is that if national tourism promotion and marketing were left entirely to the private sector, it could result in the unbalanced development of infrastructure and market expansion, with the risk of growing congestion and increased pressure on environmental resources.

Tourism is multi-disciplinary in nature and the industry affects, and is affected by, many other sectors of the national economy. It therefore makes sense for governments to maintain their involvement in the sector and ensure intra-governmental links between National Tourism Administrations (NTAs) and other ministries and government departments.

Too Many Ongoing Changes for Any Meaningful Assessment

Given the many changes that have already taken place over the past year or two in the organisation of tourism in the countries under survey — not to mention ongoing changes and those expected to be implemented in 2004 or soon after — it has been very difficult to make any meaningful assessment of the cost-effectiveness of the different NTOs under survey, or of their respective national tourism support systems.

Clearly, the absence of consistent, comparable tourism satellite account data have also been a handicap in this respect.

Reviews and Restructuring

As we initially suspected, increasing concerns over the need to introduce budget cuts have resulted in an almost continuous restructuring of some governments' and their respective NTOs' roles and activities in tourism. After many years of no or limited change, even France and Spain are likely to undergo a significant restructuring in the foreseeable future.

The Case Studies

The following chapters present the individual case studies of each of the eight NTOs. The analysis for each country is divided into five sections:

- Key facts;
- Recent tourism performance;
- Organisation of tourism;
- The NTO;
  - The NTOs are considered individually in alphabetical order by country and each section focuses on the following main areas;
    - Structure;
    - Role and activities (including marketing);
    - Staff and offices;
    - Resources and funding;
    - Additional localised case study where appropriate;
    - Additional information is also included where considered appropriate;
- Key lessons from each country.

The cases are followed by our perspectives on lessons from such a benchmarking exercise.

.

Chapter 5

Australia

Australia's Recent Tourism Performance

Inbound Tourism Trends

International tourism to Australia peaked in 2000 — the year of the highly successful Summer Olympic Games in Sydney — when Australia attracted 4.9 million visitor arrivals (VF, or total arrivals including same-day visitors). In the shadow of 11 September and the collapse of the country's second-biggest airline Ansett, the arrivals trend since then (i.e. to end-2003) has been negative (Table 5.1).

The past three years have produced even greater challenges for Australia. It used to be seen as a safe destination, relatively isolated from the impact of terrorism and other negative events occurring beyond its borders. But the combination of the terrorist attacks in Bali, the war in Iraq and the SARS outbreak propelled the country into the global arena. Instead of a continued boom in tourism growth forecast for the post-Olympics period, Australia has suffered three years of declines in arrivals — albeit much more modest decline than for some of its competitors.

In 2001, international visitor arrivals fell by 1.5% on 2000's level. 2002's arrivals stagnated (at −0.3%) and preliminary figures for 2003 point to a further 2% decline to 4.7 million. Not surprisingly, the first five months of 2003 were the most disappointing, with arrivals down 8.2% as a result of SARS and the Iraq war. Overnight volume changed little over the period 2000–2002, although data from the Bureau of Tourism Research (BTR) shows that it declined by around 4% in fiscal 2002/2003. However, anecdotal evidence suggests that growth in the second half of 2003 was positive, reducing the negative trend (Table 5.2).

Key Markets

Major markets, in terms of arrivals, are New Zealand (accounting for 16% of the market in 2002), Japan (15%) and the UK (13%), with the USA a distant fourth (9%).

In terms of expenditure, however, the ranking is different, with the UK in number one position generating 15% of total spending by international visitors in 2002, according to the BTR. The USA was ranked second with a share of 11.9%, followed by New Zealand and Japan with around 8% each.

Another big spender for Australia is China, which, in 2002, ranked sixth in terms of both spending and arrivals (Table 5.3).

Table 5.1: Australia — key facts, 2002.

Population	19.5 mn
GDP	£265.9 bn
International arrivals (TF)	4.8 mn
International overnights (total)	127.7 mn
Average length of stay (nights)	26.6
International arrivals per inhabitant	0.2
Domestic overnight trips (FY 2002/2003)	75.2 mn
Domestic overnights (total)	302.3 mn
Average length of stay (nights)	4.0
Domestic day trips	143.3 mn
Domestic spending (same-day and overnight travel)	£19.1 bn
International receipts (FY 2001/2002)	£4.1 bn
as a % of GDP	1.6%
per tourist arrival	£861
per overnight	£33
per inhabitant	£212
Tourism's total (direct) contribution to GDP	4.5%
Tourism's contribution (direct and indirect) to GDP	8.9%
WTTC estimate (for T&T industry GDP)	5.1%
NTO's total tourism budget (FY 2001/2002)	£44.3 mn (0.0)
State contribution (% share)	£35.5 mn (80.1%)
Marketing budget (% share of total budget)	£35.4 mn (80.0%)
Rate of exchange	£1 = A$ 2.76

Table 5.2: International visitor arrivals and receipts, 2000–2003.

Year	Arrivals ('000)	% annual change	Receipts[a] (£ bn)	% annual change[a]
2000	4,931	NA	3.79	NA
2001	4,856	−1.5	3.45	9.6
2002	4,841	−0.3	4.12	5.4
2003[b]	4,744	−2.0	4.29	−4.2

[a]Receipts are for FYs ended 30 June — % annual change in A$s.
[b]Provisional.
Sources: BTR and ATC.

Preliminary Results for 2003

Preliminary results for 2003 point to declines for the majority of Australia's major source markets. But a few stand out as strong performers — most notably the UK, which alone of Australia's traditional major source markets has continued to grow throughout this difficult

Table 5.3: Australia's leading international markets, 2000–2002 ('000).

Market	2000	2001	2002	2002 (% share)
New Zealand	817	815	790	16.3
Japan	721	674	715	14.8
UK	580	616	641	13.2
USA	488	446	434	9.0
Singapore	286	296	287	5.9
China	120	158	190	3.9
South Korea	157	176	190	3.9
Malaysia	152	149	159	3.3
Hong Kong	154	154	151	3.1
Germany	143	148	135	2.8
Taiwan	134	110	97	2.0
Canada	88	93	91	1.9
Indonesia	98	98	89	1.8
Thailand	73	80	83	1.7
Netherlands	61	57	53	1.1
South Africa	60	55	51	1.1
France	57	50	50	1.0
Ireland	46	52	48	1.0
India	41	48	45	0.9
Italy	58	43	43	0.9
Total (incl. other)[a]	4,931	4,856	4,841	100.0

[a]Visitor arrivals (i.e. including same-day visitors) at frontiers.
Sources: BTR and ATC.

period. Visitor arrivals from the UK increased by 10% in 2000, by 6% in 2001, 4% in 2002 and by an estimated 5% increase in 2003 to 672,800 visits. In the year when British enthusiasm for the Rugby World Cup generated additional travel to Australia, the UK overtook Japan (which produced 627,700 arrivals last year) to become the destination's second-largest source market.

Among Australia's other key long-haul markets, the USA decreased by 3% to 422,100 — the fourth consecutive year of decline for this crucial high-yield market. France increased by 4%, but this followed a 13% decline in 2001 and a 1% fall in 2002. Germany, too, grew by 2% in 2003, but this again followed a 9% decrease in 2002. Most other European source countries recorded declines.

The performance of Asia in 2003 was generally dismal. Japan fell 12%, and there were also declines for China (−7%), Singapore (−12%), Taiwan (−10%), Thailand (−11%) and Malaysia (−2%). By far the best performing Asian market in 2003 was South Korea, which increased by 9%. This market has been increasing year on year since its recovery from the Asian economic crisis in the late 1990s. South Korean arrivals increased by 45% in 2000, by 12% in 2001 and 8% in 2002. Also encouraging for Australia was a turnaround in the Indonesian market last year — up 1% after a 9% decline in 2002.

In addition, there was growth from New Zealand. After a 3% decline in 2002, arrivals from New Zealand rose 6% to 839,100 — thereby increasing its market share to 18%.

Purpose of Visit

Holiday travel dominates Australia's inbound tourism, generating 55% of all arrivals in 2000, 2001 and 2002. The share of VFR is around 20% (it declined by one percentage point in 2002). Business arrivals account for some 15%, while educational/study tourism — a sector that is growing in importance following aggressive marketing — increased its share from 4% in 2000 to 6% in 2002 (Table 5.4).

Domestic Tourism

The Australian Tourism Satellite Account (ATSA) shows that domestic tourism accounted for 76% of tourism consumption in Australia in the fiscal 2001/2002 (ended 30 June 2002). In terms of number of trips and nights, the sector has stagnated over the past five years, according to the National Visitor Survey — with 73 million overnight domestic trips in 1998 and 75.3 million in 2002. Domestic visitor nights totalled 293.5 million in 1998 and 290.7 million in 2002.

In the first six months of 2003, Australians took nearly 28 million overnight trips — a slight fall on the number taken in the first half of 2002.

Tourism's Economic Contribution

Tourism is Australia's fourth largest industry and a leading services exporter, with many regions of the country showing a growing dependence on the industry for the generation of business activity and jobs. The latest available data from Australia's Tourism Satellite Account (TSA) show that the industry directly contributed 4.5% of GDP in 2001/2002 — down from 4.8% in 2000/2001. This was attributed to the strong growth of the overall national economy.

Total tourism consumption was £25.7 billion — an increase of 22% on 1997/1998's level (in A$s), but a fall of 0.7% on 2000/2001 — of which 24% came from international tourism.

The industry was directly responsible for employing 549,000 people, or 6% of total employment in Australia, and accounted for 11.2% of total export earnings, or £6.2 billion — higher than exports of coal and iron, steel and non-ferrous metals.

Table 5.4: International tourist arrivals in Australia by purpose of visit, 2000–2002 ('000).

Year	Holiday	VFR	Business	Education	Other
2000	2,517	929	661	180	280
2001	2,416	923	632	213	245
2002	2,446	853	659	262	243

Source: BTR.

Current Forecasts

Australia's Tourism Forecasting Council believes that international arrivals will pick up in the coming months in line with the strengthening of the US, Japanese and European economies. The Australian Tourist Commission (ATC) points to strong growth in December 2003 in the US market, and is encouraged by the recovery from New Zealand, France and Germany, despite the problems of 2003.

Growth from China, which was severely impacted by the SARS crisis, is expected to continue on its pre-SARS rapid upward path — Chinese arrivals in December 2003 were 21% higher than in December 2002. India also expanded rapidly in December 2003 as cricket fans followed their team to Australia — and the ATC is hopeful that this promising emerging market will continue to grow in 2004. Barring any further disasters in the international arena, the ATC also expects 2004 to see a steady recovery from most of its Asian markets.

On the negative side, aviation capacity continues to be an issue on some routes at certain times of the year, particularly between Australia and North America. But domestically, positive developments with the continued expansion of low-fare/low-cost carriers should further improve Australia's attractiveness as an international visitor destination, facilitating visitor dispersion to regions.

However, there is some concern as to the impact of the sharp appreciation of the Australian dollar against the US currency. This partly explains the new emphasis within the industry and government on enhancing and communicating the quality of the Australian tourism product.

Longer term, forecasts from the Tourism Forecasting Council are fairly bullish, with an average annual growth of 4.8% projected over the coming decade. The best growth is expected to come from Asia (+6.3% per annum), ahead of Europe (+4.2%) and North America (+3.5%).

Organisation of Tourism in Australia

Australia's National Tourism Organisation (NTO) is the ATC, a government statutory authority (similar to the crown corporation status of the Canadian Tourism Commission), which allows it to operate as a separate entity to the federal government. It was established in 1967 to promote Australia as an international tourism destination. It is funded largely by the Australian Federal Government and reports directly to the Minister of Small Business and Tourism within the Commonwealth Department of Industry, Tourism and Resources (DITR).

Australia's basic tourism support system (Figure 5.1) has existed for over a decade, and is now about to change, following the publication of a government *White Paper* in November 2003. This was drawn up by the DITR in consultation with the State and Territorial Tourism Organisations and the industry through the many industry associations and advocacy bodies. These changes are in the process of being implemented and many details are still being worked out. However, it is useful to look at the existing framework to help understand what broad changes are being made, the reasons for these changes, and what form the new structure is most likely to take.

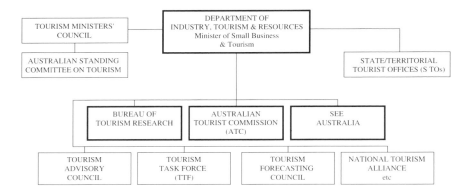

Figure 5.1: Structure of the Australian tourism support system. Note: Please see text for additional consultative and advocacy bodies.

Commonwealth Department of Industry, Tourism and Resources

Tourism in Australia is now the responsibility of the DITR. this has not always been the case, however. In the mid-1990s, the ministry responsible for tourism was that of Tourism, Communication & the Arts and tourism was then moved to the Department of Industry, Science and Resources — alongside sport — before the latter was changed to the Department of Industry, Tourism and Resources in 2002. The department has two ministers — the Minister of Industry Tourism and Resources, who sits in the Cabinet, the key decision-making body of the federal government, thereby ensuring that tourism is represented at the highest level of government. He is supported by a junior Minister for Small Business and Tourism, currently Joe Hockey.

Hockey, a member of John Howard's National Coalition party, is a firm supporter of tourism and has done much to ensure that it has a high profile in government.

The DITR is directly involved in a wide range of tourism matters, including bilateral tourism relations with other countries (e.g. the approved destination status (ADS) negotiations with China), visas and passenger processing, transport and security, taxation and assistance, education and training, industry standards and regulation, and regional and niche tourism development. It is also responsible for negotiations with the World Tourism Organisation regarding its recent renewal of membership — an organisation from which it withdrew in 1989.

Within the DITR's tourism division are the Tourism Market Access Group, the Tourism Business Development Group, the Tourism Strategy Group and the BTR (see below).

In the fiscal 2002/2003, following the downturn in visitor arrivals, the DITR implemented a National Response Plan in conjunction with Australia's states and territories. This *Green Paper* on tourism development has in turn led to the development of a new medium- to long-term tourism strategy for Australia's tourism industry — published as a *White Paper* in November 2003.

Other DITR activities in 2002/2003, which illustrate the scope of the department's tourism involvement, include a range of regional and niche tourism initiatives. One initiative was to increase Japanese and Chinese tourism, for instance, and funding was also provided for the development of wine tourism over a three-year period starting in 2002/2003. The DITR established a Major Events Co-ordination Unit — to facilitate the Rugby World Cup and other large-scale events — and gave policy advice and support to help advance indigenous tourism.

The DITR also worked on issues such as air services liberalisation, land transport development, and the Restaurant and Catering Industry Action Agenda in 2002/2003. Tourism accreditation, and strategies to improve Australian tourism standards are the remit of the DITR rather than the ATC, and it is concerned with action that will improve tourism product quality such as the recent move to develop a national registration system for tour guides and an associated code of conduct.

In addition to funding the ATC (see Table 5.5), the DITR commits government funds to tourism through its regional development and business assistance programmes. In 2002/2003, the Australian Federal Government gave around £18.9 million for tourism over and above its contribution to funding of the ATC — much of it channelled through the DITR — or a total of £58.3 million.

National Tourism Accreditation Programme

As an initiative of the *Tourism White Paper*, the Australian Government announced in mid-February that it would provide £0.8 million towards setting up a national tourism accreditation programme. The funding, to be directed at developing a national framework for voluntary tourism accreditation, will be available over two years from 1 July 2004, after which the industry will take over the financing.

Table 5.5: Direct tourism-related spending by the Australian Government, 2002/2003.

Funding activity	(£ mn)	Government agency
ATC	39.4	DITR
Export market development grants	6.7	Austrade
Regional tourism projects	3.5	DITR
See Australia	0.8	DITR
Bureau of Tourism Research	6.8	DITR
Co-operative Research Centre for Sustainable Tourism (*crc*Tourism)[a]	1.2	Department of Education, Science & Training
Australian Bureau of Statistics	0.8	Australian Bureau of Statistics
Conservation of rural and historic hotels	1.6	Department of Environment Heritage
Tourism policy	3.5	DITR
Total	58.3	—

[a]In future, it will be known as Sustainable Tourism CRC.
Source: White Paper, November 2003.

The system will help lift industry standards by setting up benchmarks for business practices that can be adopted by all tourism industry sectors and across all categories of product. Australia's competitors overseas, such as New Zealand with its Qualmark brand, actively sell their brand and product in the market using national accreditation programmes. The reality is that Australia will never be the cheapest or closest destination for most tourism markets so, according to Minister Hockey, 'Australia must compete on increasingly important intangibles like quality, value, consumer expectations and visitor satisfaction'.

The new National Tourism Accreditation Working Group (NTAWG), drawing on a membership of 20 industry representatives, is now developing an effective, sustainable accreditation framework for implementation.

'For industry to embrace accreditation,' said Hockey, 'benefits must exceed compliance costs. Key benefits are likely to include more efficient and effective business practices, marketing leverage through the quality mark or brand recognition, and preferential access to national parks and other protected areas due to better environmental management standards.'

Mr Hockey said a 'big-ticket' item, particularly for small businesses, would be access to better or cheaper insurance due to superior risk-management practices of accredited businesses.

Co-ordination with Australia's States and Territories

Australia's federal system of government, with powers distributed between the national government and the governments of the country's states and territories, enables each state and territory to develop its own tourism authorities and organisations.

Australia's six states — Western Australia, South Australia, New South Wales, Victoria, Queensland and Tasmania — and the Northern Territories and Australian Capital Territory, each have their own tourism boards, tourism ministers, strategies, marketing and promotion programmes and overseas representation. The tiny, sparsely populated Norfolk Island, Australia's third territory, also has its own independent tourism organisation, but obviously on a much smaller scale.

The need for liaison and co-ordination between the State and Territory Tourism Organisations (STOs) and the tourism regions within them, and the NTO has long been a key concern of the central tourism authorities, and various attempts to tackle the situation are already in place. Nonetheless, improved central/STO/regional co-ordination remains a key strategy in the new government *White Paper*.

Bureau of Tourism Research

The BTR is a non-statutory, inter-governmental agency, funded jointly by the federal government and the STOs and located, for administrative purposes, within the DITR. For policy matters and use of its core budget, the BTR reports directly to the Minister for Small Business and Tourism and to the Tourism Ministers Council (TMC). Its annual budget is around £1.8 million (with federal government funds supplying roughly half of this), and it has a staff of around 20.

The BTR's mission is 'to provide independent, accurate, timely and strategically relevant statistics and analyses to the industry, the government and community at large'. Its core activities are its two major travel surveys — the *International Visitor Survey* and the *National Visitor Survey* — as well as its analytical and forecasting work, which includes forecasts for the Tourism Forecasting Council (see below). It is a cost-recovery operation, but releases useful basic statistics free of charge on its website.

The BTR works fairly closely with the national statistics agency, the Australian Bureau of Statistics (ABS), especially in the area of research into tourism's economic importance — e.g. for the ATSA. The ATC and See Australia (see below) are also active in research — the ATC within its Market Development division. Although most of this focuses on consumer research and on market insights and product viability — so there is no real overlap — one of the reasons the tourism *Green Paper* was produced by government was to try to minimise the number of different bodies involved in research and other key areas.

According to the ABS, total R&D spend with a tourism objective is estimated at £7.7 million a year. This is split across business (£3.8 million), universities (£3.4 million), Commonwealth agencies (£0.4 million) and state government agencies (£39,370).

Tourism Forecasting Council

Established in 1993, the Tourism Forecasting Council (TFC) is a high-profile body that provides forecasts of activity across all tourism sectors — inbound and outbound — to the federal government, STOs and international and domestic tourism investors and operators. The council's membership is drawn from both the public and private sectors.

There are eight members of the TFC's Observer Organisation and ten members of a Technical Committee that assesses the forecasts, recommending adjustments if necessary, before they are considered by the TFC. The BTR manages the forecasting unit and chairs and provides secretariat support to its technical committee. This will clearly change once the *White Paper* is fully implemented and both the BTR and the TFC come under Tourism Australia.

See Australia

Traditionally, little emphasis has been placed on the promotion of domestic tourism, which was growing at less than 1% a year in the 1990s. It was not until 1999 that a separate body, See Australia, funded by the federal government, was established to boost the domestic sector.

Under the aegis of the DITR, See Australia is guided by a board of directors made up from representatives of the federal government, the STOs and the Tourism Task Force (TTF) (see below). Private sector sponsors for See Australia initiatives include airlines, hotel groups, online agents, car-hire companies and credit card companies, etc.

See Australia's remit was to develop and implement strategies to encourage Australians to travel more in their own country, and make it easier for them to find information to book and pay for Australian holidays. A public–private sector campaign was created — with sponsors such as MasterCard International, AAA Tourism, Accor Asia Pacific, Avis, Best Western, Lastminute.com, Qantas, travel.com.au and Trendwest — to attempt to change attitudes and behaviours towards holidays, and overcome barriers to domestic tourism growth.

These barriers include job insecurity, time poverty, the forgotten role and value of holidays in terms of re-energising, etc. The backbone of the initiative is research on

Australians' decision-making processes, and the needs and requirements for national tourism experiences.

In May 2003, £2.8 million was allocated to boost domestic tourism and counter the international downturn following SARS and the Iraq war. This initiative was a result of See Australia research, which showed that 22% of Australians were changing their holiday plans for the next 12 months — just as they did after 11 September — or even deferring their holidays altogether. See Australia also ran a campaign to encourage an estimated 100,000 Australians to travel interstate to watch World Cup matches — a £39.4 million boost for the economy.

Note: Following the implementation of the government's *White Paper*, domestic marketing will become a key responsibility of the new NTO, Tourism Australia, but at a top level only — i.e. it will not be responsible for promoting specific products, as this is the responsibility of STOs and regional tourism authorities. Domestic tourism will receive a budget allocation of £7.5 million in 2004.

Consultative and Other Related Bodies

The TMC, set up in 1959, is the highest-level co-ordination body, comprising portfolio ministers from the federal government, from the six states and two territories (currently Australia Capital Territory and Northern Territories) and from New Zealand, with Norfolk Island and Papua New Guinea holding observer status. The TMC's main role is to facilitate consultation and policy co-ordination between members.

Each ministerial council operates in conjunction with a standing committee. The Australian Standing Committee on Tourism (ASCOT) — founded in 1976 — which meets twice a year, is the forum for senior officials to discuss issues at an operational level. It comprises representatives from relevant ministers' departments, from the ATC and the BTR. Decisions are taken by ASCOT and then passed to the TMC for consideration.

The TMC meets once a year, or more frequently if necessary, and the chair rotates annually. The DITR provides the secretariat for the TMC and briefs the ministers and senior officers who participate in ASCOT.

Note: A TMC meeting was scheduled for 13 February to commence discussions on the development of a new inter-governmental agreement on tourism. This is intended to clarify roles and responsibilities and provide a basis for improved co-ordination between the federal and state and territory governments. The agreement will be developed in consultation with all government representatives.

National Tourism Alliance

The National Tourism Alliance (NTA) was formed to create unity within the tourism industry through a common, cohesive platform and a single voice to federal government. Its role is to co-ordinate policy and representation to the government on behalf of the Australian tourism industry. Membership of the NTA is open to national industry associations and state tourism industry councils. Members represent over 90% of tourism industry operators covering accommodation, airlines, car touring, inbound tourism, retail travel agencies, business tourism, the meetings, incentives, conference and exhibition tourism (MICE) sector, farm and country tourism, youth hostels, retail, adventure operators and the caravan and camping industry.

Tourism Task Force

TTF Australia is the peak industry group developing tourism and infrastructure. A non-political, independent body, it represents the chief executives of 200 of the most prestigious investors, operators, regulators and developers in Australia's tourism, transport and infrastructure industries. It was established in 1989 during the pilot's strike, to act as an advocate for its members to federal, state and local governments. Since then, it has fought for its members' interests during and after every crisis that has faced the industry including, for instance, the Asian financial crisis, 11 September and the Ansett collapse, SARS and the Iraq war.

The TTF has been one of the most aggressive organisations in terms of lobbying on behalf of the ATC for increased marketing funding over the past decade. It also claims to have been a driving force behind the establishment of See Australia, and it has been one of the main proponents for structural reform to reduce the duplication of federal, state and local agencies. The TTF has an executive staff of 17 people, and a board of 16 (including its chairman and three deputies).

Australian Tourism Export Council (ATEC)

ATEC represents the interests of over 1000 tourism export companies throughout Australia and has a proven history of building better business opportunities for Australia's tourism industry. Formed in 1972 as the Australian Incoming Tour Operators Association (ITOA), it later became the Inbound Tour Operators Association and carried the name ITOA until 2000.

In recognition of the selling of Australia overseas and the £6.7 billion contribution its industry members make to the nation's export economy, the operating name was changed to the ATEC in late 2000. ATEC is now one of the major tourism industry associations and has an interface with federal and state governments and other industry bodies such as the ATC.

Membership of ATEC comprises over 150 inbound tour operators who collate, contract, book, administer and service fully independent travellers (FIT), group, incentive, conference and cruise ship business around Australia. It also represents Australian tourism product suppliers including accommodation providers, tour companies, attractions, airlines, cruise lines, transport, food and beverage outlets and tourism services. ATEC's primary role is to optimise the business success of members so that the resulting economic and social impact of tourism exports for Australians is maximised.

There are a number of other consultative and advocacy bodies that, although not directly involved in tourism, work closely with the DITR and the ATC. These include Austrade and Invest Australia — which respectively focus on trade and investment facilitation — Environment Australia and *crc*Tourism (now being renamed Sustainable Tourism CRC).

The following three DITR-initiated advisory groups should also be mentioned:

The ADS Joint Monitoring Group meets to discuss issues relevant to the development of the China inbound market and, especially, the leisure sector stimulated by the country's ADS. The group includes the federal government's Department of Immigration and Multi-cultural and Indigenous Affairs, the DITR, the ATC, ATEC, Tourism Victoria and ADS operators.

The Japan–Australia Advisory Group, which was the first tourism-related advisory group to be set up, includes the highest level of representation from travel agents (Japan Travel Bureau, etc.) and trade organisations.

The Indigenous Tourism Leadership Group is supporting the bid to develop this unique sector of Australian tourism, and is made up of individuals experienced and involved in the sector. The ATC plays a consultative role.

Background to the White Paper

The major catalyst for structural and strategic change in the way Australia's tourism is marketed and promoted has been the disappointing performance of the industry since the 2000 Summer Olympics. Arrivals, nights and receipts have been below target since 2001. However, the change in strategic direction was also stimulated by a change in CEO at the ATC.

The former CEO, John Morse, was credited with masterminding the huge publicity for tourism before and during Australia's hosting of the Olympics. Under his leadership, the ATC successfully leveraged the Olympics to put Australia on the world tourism map, thereby generating billions of dollars in free PR in the world's leading media. His successor, though no less dynamic, has adopted what is seen as a much more business-like approach to sustainable tourism development.

The tourism *Green Paper*, developed in response to pressure from the ATC and industry — and in consultation with all stakeholders — canvassed the major issues for developing a medium- to long-term strategy for Australia's tourism. It had five key themes:

- diversification of Australia from a travel destination into a lifetime experience;
- diversification of the Australian tourism product;
- focus on business yield and niche markets;
- enhancing business profitability to better position the industry against volatility and global uncertainty; and
- improving asset utilisation and co-ordination across public and private sectors.

The resulting *White Paper*, the culmination of a process characterised by an unprecedented level of industry and government partnership, concluded that the existing tourism structure was neither strategic nor responsive enough. Brand Australia, it said, is not perceived as a sufficiently unique brand, and marketing to the domestic sector is not fully integrated into the general marketing effort. It is felt that regional dispersal of international and domestic tourism is uneven.

The industry also needs improved forecasts — especially at a regional level — and better relationships between the public and private sectors and between federal and regional bodies. As already noted, the *White Paper* shows that there is continuing concern over the duplication of efforts, especially in the areas of marketing and research, by the ATC and STOs, as well as over the large number of bodies — from both the public and private sectors — acting as independent lobbyists in the tourism sector. A simpler structure is critical to the effectiveness of the different players, the report noted.

Unlike past tourism strategies, the new *White Paper* sets clear targets and goals and is matched with funding. It recognises the importance of visitor yield over visitor numbers.

Niche-market tourism programmes will be developed in a range of areas, such as — but not limited to — food and wine tourism, study tourism, caravanning and business tourism.

The *White Paper* also sets out a clear strategy to increase domestic tourism, and this will stimulate growth in regional areas that rely heavily on tourism for their economic development.

The *Tourism White Paper* took almost two years to develop. Implementation kicked off in early 2004, starting with increased international marketing of Australia as a destination to capitalise on the goodwill and media exposure generated by the Rugby World Cup. It should be completed by the middle of this year.

Tourism Australia and the New Tourism Support System

Structurally, the major change resulting from the *White Paper* will be the creation of a new body, Tourism Australia, which will incorporate the ATC, See Australia and the two research bodies, the BTR and the TFC, under one umbrella. The rationale behind this major upheaval is to better harness all the skills and knowledge of the four organisations.

Also important is the move to bring domestic tourism, which is currently not in the ATC's remit, into the new Tourism Australia, so that marketing the sector will become a key responsibility, albeit at a top level only. Specific product marketing will remain the responsibility of the STOs and regional tourism authorities.

The Australian Government will provide a funding package of £92.5 million over four and a half years to boost Australian tourism. Funding will commence in the first quarter of 2004.

Structural reform and funding Tourism Australia will be responsible for international marketing, including the launch of a revitalised Brand Australia. It will receive an additional £47 million over four and a half years to attract high-yield international tourists to Australia. This will bring the total international marketing spend to around £207 million by July 2008.

The new NTO will also include two new units — Tourism Events Australia and Tourism Research Australia. Tourism Events Australia will focus on branding and promoting Australia as a business and events destination, providing assistance to state and territory event agencies. It will also develop a National Events Calendar. Branding will take a more distinctly Australian approach than the previous, more generic campaigns and will feature regional Australia.

Tourism Research Australia will have a significant capacity to address identified gaps in tourism research and statistics and more effectively prioritise funding for tourism research. It will provide more comprehensive International and National Visitor Surveys, and will provide an information dissemination service, including a tourism statistics regional advisory service. Additionally, it will undertake new research into yield and niche markets, with a focus on tourism impacts in regional Australia.

Tourism Research Australia will also focus on educating investor markets by providing up-to-the-minute analysis and forecasting information. The DITR will work with the ABS to improve tourism-related data collections. These include continued production of the ATSA and expansion of the *Survey of Tourism Accommodation.*

Domestic tourism In a significant boost to regional tourism, £17.9 million will be provided over four and a half years to See Australia, as part of Tourism Australia, to help stimulate growth in domestic tourism.

In addition to marketing campaigns to encourage more Australians to holiday at home, regional Australia will benefit from a new initiative that will better identify high-yield niche markets. Funding under this initiative will be provided on a matching basis from individual regions that enter into partnerships with See Australia, and will reinforce the national, state and territory domestic marketing efforts.

Australian Tourism Development Programme   To encourage the development of tourism across Australia, particularly in regional areas, funding for a new programme will be provided — the Australian Tourism Development Programme. This will build on the successful Regional Tourism Programme by targeting innovative projects that enhance tourism products in regional and metropolitan destinations.

Indigenous Tourism Business Ready Programme   The Australian Government will create an Indigenous Tourism Business Ready Programme to assist individuals or new businesses to develop a viable indigenous tourism product or business. The programme will encourage the development of management skills, business and strategic plans, market research, and an understanding of tourism distribution networks and commercial practices in the tourism industry.

Tourism in protected areas   The Australian Government will provide funding to boost nature-based tourism for the economic benefit of local communities, while increasing capacity to protect and conserve the environment for the future. The close co-operation of states, territories and industry will be sought.

Accreditation   To ensure international and domestic tourist expectations are met, the Australian Government will provide one-off assistance to industry to establish an effective national, voluntary accreditation system. A working group comprising industry, states and territories will assist the government to develop this national system.

Strengthening relationships   The Australian Government is looking to strengthen relationships between governments, within government and with industry by:

- forming an Industry Implementation Advisory Group (IIAG) to assist in implementing the *Tourism White Paper* initiatives;
- preparing an Implementation Plan in consultation with the IIAG;
- establishing an Australian Government Ministerial Council on Tourism;
- hosting an annual consultative forum between government and industry;
- developing a new intergovernmental agreement between the Australian Government, States and Territories; and
- publishing regular newsletters and annual progress reports on the implementation of the *Tourism White Paper.*

Note: The new IIAG: Research & Statistics sub-group held its first meeting on 21 January in Sydney. Matters discussed at the meeting included stakeholder expectations and identification of research and data priorities. The IIAG sub-group has been convened to advise on *White Paper* research and data issues, including budgetary, structural and tasking priorities.

Future Role of the DITR

The *White Paper* indicates that the DITR will continue to be the primary source of tourism policy advice to the Australian Government. In addition to the above, it will continue to focus on initiatives concerning tourism quality, as well as encouraging sustainable tourism in national parks and protected areas, and influencing policy settings on tourism transport and infrastructure — particularly a proactive approach to air services and policy and agreements.

The Australian Tourist Commission

Structure

The ATC is a statutory authority governed by a board of directors and directly responsible to the Minister for Small Business and Tourism. Its principal objectives — set out under the ATC Act in 1987 — are to:

• increase the number of international visitors to Australia;
• maximise the benefits of international tourism for Australia;
• work with other relevant agencies to promote the principles of ecologically sustainable development; and
• raise awareness of the social and cultural impacts of international tourism.

In addition to marketing and promotion, the ATC is involved in trade relations (events and industry), consumer research and brand tracking, industry liaison and segment development. It has also developed a sustainable tourism plan that involves:

• developing partnerships that contribute to the long-term environmental, social and economic sustainability of the tourism industry;
• developing a reliable knowledge base to enable effective decision-making processes, which integrate both long- and short-term economic, environmental and social considerations;
• creating a sustainable tourism focus for the ATC's marketing activities;
• creating a high profile for best practice sustainable tourism products; and
• ensuring continuous improvement of the ATC's corporate environmental performance.

Board of Directors

The ATC is governed by a 10-member board, which includes the ATC CEO and a DITR representative. The remaining eight members are from industry, bringing to the board a range of tourism skills and experience. The Board meets at least six times a year.

Relationship with the STOs and Other Government Bodies

The ATC has working agreements with all Australia's State and Territory Organisations (STOs). It also works with the CEOs' Forum and the Destinational Marketing Alliance (DAMA) — both organisations ensuring that all activities and programmes are aligned in offshore marketing. DAMA groups also exist in key regions where the STOs have a presence, such as Europe, the USA, Asia and New Zealand.

The ATC has also developed partnerships with two other Australian government agencies — Austrade and the Department of Education — to market Australian education and trade in conjunction with tourism.

Industry Advisory Panels (IAPs)

The ATC keeps in touch with the industry through IAPs for each of Australia's five major inbound regions (i.e. Japan, Asia, the Americas, New Zealand and Europe). These meet in November (before the next planning cycle) and provide a forum for the ATC to listen to feedback from stakeholders on how the ATC could better impact issues.

Other advisory panels include the Backpacker Tourism Advisory Group, which was formed to strengthen partnerships in the backpacker industry through communication and consultation. The group, which acts as a conduit between industry and the ATC, comprises 12 industry representatives, including one representing STOs and one the ATC. There is also a Rugby Tourism Advisory Group — a joint initiative with the ATC, the Australian Rugby Union and the TTF — which ensured that the whole industry capitalised on Australia hosting the Rugby World Cup.

Staff and Offices

ATC headquarters   There are currently 80 staff working at the ATC's HQ in Sydney. The executive board of six members comprises the ATC CEO and the executive general managers of Marketing Development, Eastern Hemisphere, Western Hemisphere, Corporate Services and Organisation Development (Figure 5.2).

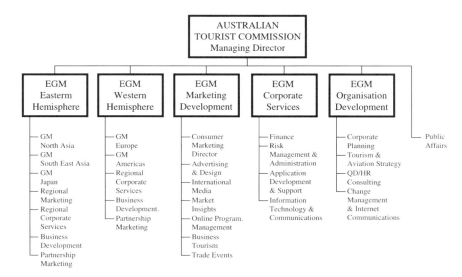

Figure 5.2: The Australian Tourist Commission's structure at HQ.
Note: EGM = Executive General Manager; GM = General Manager.

The operation at HQ is divided into five areas:

Marketing development, with a staff of around 40, responsible for:

- visiting Journalist Programme;
- marketing (including brand development), advertising and design;
- trade event organisation and management (for events in Australia and overseas);
- business tourism programmes (brand and advertising development and marketing activities);
- 'market insights' (consumer research for all key markets, product viability research, consumer segmentation research); and
- online marketing (australia.com management and development, online campaign and content development, database management).

Hemispheres (13 staff), responsible for developing and implementing marketing strategies in their own regions. There are two general managers in this operational area — one overseeing the Eastern Hemisphere and the other, the Western Hemisphere. This division also acts as an interface between overseas and Australian operations so that the ATC and industry better understand the conditions in-market. It has four operational areas:

- Eastern Hemisphere (developing international marketing strategies in China, Hong Kong, India, South Korea, Malaysia, Singapore, Taiwan and Thailand);
- Western Hemisphere (developing international marketing strategies in the Americas, New Zealand, the UK/Europe and the Middle East);
- trade development (advising and liaising with key Australian industry stakeholder groups, with inbound tour operators and specific suppliers in segments such as backpacker/youth/adventure and education and industry associations); and
- partnership marketing (servicing and advising Australian suppliers to international markets).

Organisation development (nine staff), responsible for building optimum organisational performance, developing strategic direction and driving change. It is also responsible for human resource activities and development for ATC staff worldwide, as well as for improving internal communication practices.

Public affairs (six staff), responsible for increasing awareness of the ATC and Australia's inbound tourism industry in Australia, and for the ATC's communications strategy.

Corporate services (12 permanent plus 28 temporary/freelance staff contracted to work on online programmes) responsible for finance, administration, IT & communications.

ATC Offices Abroad

Australia now has 12 offices abroad, having closed one (a second office in Japan, in Osaka) in 2003. From these bases the ATC says it is active in some 20 countries.

- Europe — London (regional HQ) and Frankfurt;
- Americas — Los Angeles (regional HQ);
- Asia Pacific — Auckland, Bangkok, Hong Kong (regional HQ North Asia), Kuala Lumpur, Seoul, Shanghai, Singapore (regional HQ South and Southeast Asia), Taipei and Tokyo.

The ATC has been reducing its overseas presence in recent years and, in addition to the closure of Osaka, it has cut its presence in Denmark, Sweden, Philippines, Indonesia, South Africa and Latin America. Representative offices in France and Italy have also closed and have been replaced with single representatives.

None of the ATC overseas offices are shared with Australian Embassies or Consulates, but the ATC has linked with other organisations where it has deemed this to be advisable and practicable. Its offices in Singapore, Los Angeles and Tokyo are shared with STOs, for instance, and in London various STOs have been located in the ATC office for short periods. In Tokyo, the ATC is in the same office as Austrade.

There are 120 staff employed overseas, of whom 100 (83%) are local. None of the ATC's offices are open to the public, and in many cases they are located in areas away from the town/city centres where rents are cheaper.

Resources and Funding

The ATC's total budget fell by 0.3% in fiscal 2002/2003 (ended 30 June 2003) to £48.0 million. Of this, 82% was funded by the federal government. The total budget for 2003/2004 still has to be confirmed but preliminary estimates put the federal government share (before the switch to the new Tourism Australia is taken into account) at £39.9 million (+1.4%).

Additional one-off funding was awarded in 2002/2003 as a response to the downturn in visitor arrivals. The DITR allocated £0.8 million for a promotional campaign estimated at £2.8 million, run in partnership with the STOs and industry. It also gave an additional £3.9 million to the ATC in 2002/2003 to implement strategic marketing initiatives in key international markets. With the funds, the ATC was able to boost campaigns in the USA, UK, Europe and Asia as well as launch a new campaign in Japan.

Marketing takes the lion's share of ATC's budget — 80% — with just 20% allocated to administration (including salaries) in both 2001/2002 and 2002/2003. In 2003/2004, the ATC projects that a higher percentage, 84%, will be spent on marketing (Table 5.6). This excludes any additional funding that will come as a result of the *Tourism White Paper* — most of which will make an impact as from 2004/2005.

As already indicated, additional funding of £93 million will bring total direct funding over the next four and a half years to over £236 million. International marketing will get an additional £47 million while domestic marketing will get an extra £18 million. A further £27 million will go to structural initiatives such as research and statistics and events promotions.

Role and Activities

ATC's Marketing Strategy

After the downturn following the events of 11 September 2001, the ATC reviewed all its activities overseas and in Australia. The main challenges identified were: costs of marketing, media costs, competition from other destinations, changing consumer attitudes and preferences, changing distribution systems and aviation capacity. As a result of the survey, a number of

Table 5.6: The ATC's annual budget, 2001/2002 to 2003/2004[a] (£ '000).

Source of funding	2001/2002	2002/2003	% annual change[b]	2003/2004[c]
Federal government	35,473	39,341	2.1	9,881
Advertising	4,508	4,642	−5.2	NA
Sale of goods & services	142	107	−30.7	NA
Industry contributions	3,347	3,104	−14.6	NA
Interest	339	524	20.8	
Net foreign exchange gains	—	45	115.0	NA
Revenue from sale of assets	12	4	−72.7	NA
Other	424	210	−54.4	NA
Total	44,306	47,798	−0.3	NA
Of which				
% share to marketing	80	82	—	84
Actual M&P budget	35,445	38,382	−0.3	NA

[a]FY from 1 July to 30 June.
[b]% change in A$s.
[c]Provisional.
£1 = A$2.76 in 2002 and A$2.54 in 2003 and 2004 (estimated for 2004).
Source: ATC.

important changes in marketing strategy were introduced. The core marketing strategies, now being implemented, were outlined as 'four key strategies for 2003 and beyond' in the ATC Corporate Plan 2003–2008, published in May 2003. These are:

- focusing efforts on areas/sectors where the ATC can make the most impact;
- improving insights and understanding of changing consumer needs and priorities;
- strengthening the brand and differentiating Australia from other destinations; and
- creating better synergy between the ATC and its partners — the STOs, regions and industry.

According to the plan, the ATC activity was to be apportioned with the following emphasis: insights into markets and consumers (15%); facilitating development of appropriate products (20%); ensuring accessible and competent distribution outlets (10%) and promoting Brand Australia (50%). Crucially, promoting individual products and destination details, and converting these to sales, are excluded from the ATC's activities.

The key strategies in the *White Paper* expand on the four strategies already outlined above. They are:

- grow international tourism to Australia through vigorous marketing of Brand Australia in key global markets;
- leverage promotion of Australia through strategic partnerships with STOs and the industry;
- help attract major events to Australia and assist with the growth of business tourism;
- conduct an expanded range of research and analysis tailored to meet government and market needs;

- analyse and disseminate trends in global and domestic tourism to help with strategic planning, including regional tourism; and
- develop strategies to promote growth in the domestic tourism industry and encourage regional dispersal of international tourists.

A New Brand Australia

'Brand Australia' — the image of the country and its experiences that the ATC conveys through advertising, PR and online campaigns — is the concept that underlies the ATC's, and the future Tourism Australia's, whole marketing strategy. It should guide the tone, design and imagery for all communications to both consumers and the trade in all types of media advertising and communication.

The ATC's introduction of Brand Australia back in 1995 was an innovative move for the travel industry, and the ATC has continued to keep the concept of a country brand at the forefront of its marketing. Brand Australia aims to strengthen the emotional bonds that people overseas have with Australia, and increase the strong aspirational appeal of a holiday in the country. It is based on a combination of Australia's spectacular natural environment, the distinctive personality of the people, and the free-spirited nature of the country's lifestyle and culture. It aims to promote the personality of Australia as a free-spirited, optimistic, fun and liberating destination offering a range of experiences.

However, recent research and focus groups in some of Australia's core markets revealed that the knowledge of Australia's diverse geography and climate, its main cities and the variety of experiences on offer, has not fully been conveyed to many markets and segments, even the UK. As a result the ATC is working to 'refresh' the brand, ensuring it better communicates the unique attributes that differentiates the country from other destinations.

In an important change in approach, the ATC has made the decision to focus on brand marketing, featuring experiences that create awareness and desire for the destination of Australia as a whole. It will not be involved in promoting specific products and places. This will be left to the STOs and tourism regions, which now have the responsibility of converting the awareness created by the ATC into visits.

Note: In June 2003, the Marketing Development department was restructured, with a renewed emphasis on the development of Brand Australia. A new job — Consumer Marketing Director — was created to work closely with the regional marketing directors to ensure consistency of the brand positioning.

The *White Paper* calls for further refinement of Brand Australia as a 'Platinum Plus' destination — explained as a destination that is a market leader in both quality and value. At the heart of the new branding is the consumer website www.australia.com, which was upgraded in 2002/2003 and will continue to receive substantial investment.

Rationalising Marketing Partnerships

As already indicated, the ATC is looking for ways to improve synergy and leverage with industry partners and with the STOs and regions. The ATC already has dedicated account managers for each state and territory to liaise with and assist the trade with marketing needs, but there is still overlap in ATC/STO activities, both in Australia and overseas. The ATC's decision to focus only on marketing which supports Brand Australia is seen as one step, but other solutions are also anticipated once the *White Paper* is implemented.

More and Improved Research

As noted above, initial announcements confirm that Tourism Australia will receive more funding for research to ensure better targeted marketing, especially for research into global customer segmentation. This is essential if its strategy and activities are to be insights-driven, and its online marketing capability developed to target segments through direct and personalised communication. The new organisation will also put more emphasis on sharing the results of its research with its partners and with tourism businesses in general.

Reducing Target International Markets

In 2002/2003, the ATC decided that too many international markets were being targeted, and resources were spread too thinly, thereby limiting the ATC's ability to properly develop opportunities in the most promising markets. It has therefore limited its target markets to 20 — which represent 90% of international arrivals (and it has offices in only 12 countries). The identification and ranking of these target markets is based not simply on their current size and value, but also on their potential. Thus China — which ranks sixth in terms of visits and expenditure in Australia — is identified as one of the top three priority markets. The potential opportunity has been balanced with the level of investment required to realise that opportunity.

The ATC's market prioritisation is set out in the ATC Corporate Plan 2003–2008. Key markets are:

- *USA, China, UK* — top priority markets — maximise yield and visitation potential;
- *Germany, Singapore, South Korea, Japan, New Zealand, Canada* — encourage growth potential. There are segments within these markets that have strong growth potential. The ATC will identify and selectively target those segments;
- *Italy, Ireland, France, India, Hong Kong, Switzerland, the Middle East* — maintain support and develop. These markets offer some specific opportunities over the next five years. Marketing will be limited to supporting and developing those opportunities;
- *Netherlands, Malaysia, Thailand, Taiwan* — limit to supporting industry initiatives. These markets have limited growth potential. ATC activity will be limited to trade support;
- *Latin America, Sweden, Denmark, Philippines, Indonesia, South Africa* — provide strategic support as required. The ATC has no direct presence in these markets, but will continue to service them through other channels, particularly through the website.

Higher Profile for MICE and Events Tourism

Over the past three years, the ATC has increasingly paid attention to the MICE and, once the *White Paper* is implemented and the new Tourism Events Australia unit is established within Tourism Australia, the sector will become a key priority.

The ATC seeks to position Australia as a 'unique, desirable and achievable destination' for MICE business. It also conducts campaigns to reinforce the idea of Australia as 'a great place to do business'.

The ATC launched its first business tourism global brand awareness campaign in 2001, with a second phase in 2002, generating confirmed MICE events worth £333,000. However, the sector faces tough competition — in 2002 Australia fell in ICCA's world ranking from fifth to seventh in attracting international conferences — and, in July 2003, a separate Business Tourism unit was created in the ATC's Marketing Development group.

The ATC promotes business tourism through international campaigns, and also tries to generate positive international media coverage about Australia, showcasing the country's achievements in commerce and industry. The ATC distributes a business tourism online newsletter, and organises Dreamtime — an annual event for the international incentive travel sector held in Australia.

The ATC provides a range of resources to assist business planning (a downloadable motivational video, for instance, best practice case studies, incentive itineraries, etc.) and collateral material for events' organisers. It has been working particularly hard in Asian markets — it runs Team Australia Business Events Educational (it has been an annual event for the past five years) and in 2003 it ran its first Asian Corporate Familiarisation with 12 potential corporate customers.

Team Australia — a driver in business tourism promotion (it has 14 members at the time of writing this report) — is an international marketing collaboration between the ATC and members of the Australian Association of Convention Bureaux. Its activities include sales missions (it ran one to London and Paris in September 2003), and participation in events such as Pacific Rim Incentives and Meetings Exchange (PRIME).

Market Segmentation

The ATC's key areas for product segment activities are: indigenous (Aboriginal) tourism, backpacking, ecotourism, education, food and wine, gay/lesbian and special events — particularly sporting events such as the 2006 Commonwealth Games and annual arts festivals like those in Adelaide and Perth. These segments were handled by a 'segment development unit' at head office, but this was disbanded in July 2003, with the activities divided between Marketing Development and Hemispheres.

Indigenous tourism is the most recent segment to be launched — it was not until 2001/2002 that the government-funded body Indigenous Business Australia first started acquiring equity in a number of tourism ventures. For political and economic reasons, as well as its viability as a unique tourism attraction, the indigenous segment looks set to expand, and is highlighted in the *White Paper* as 'offering a pathway to economic independence for some remote regional areas'.

ATC Marketing Activities and Industry Buy-in Opportunities

Marketing to the Consumer

Four key mediums are used by the ATC HQ to reach the consumer and encourage them to visit Australia:

- *australia.com* — The website is regarded as the key response mechanism for ATC consumer marketing activities worldwide, and is integrated into print and TV advertising, publications and PR programmes. The website offers over 60 language/country combinations, with over 10,000 consumer pages. It has recently been 'revitalised'; the design has been improved and sections added on aboriginal tourism, backpackers, families and island experiences.

  The website offers suppliers a range of opportunities to buy-in at very different levels and costs. The cheapest option is to list a product on the Australian Tourism Data Warehouse, which is accessed through destination pages in 'Places to Go', 'Things to do', 'What's on'. Also offered are advertising banners and squares, or content pages, giving more detail for single or for multiple products. The content pages' options vary to include a whole range of packages with, for instance, a specified number of related links or highlighted text;
- *E-mail travel clubs* — These are made up of e-mail members who have indicated that they want more Australian product information. For the moment they are only offered in North America and Europe. Membership is around 100,000 in the USA, 10,000 in Canada, 26,000 in the UK, 9000 in Germany, 4000 in Italy and 1300 in France. Products can be advertised as a product feature in a regular e-mail newsletter, or exclusive e-mails related to a specific product can be sent out;
- *Essential Australia travel guides* — Hard copy brochures, only offered in Europe. In 2004, 300,000 will be distributed in Europe in five languages — English, German, Italian, Dutch, French — and will be distributed throughout Europe at shows, ATC offices, workshops, embassies, consulates, airline offices and in travel agents. Suppliers are encouraged to advertise and/or join a website listing;
- *International publicity programmes* — Over 20 PR companies are employed around the world for this. Activities include press trips, international media relations — servicing enquiries, proactive stories to media, crisis management, negotiating multi-faceted promotions with the media and industry.

Marketing to the Trade

The ATC adopts a number of methods to reach wholesalers and travel agents who sell Australian holidays and business travel. Key activities are:

- Participation in trade events, and organising trade missions, workshops, seminars, etc;
- Running an Aussie Specialists training programme in North America and Europe and, more recently, in China. The programme run by the ATC and STOs, educates and trains travel agents so that they develop an in-depth understanding of Australia. Various

resources are distributed to qualified Aussie Specialists on a regular basis to improve product knowledge and motivate them to sell Australia. There are around 1000 Aussie Specialists in the USA, 1500 in Europe and 165 in China. Suppliers are encouraged to advertise in the specialist programme website newsletter. The ATC also sells the membership list and e-mail blasts;

- Running a special website for North American travel agents — Travelagent australia.com. This is the main resource for US travel agents selling Australia, with around 1000–1500 visits by US travel agents per week. Suppliers can buy homepage advertising, banners and e-Bulletin features;
- As noted above, the ATC has a range of activities specifically to promote business tourism to Australia, targeting key international corporate decision-makers and event planners. The ATC has a sector-specific website — meetings.australia.com — which has recently started to offer advertising opportunities to suppliers. There is also a quarterly online newsletter for North American (2500 subscribers) and European (1000) business tourism markets. This also takes sponsorship with direct links to product websites and has an e-mail response mechanism;
- The ATC stages the one major trade event, Dreamtime, in Australia, which targets international incentive buyers. Their staff also attend major international and national business tourism trade shows — 34 in 2002/2003;
- International publicity programmes — as for consumer programmes.

Note: The ATC marketing opportunities are eligible activities within Australia's Export Development Marketing Grant Scheme that allows companies to claim up to 50% back on their marketing expenses (less the first £5900).

Among more original methods the ATC has adopted is celebrity endorsement of Brand Australia. Using different celebrities for different source markets, the ATC has found its Tourism Ambassador programme to be successful, and Tourism Australia will develop it further. This began in 2001/2002 with Ian Thorpe in Japan, and in 2002/2003 Italy-based model Megan Gale was used in Italy, and surf champion Layne Beachley became the ambassador for the youth market in the USA.

New Media, E-Marketing and Customer Relationship Management (CRM)

As already indicated, the intention is for the web to be increasingly positioned at the heart of Australia's international marketing effort, driving the whole programme. The consumer site www.australia.com has over 10,000 consumer pages, and offers 60 language/country combinations. The ATC also runs a vast and very comprehensive corporate site www.atc.net.au.

In 2002/2003 australia.com delivered 42 million pages to consumers — 45% in the USA, 21% in Europe, 13% Japan and Korea, 13% rest of the world (of this 13%, 'other Asia' was 6% and New Zealand together with the Pacific 2%). In March 2003, the website won the Travel & Tourism award at BTTF in Birmingham for the best tourist board website. One of its main attractions in the UK is the Ozplanner™, a new interactive tool that was launched in the UK to help first-time visitors in the planning of their trip to Australia.

According to the *White Paper*, www.australia.com will become a portal for domestic as well as international tourism. There are also plans to expand the Australian Tourism Data Warehouse (supplied by the STOs), which is already an impressive resource.

Meanwhile, CRM is also seen as a growing priority for the ATC and industry to improve knowledge and understanding of customers and better target potential business.

Case study — The UK office of the Australian Tourist Commission

---

Staff and Responsibilities

The London office is ATC's European HQ as well as the UK office. There is a satellite office in Frankfurt and individual representatives in France (Paris) and Italy (Milan). This is a much smaller European representation than a few years ago when there were offices in France and Italy and a larger representation in Germany. The Swedish office (which covered Denmark and Scandinavia) has been closed altogether, and marketing to the Swedish market is largely carried out via the Internet.

Within the London office, some staff handling advertising, PR and the servicing of requests for information have responsibilities for all target European markets (the UK, Ireland and the Netherlands, France, Italy, Germany and Switzerland). There is a multi-lingual team to respond to European trade enquiries.

Other staff focus specifically on UK and Ireland, particularly business and trade development. For the past 18 months, the London office has employed an in-house researcher who handles market research and intelligence gathering, and focus and testing groups and developing strategic plans.

Budget Allocation

In Europe, the ATC's major expenditure is on advertising — with or without industry partners. The second most important expenditure items are PR activities — the ATC has four PR agencies in Europe. Third comes information servicing and e-marketing, which involves handling calls to action (brochure distribution), and phone calls from the trade.

Ranked fourth in terms of expenditure is trade development. This involves road shows, industry for a (MAIT), trade events, Aussie Specialists, and one-to-one training. While some of the trade development activities involve considerable outlay, others are virtually self-funding through partnerships, either with the STOs or industry — e.g. the ATC's presence at major international tourism trade shows such as International Tourism Exchange (ITB) (where for the second year running it will share a stand with New Zealand) and the World Travel Market (WTM).

Enquiries

The underlying intention is to lead all callers back to the ATC's websites — www.australia.com for consumers, www.atc.net.au and www.meetings.australia.com for the trade.

The London office has virtually no walk-in consumer enquiries — its large office is rather out of the way in Putney where rents are cheaper — but it has a policy not to turn people away if they do drop in. A few consumer enquiries still come by letter, but the number of e-mail enquiries has grown rapidly in the past year or so.

For consumer phone calls, a voice response service offering a brochure is used. The call centre is based in Sunderland. The ATC London office decided to use this off-site service recently because the volume of calls was becoming too large to handle in-house. However, for trade enquiries, the London office mans a telephone service with three operators who speak several languages. They take pan-European calls from the trade and from Aussie Specialist agents.

Public Relations, Advertising and Promotions

Most marketing campaigns are carried out in partnership with the industry, or with some element of industry buy-in, although ATC London is prepared to do some advertising/PR on its own if funds are available. One example when it bore all costs was an additional (unscheduled) newspaper advertisement following the UK's victory in the Rugby World Cup, designed to take further advantage of Australia's high profile in the UK at that particular moment.

In Europe, the ATC partners extensively with airlines but there are also numerous other partners — tour operators, hotels, car rental companies, venues, etc. — although few from non-tourism sectors.

Trade and Consumer Activities

Among the different travel trade activities in the UK in 2003/2004, the following should be mentioned:

- a new campaign to encourage travel agents to become Aussie Specialists (which also lets the trade know the programme is now free of charge);
- co-ordinating the Australian delegation at WTM and the Adventure Travel and Sports Show (the latter for the first time); and
- the Corroboree UK, 2004 — a new training event to replace Oztalk, based on extensive discussions with tour operators, wholesalers and retailers in the UK. It will provide various opportunities to train frontline staff through workshops.

Consumer marketing activities in Europe for 2003/2004 are focused on aboriginal tourism, the luxury segment, backpackers (a new campaign has just been launched in Germany) and the World Cup. Among the campaigns being launched in the UK are:

- A Boomerang Track promotion at the start of 2004, supported by the Aboriginal Tourism Association, Qantas, various tour operators and hotel groups. Using a *Sunday Telegraph* supplement as the launch of a competition to win an Aboriginal adventure tour, the promotion was followed up with further supplement distribution at consumer shows (destinations, etc. with an Aboriginal dance group performance), a Travel Trade Gazette (TTG) supplement and new Internet pages;
- Targeting the UK luxury segment, the London office used advertorial in the *Tatler Travel Guide 2004* and added wine-tasting events to the campaign;
- Partnering with Singapore Airlines through an advertising campaign in Southeast England and the Manchester area is designed to motivate consumers (25–35 year-old professionals) to choose an Australian holiday flying Singapore Airlines;

- In the final quarter of 2003, the London office co-ordinated a multi-faceted promotion linked to Disney's film *Finding Nemo*, with partners Tesco's (where leaflets were distributed), the *Sun Online*, *Mail on Sunday*/AOL and specially themed web pages on www.australia.com.

Barriers to Effective Marketing

The major barriers to selling Australia in the UK and Europe continue to be the time difference, the huge distance to travel and the cost of getting to Australia. There is also fairly widespread ignorance of the range of destinations in Australia, and most people looking to take a holiday there feel that this is a once in a lifetime visit. For the past two years the ATC has been working on these barriers with some success by conveying the idea that a two-week holiday in Australia is a viable option.

Dealing with Negative Publicity

Negative events relating to Australia and the reporting of them are monitored overseas and in Sydney. The initiative to deal with them — by deflecting attention or seeking positive advertorial, etc. — may be taken by HQ or by the overseas office. On the current security issue, the ATC in London is not pushing Australia as a 'safe' destination — it is leaving the consumer be the judge of that.

Lessons from Australia

Widespread Recognition of Tourism's Economic Importance

Of all the countries studied — both in terms of the overall tourism support system and the NTO's effectiveness, Australia is an exemplar of good practice.

In Australia, the Minister of Industry, Tourism and Resources is a Cabinet-level post and the Prime Minister put his name to the *White Paper*. As in Canada, tourism is treated as a business. Tourism's contribution to economic growth and employment is regularly monitored by the ABS in the context of the country's TSA and, thanks to the pioneering efforts of the ABS and BTR, Australia is considered by OECD to have been one of the first countries to develop meaningful measures for ROI in tourism.

Although the country's opposition Labour party is against what it sees as excessive support of tourism, the current National Coalition is by no means the first party in power to give a high priority to tourism.

The large number of aggressive lobbying industry bodies in Australia has no doubt helped to stimulate public–private sector partnership in tourism development, management and promotion, and this has resulted in frequent and widespread media coverage about tourism, in turn stimulating stakeholder buy-in from the public as well as the industry and different levels of government.

A Proactive Approach from Both Government and Industry

The strategic and structural changes currently being implemented by government reflect the pro-active stance of both government and the industry. Like the ATC before it, Tourism Australia is likely to continue to be one of the industry's most effective NTOs since its new strategy for tourism takes account of the changing marketplace and aims to provide equitable benefits for all stakeholders.

The focus on solid, scientific research as the basis for developing marketing strategy and practice can also only add to the ATC's/Tourism Australia's credibility and efficiency both at home and internationally. The close relationship between research and marketing will be highlighted when they are brought together under the Tourism Australia umbrella. Australia also has a head start in terms of monitoring the economic value of tourism, having been one of the first countries to develop a TSA.

The decision to lead research further into market segmentation will help ATC/Tourism Australia fine-tune its marketing focus — over the medium to long term it can expect more interest from an expanded variety of source markets and niche market segments. Tourism Australia plans to provide a structural framework that will allow industry to identify opportunities quickly and to develop strategic plans for high-yield niches.

It is interesting to note that Tourism Australia will receive more funding from government for research to ensure better-targeted marketing, especially for research into global customer segmentation. It believes this is essential if its strategy and activities are to be insights-driven, and its online marketing capability developed to target segments through direct and personalised communication.

Brand Development

Despite Australia's current concern that its brand needs revitalising, it is important to note that the ATC has already achieved a strong brand image of Australia in many markets as a result of eight years of brand marketing — and is very much ahead of the pack in this respect. The Premium Plus brand should further strengthen Australia's brand position as its strong logo is also highly rated by the industry and by competitors.

The ATC's decision to focus on brand marketing, featuring experiences that create awareness and desire for the destination of Australia as a whole, is an important change in approach. The ATC/Tourism Australia will not be involved in promoting specific products and places. This will be left to the STOs and tourism regions, which now have the responsibility of converting the awareness created by the ATC into visits.

Some 50% of the ATC's activity is allocated to promoting Brand Australia. While facilitating the development of appropriate products is also seen as important (accounting for 20% of activity), promoting individual products and destinations, and converting these to sales, are excluded from the ATC's activities.

Partnership with the Regions

In line with trends in parts of Europe — notably the Nordic countries — the decision to sharply differentiate the marketing focus of the NTO (in favour of focusing on the country brand) and the STOs (marketing destination and products) should improve the already good partnership between the ATC and the states/territories.

A High Priority to E-marketing

The concerted effort to steer all marketing activity through www.australia.com makes a lot of sense, both from the point of view of cutting costs and increasing the NTO's effectiveness. It now remains to be seen how skilfully Tourism Australia can manage its customer/potential customer base.

Among the ATC's practices that help build relations with the industry, one important strength is the way the ATC explains to the trade what it is doing and why, and clearly sets out (largely via the website) opportunities for partnership/buy-in via the industry website.

The industry also appreciates the ATC's generous approach to its research data. A huge range of timely consumer surveys of various source markets, segment surveys, ATC and government strategy papers etc., as well as a range of visitor surveys from BTR, are easily accessible through the website — and the *White Paper* promises this will improve!

Another successful way to engage the trade is the Aussie Specialist Programme, which improves travel agent knowledge in target markets, encourages more sales, and provides an easy conduit for new products/destinations to be launched.

Chapter 6

Canada

Canada's Recent Tourism Performance

Canada is a federation of 10 provinces and three territories with the federal government responsible for national issues. The country offers significant diversity including strong urban products, cultural attractions, festivals, national parks, world class resorts, hotels, restaurants and theatre. This is feasible given the range of product and diversity on offer. Canada also benefits from a range of city destination products including Toronto (major airport hub and provincial capital), Vancouver (reputation as one of the most attractive cities in North America), Quebec City (a UNESCO world heritage site), Montreal (the largest French speaking city in the world outside of Paris) and Ottawa (the Federal government capital).

Tourism is the eleventh largest industry sector in Canada (See Table 6.1). The National Tourism Organisation (NTO) for Canada is the Canadian Tourism Commission (CTC), which is supported by a provincial structure throughout the country.

International and Domestic Tourism

The USA represents the crucial segment of demand in international leisure, business and VFR. Downturns in the US economy impact significantly on Canadian tourism performance but good iconic marketing featuring the natural, wilderness and urban products along with unusual strategic alliances in marketing campaigns can help. This coupled with strong communication between Provincial and National marketing is supposed to have helped drive a coordinated use of resources.

Canadian tourism will always be strongly supported by very strong domestic demand. Canada's largest market is the Canadians themselves, who account for 70% of tourist expenditure. In terms of non-domestic tourism, Canada is one of the world's top destinations, and for the past five years has made the top 10 lists of destinations as compiled by World Tourism Organization (number 8 in 2002).

The domestic tourism market is the biggest sector of the Canadian market and many Canadians opt to explore their own country as an alternative to overseas travel (the major exception here is visitation to the USA). Canadians are highly mobile, and VFR traffic is significant amongst a nation spread across such a wide geographical area. CTC focuses on the inter-provincial data whilst the 'intra-provincial' data is the responsibility of the provinces and territories. The inter-provincial spend is four times higher than that of the 'intra-provincial'.

The relative strength of the Canadian dollar became a major factor in Canadian overseas travel, and the relative strength against the US dollar caused tourism to the USA to

Table 6.1: Canada: key facts — 2002.

Population	31.4 mn
GDP	£477 bn
International arrivals (TF)	20 mn
International overnights (TCE)	122.1 mn
Average length of stay (approx.)	2.2
International arrivals per inhabitant	0.64
Domestic arrivals	95.2 mn
Domestic overnights	187.9 mn
Domestic receipts	£13.2 bn
International receipts	£6.5 bn
– as a % of GDP	1.3%
– per international tourist arrival	£325
– per international overnight	£145
– per inhabitant	£207
Total tourism receipts	£19.7 bn
– as a % of GDP	4.1%
– per total tourist arrival	£171
– per total overnight	£85
– per inhabitant	£627
Tourism's total contribution to GDP	2%
WTTC estimate for T&T industry GDP	3.8%
NTO's total tourism budget	£54.1 mn (plus £40 mn from joint marketing and research partnerships)
State contribution	£47.0 mn (50% of £94.1mn as above)
Marketing budget	£44.9 mn (83%)
Exchange rate	£1 = C$2.35

increase. Figures for 2001 showed a significant downturn across all categories, which was significantly influenced by the events of the final quarter of 2001. Similarly, both leisure and business travel was badly affected by 11 September 2001, and it was only in 2002 that any significant revival in tourism numbers was evidenced. Thus the later part of 2001 saw subdued business travel and much reduced leisure travel (Table 6.2).

Canadian domestic tourism accounts for approximately two thirds of all travel expenditure, with the largest outlay being air transport. Similarly for international tourists, the largest item of expenditure was air transport. Yet the consequences of 11 September 2001 for the national flag-carrying airline Air Canada and its internal domestic airline Jazz were particularly hard. The situation is so serious that the state-operated carrier has moved into voluntary receivership pending restructuring (the Canadian equivalent of Chapter 11 debt restructuring). The airline is slowly restructuring with significant private sector investment and restructuring in part at least as a low-cost carrier. Domestic demand

Table 6.2: Inbound trips to Canada 1999–2002.

Country/ Area	2000 (000s)	1999–2000 (%)	2001 (000s)	2000–2001 (%)	2002 (000s)	2001–2002 (%)
USA	15,224	+0.3	15,589	+2.4	16,168	+3.7
Overseas	4,393	+4.9	4,034	−8.2	3,796	−5.8
Total Inbound	19,617	+1.3	19,623	+0.03	19,964	+1.7

Source: CTC.

for operations such as WestJet, the Calgary-based budget airline rose significantly over this period of adversity.

US Tourism to Canada

Trade and traffic between Canada and the US has been positively affected by the introduction of the North American Free Trade Agreement (NAFTA) in 1995, which stimulated economic activity and business tourism.

The US is the vital component of inbound travel and the US visitor is vital to Canadian tourism. In the late 1990s, the currency situation (weak Canadian dollar — strong US dollar) saw an increase in US visitation and an increase in visitor expenditure. Despite good growth evident in 2002 from the US market, the downturn following 11 September 2001 was considerable. Overseas markets were also badly affected in 2001 by a combination of factors discussed in the section below.

Business tourism from the US is also showing positive growth with the main catalysts of growth being conventions, meetings and incentive travel. The expenditure profile of US business visitors (almost twice that of leisure visitors) makes them highly sought after. Canada attracts almost 33% of non-US-based corporate meetings and more than 33% of non-US-based association meetings. Canada represents a relatively close, secure and comparable destination, which offers the US a predominantly similar language, comparable currency and a range of urban convention, and conference destinations that cluster around the southerly border with their country. Such cities are particularly attractive to US delegates and conference organisers interested in a change of destination but who are limited in terms of travel times.

International Visitors to Canada

Canada's top international markets in 2002 (2001) are given in Table 6.3.

The top five nations listed above together with Canada account for 90% of the total overnight travel receipts. During 2002 there was an increase in tourists from the USA (3.8%) with a resultant increase in expenditure of 6.3%. However, other international tourist arrivals dropped by 5.3% with spending down by 3.3% (Table 6.4).

For the year November 2003, the top five source countries for international visitors are contained in the following list. It is evident that 2003 has been a difficult year for Canada

Table 6.3: Canada's Top international markets in 2002.

1. USA (1)
2. UK (2)
3. Japan (3)
4. France (4)
5. Germany (5)
6. Mexico (7)
7. Australia (6)
8. South Korea (8)
9. Hong Kong (–)
10. Netherlands (10)
11. Taiwan (9)

Source: CTC.

Table 6.4: International tourist trips to Canada.

Country/Area	2000 (000s)	2001 (000s)	2002 (000s)	2001–2002 (%)
UK	862	826	721	−12.7
Japan	493	410	423	+3.1
France	402	357	312	−12.5
Germany	380	330	292	−11.5
Total Europe	2,463	2,267	2,044	−9.8
Total Asia Pacific	1,421	1,285	1,287	+0.2
Total Latin America	396	377	392	+4

Source: CTC.

as all generating markets reported a reduction in visitation in comparison with the same period in 2002. The total overnight overseas volume was down 15.6% year on year. Similarly travel from the USA over the period from January to November 2003 has dropped to its lowest for five years.

However there are some positive signs emerging. Statistics Canada reports that tourism spending grew by 1.5% in the third quarter of 2003, an improvement over the 4.2% drop experienced during the second quarter as a result of the outbreak of SARS. After receding for five consecutive months, the decline in total overnight international travel to Canada registered a reversal in November 2003, falling 10.0% when compared to November of 2002.

In the past few years, international visitation has been badly affected by the prolonged impact of the Asian Financial Crisis (particularly in Japan), which has led to a downturn in visitation. Europe was similarly affected by economic uncertainty and impacts were evident in French, German and UK generating markets. 11 September 2001 also caused significant reduction in final quarter traffic to Canada. In 2003 the main impacts were the war in Iraq and SARS virus, which catapulted Canada, and particularly Toronto, onto the world stage for the wrong reasons in terms of tourism.

The MICE Market

Business tourism accounts for 19% of all international tourism revenue with 13% attributable to the USA and the remaining 6% to European business travellers. The returns from business tourism equate to 6% of the total marketing and sales budget. There has however been a decline in the business tourism emanating from the USA, which pre-dates 11 September. Steps have been taken in an attempt to reverse this trend by including within the strategy a campaign to raise awareness of Canada as a business tourism destination. As regards the overseas market in Europe, Canada is increasingly being regarded as a viable meeting and incentive market for business travellers, especially in the case of France, Germany and the UK (Table 6.5).

The CTC's meetings, incentives, conferences and events (MICE) programme is committed to raising awareness of Canada as a premier four-season destination for meetings, conventions and incentive travel in the US corporate and association markets. The programme has been designed by an industry-led marketing committee with the primary objective of providing partnership opportunities for the Canadian tourism industry and sales development in-market. There is a strong focus on sales development with the main goals being to:

- entify and develop new sources of business;
- crease growth within current account base;
- identify new business opportunities;
- expand underdeveloped markets;
- create platforms to showcase product focus; and
- generate short-term programmes for immediate/crisis opportunities.

A further objective is to identify and maintain a development account database of 1,000 top accounts in the US through a series of initiatives, detailing activities and results within each project, initiating familiarisation/site inspection trips with a focus on specific products,

Table 6.5: Purpose of international visit analysis by arrivals (%): 2000–2002.

Purpose	2000	2001	2002
	() = USA	() = USA	() = USA
Business Travel	18(15)	15(12)	16(12)
Holiday	49(56)	52(59)	48(60)
VFR	28(19)	26(19)	28(19)
Other	5(10)	7(10)	8(9)

Source: CTC.

develop new business accounts (target 25% conversion over three years), confirm and track leads/pitches from current and new sources of business, partner with key industry associations to create awareness and sponsorship opportunities, and work with partners to identify account and promotion opportunities in-market to address short-term need periods or market shifts. The overall goal is to increase revenue from the meetings and incentive travel market in the United States. This will be accomplished by:

• positioning Canada as the preferred destination with meeting planners;
• continuing to build awareness of Canada as a meeting destination;
• increasing database marketing to identified, qualified leads;
• increasing the number of partners in the programme.

The MICE programme targets meetings, conventions and incentive travel decision makers with two main strategies: relationship building and advertising.

Relationship Building

The aim is that existing relationships will be strengthened whilst new ones developed through

1. Direct mail
2. Relationship marketing using a CTC database of qualified meeting planners and/or partner lists/outside lists
3. Business Development
4. Creation/enhancement of working relationships with key accounts by the CTC Sales Force
5. Familiarization tours and site inspections under the visit Canada programme
6. Trade Shows/Special Events
7. Canadian presence (CTC plus partners) at major industry trade shows
8. Hosting of special marketplace where Canadian suppliers are featured exclusively
9. Public Relations and Media
10. Through leveraged activities linked to the US Leisure Marketing programme, increase the quantity and quality of unpaid media exposure and public relations.

Advertising

Canada's low awareness levels among American meeting planners will be addressed through direct-response advertising in key US business travel publications and websites.

For example, prior to the establishment of CTC, individual participants invested in trade shows separately. Now with the implementation of a 'Canada Stand' at major US trade shows, the participants form part of the CTC integrated partner participation. Committees of partners are formed to achieve an overall Canadian presence while maintaining the uniqueness of each destination. CTC takes the lead in staging the national 'Canada Stands' at key US trade shows.

Future Concerns

In recent years Canada has been losing its competitive position in major markets, for example in Japan, the share of tourists going to Canada reduced by 27% over the period from 1996 to 2002. This will be further reduced in view of the large drop in visitors during 2003. The UK market share has also reduced by 22% over the period from 1996 to 2002.

Aggressive competition from Canada's main competitors, USA, Australia, New Zealand and South Africa is a factor. CTC recognises that their marketing investment is low in comparison with its rivals. CTC has one of the lowest ratios of marketing invest-ment to international receipts, as shown in Table 6.6 for 2001.

Canada also needs to reconsider the USA market, which comprises no less than 60% of the total international market. It is considered a fairly secure market although it has been shown to be vulnerable. Canada has recognised that it must:

- Secure existing visitors;
- Expand on the alternative visitors it can attract beyond the top 6 that make up the majority of its international receipts. For example, the CTC Argentinean office was closed due to lim-ited return on investment but there are serious discussions about opening an office in China.

Market Portfolio Analysis can assist in identifying where CTC's priorities should lie. This analysis is based on the size of the market, the performance and the potential for future success. It includes an analysis of receipts potential, VFR proportion, 'shoulder sea-son' visitation, air seat capacity and outlook. The UK has been given a high ranking of '100' by CTC and is placed in Tier 1 of three tiers with Japan (ranking of 67), Mexico (ranking of 54), France (ranking of 40) and Germany (ranking of 39). Tier 2 consists of nations such as Australia and China with Tier 3 comprising others such as Spain and India, where the market is not deemed to be significant for Canada.

Canada's international travel deficit reached its highest level in more than nine years in the third quarter of 2003. Estimated at £0.511 billion, it grew by £71.5 million over the previous quarter. The main causes have been attributed to the lagging effect of SARS and the appreciation of the Canadian dollar against the US dollar.

Other factors of concern for CTC includes Canada being regarded as a 'cold and bor-ing' destination. To overcome such perceptions, it is acknowledged that time and money

Table 6.6: Marketing investment to overnight receipts.

Country	Marketing investment (£ mn)	Marketing investment as a percentage of overnight travel receipts (%)
Australia	46	0.97
New Zealand	18	1.40
South Africa	9	0.51
Canada	22	0.32

Source: CTC.

needs to be made available. CTC also faces the challenge of understanding what customers want from a holiday, and CTC must continue to provide the infrastructure and support to enable the 'product' offerings to be refreshed on an ongoing basis.

Organisation of Tourism in Canada

Tourism is included within the responsibilities of Industry Canada, the structure of which is as follows, see Figure 6.1 (Source: Industry Canada).

CTC is one of the 14 federal departments and agencies that make up the Industry Portfolio section of Industry Canada. Together, these organisations further the Government of Canada's goal to build a knowledge-based economy in all regions of Canada and to advance the Government's jobs, growth and innovation agenda. This involves creating a dynamic economy that

- provides more and better paying jobs for Canadians;
- supports stronger business growth through continued improvements in productivity and innovation performance;
- gives consumers, businesses and investors confidence that the marketplace is fair, efficient and competitive; and
- ensures a more sustainable economic, environmental and social future for Canada.

Through agencies, branches and directorates as well as the Industry Portfolio, the Minister of Industry has jurisdiction over policy issues regarding: industry; trade and commerce; science; consumer affairs; corporations and corporate securities; competition and restraint of trade, including mergers and monopolies; bankruptcy and insolvency; intellectual property; telecommunications; investment; small businesses; and regional economic development across Canada.

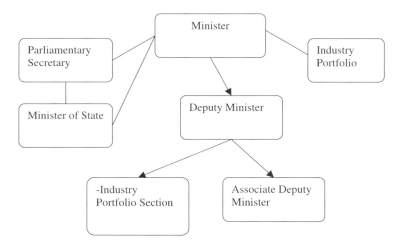

Figure 6.1: The structure of tourism in Canada. *Source*: Adapted from Industry Canada.

Canadian Tourism Commission meets with various government ministries on topics of common interest such as statistics. In addition to CTC (which will be considered in detail below) many additional agencies have some responsibility for tourism within the country. For example, Canada has four federal regional economic development agencies together with the provinces and territories that have their own tourism agencies. In addition, there is a national tourism industry association and provincial/territorial counterparts that operate in most jurisdictions. There are also various regional economic development agencies across Canada with tourism responsibilities. Depending upon their marketing and objectives, the Provinces and Territories may work together with CTC or they can develop separate individual programmes. Destination Marketing Organisations (DMOs) such as visitor bureaus may also choose to work in partnership or alone. The individual tourism businesses have a choice of working alone or with their DMO, industry association, Province, Territory, Municipality or with CTC in partnership.

Canadian Tourism Commission

CTC Tourism Vision and Mission

CTC's industry government formula is directed at:

- raising consumer awareness;
- developing a world-class tourism industry;
- responding to the needs of increasingly discriminating tourists;
- promoting win-win co-operation amongst the thousands of organisations that make up the industry;
- building firm, research-based foundations on which to make business and policy decisions;
- heightening awareness of tourism's scope and scale;
- earning recognition for the contribution of tourism to the economy.

CTC has a clear jointly developed vision and mission detailed below:

Canadian Tourism Industry Vision

Canada will be the premier four-season destination to connect with nature and to experience diverse cultures and communities.

Canadian Tourism Industry Mission

Canada's Tourism industry will deliver world class cultural and leisure experiences year-round, while preserving and sharing Canada's clean, safe and natural environments. The industry will be guided by the values of respect, integrity and empathy.

In 1995, the CTC was created as a 'special operating agency' within the Federal Government Department of Industry Canada. Over the period 1995–1998, the Federal government invested some £94 million, and a further £110 million was raised in matching contributions from the private sector and other relevant government departments for CTC activities. In 2001, a total amount of £35.5 million was raised from partnership investment.

During 2001, CTC became a Crown Corporation that allowed greater financial independence from federal government. CTC enjoyed greater legal, financial, managerial and administrative flexibility and influence. It does however remain publicly accountable. The CTC partnership with industry is reflected in the make up of the main CTC Board, which includes majority representation from the tourism sector as well as from the federal, provincial and territorial governments. Of the total number of 26 directors, no less than 17 are from the private sector with appointments held for up to three years. A range of partners from the tourism sector is present including:

- destination marketing organisations;
- transport carriers;
- hotels and restaurants;
- food, beverage, recreation, leisure suppliers;
- travel trade;
- visitor attractions.

CTC's relationship with the private sector is mainly through provincial, territorial and national tourism industry associations such as the Tourism Industry Association of Canada, the Canadian Tourism Human Resource Council and the Hotel Association of Canada. As an example, in 2003, provinces and territories worked together with the federal Minister of Industry and CTC to review the national marketing strategy.

Tourism Satellite Account

In 2002, CTC completed a five-year project with Statistics Canada to produce the first provincial and territorial satellite accounts. Canada was in fact the first country in the world to publish a tourism satellite account. Canada was also the first country to develop and publish national tourism indicators based on the tourism satellite account which permit monitoring that was not previously possible.

Research

Research is considered critical to Canada's continued industry growth and competitiveness. CTC's Research programme is a cornerstone of the Commission — a foundation of information upon which the marketing committees can build their action plans. The programme looks at both the demand and supply sides of the equation, helping industry make more informed decisions. Research has been recognised as complementary to marketing and sales, and is considered equally important. Information is critical to the success of the NTO. In the strategy document, CTC aims to

- become a world leader in the partnership-based industry approach and industry research;
- provide information to influence key external factors limiting growth;

- develop strategic alliances with academic institutions;
- provide virtual access to research data.

The Research programme collectively conducts key studies such as: financial analysis for tourism operators; reports on the tourism satellite accounts; national tourism indicators; the Canadian Travel Survey; and the International Travel Survey.

Staff and Offices

The NTO has 159 staff operating in one national office (based in Ottawa) and international offices based in:

- USA — Washington and Los Angeles plus various locations as US Leisure and US MC&IT;
- France — Paris;
- Germany — Dusseldorf;
- UK — London;
- Italy — Milan;
- Mexico — Mexico City;
- Australia — Pyrmont;
- Taiwan — Taipei;
- South Korea — Seoul;
- Hong Kong;
- China — Beijing;
- Japan — Tokyo.

The staff responsibilities are divided as follows:

Activity	Number of staff
Marketing and Sales	120
Research	12
E-marketing	2
Other	25
Total	159

A total of 96 staff work in the head office in Ottawa, with 63 working abroad. CTC engages local staff to work in their foreign offices, with the exception of those offices in the USA where some Canadian staff are based. However, for example, no Canadian nationals work in CTC offices in the UK. The offices do not serve the public, they deal with local tour operators and CTC marketing partners.

Three of the foreign offices are shared with Embassies etc but these offices will be vacated by the end of March this year. CTC has already closed offices in New Zealand, Singapore and the Netherlands with large staff reductions having been implemented in USA. A new structure involving the use of private sector offices is being tested in India.

In 2002, the Human Resource Committee identified the need to implement a new performance management system. A staff survey was produced to ensure staff involvement and a report of a succession plan was produced.

Table 6.7: Budget allocation 2002–2004.

Year	Total budget (£ mn)	% change in C$	State contribution (%)
2002	54.1	NA	87
2003	51.0	−7	91
2004	41.0	−21	88

Source: CTC.
Exchange Rates: £1 = 2.35 (2002), 2.31 (2003), 2.30 (2004).

Resources and Funding

Tourism is a significant contributor to the Canadian economy. For every tourism dollar spent, 31 cents goes to the Government, which equated to £7.25 billion in 2002.

Regarded as fundamental to CTC, partnership contributions match core government funding. In 2002, around £40 million was received in partnership contributions. The total funds available from Government were £47 million comprising £36 million of core appropriations, £6 million one-off payment and £5 million from the previous year. Of this budget 83% went towards marketing, 6% for information services and 11% for corporate.

For the period 2002–2004, the budgets were as follows (Table 6.7).

Expected industry contributions were expected to be 13.5% (2002), 9.9% (2003) and 10.0% (2004). In addition to the above funds, a total of £40 million (2002) and £25.3 million (2003) is available from industry *joint* marketing and research partnership funds.

Role and Activities

CTC is in theory industry led, market driven and research based. Its objectives are to:

- sustain a vibrant and profitable tourism industry;
- market Canada as a desirable tourist destination;
- support a co-operative relationship between the public and private sectors in the provinces and territories;
- provide relevant tourism information to the public and private sectors.

The Commission's two main areas of business are therefore marketing and sales together with Information provision. Depending upon their markets and objectives, the provinces and territories may work with CTC or independently. Destination marketing organisations also have the choice to work independently, with the relevant province or with CTC. The emphasis is on tourism being a 'shared responsibility'. It is the primary national tourism–marketing agency and this is the main use of the majority of its budget.

There are six marketing committees covering:

1. US leisure
2. US business
3. Europe

4. Asia-Pacific
5. Latin America
6. Canada (domestic).

Two other key committees oversee other strategic interests namely: the Industry and Product Development Committee (development of packages, all year tourism etc) and the Research Committee (oversees development of econometric and economic analysis tools for decision making). This committee works closely with the government statistics department (Statistics Canada) and the Canadian Tourism Research Institute. In addition to past records and Tourism Satellite Account data, the National Tourism Indicators are provided jointly by CTC and Statistics Canada, and these track overseas and domestic tourism. They provide quarterly and annual estimates of the main components of Canadian Tourism and are amongst the most developed in the world. They provide the basis for review of current performance, reviews of trends and structures and offer a foundation for policy and strategy decision.

A range of sub-committees also exists for various requirements and those currently in operation include Winter Tourism, Cultural and Heritage Tourism, and Adventure Travel and Eco-tourism. Such committees depend heavily on industry membership and industry chairs in order to locate them strategically with the trade they seek to serve and seek to bring them closer to the tourism consumer.

Planning Cycle

The CTC planning cycle flows from September to March. In September, consultations take place in the market and through working committees. This is followed in January– February with the first draft of a strategic plan to the board of directors. In March, the strategic plan and notional budget are approved. The planning cycle is represented in Figure 6.2.

The 2002–2003 strategy focused on the following objectives as shown in Table 6.8.

A National Tourism Strategy is also being developed at this time. Industry stakeholders including the Association of Canadian Travel Agents (ACTA) are liaising with Industry Canada. Consultations will also take part at the provincial level.

Future strategy documents highlight the importance of:

- Partnership
- Raising Canada's international profile
- Providing strategic information to industry through:
    - Research
    - The Industry Development Programme
    - Communications
    - The Tourism Reference and Documentation Centre comprising
        - A resource for CTC staff and
        - Industry (6000 books and 400 journals)
- A proper infrastructure to deliver the service including finance, human resources and technology.

The year 2003 was considered to be 'The Year of Challenge' (characterised by SARS and implications from the Iraq conflict) followed by 2004 as 'The Year of Rebound' and 2005 as 'The Year of Growth.'

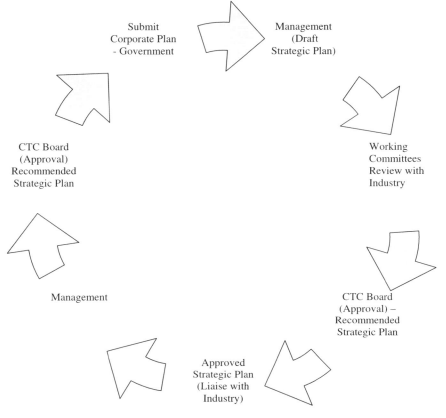

Figure 6.2: CTC planning cycle.
Source: Adapted from CTC Planning Cycle.

Tourism Development and the Product Club Approach

This system of development and upgrade of assets is almost unique to Canada. It is also one of CTC's most successful development initiatives. It provides development around core areas such as marketing, product development or innovation in thematic and market focused 'clubs'. CTC is a minority-funding agent, maintaining membership and consultation through financial input. France is credited with the original idea of Product Clubs (see the France section of the report for further information). There have been 44 Product Clubs created (as of January 2004) in Canada (involving some 5500 businesses), and they primarily consist of a partnership of entities with a common vision to undertake developments to introduce market ready packages for the tourism industry. It is one way for CTC to co-operate with the small- and medium-sized enterprises (SME) sector to ensure acceptable levels of quality of growth and product innovation. Product Clubs provide an opportunity for small businesses to share information, enhance existing products and develop

Table 6.8: CTC strategy for 2002–2003.

Objectives	Strategies	Target groups
Overcome the negative perception of Canada	Position Canada as an exciting dynamic and trendy destination	Consumer Trade Media Meetings and Incentives
Encourage shoulder season visits and spread visits throughout the year	Promote off-season products and packages	Consumer Trade Media Meetings and Incentives
Increase awareness of Canada and build a strong brand image to remain competitive	Use of a mix of complementary media to build brand and increase awareness	Consumer Trade Media Meetings and Incentives

Source: CTC.

new products. There were a record number of applications for Product Club assistance in 2002, with the current search proposals for 2004 now underway. There are two types of product: 'Tourism Products' (for example, resorts, festivals) and 'Promotional Products' (such as marketing literature). There are also 'clusters' that have been developed for specific attention such as: Outdoor Tourism; Culture; Winter and Tourism and Cities.

Partnership: The Way CTC Does Business

The principal of partnership also underpins the Popular Partnership Programme. It is an approach to regional and provincial marketing that appears to have gained some success in recent years. The objective is to encourage incremental, inter-provincial travel by Canadians. This is achieved by a combination of CTC and provincial authorities working in partnership in a targeted manner. Marketing is directed at traditional downtimes in the tourism calendar.

At a provincial level, partnership is evident in the investment and development offices (IDOs), which are the primary state and private sector forums for product development, quality improvement, and gateway and travel information centre management. IDOs act primarily to broker partnerships rather than being a direct funding agent although they will give advice on venture capital funding and relevant state sources.

Since 1999 the number of partnerships has grown as evidenced by Table 6.9 below although there are notable fluctuations.

The investment ratio of partner's contributions to CTC investment is aimed at 1:1. In 2001, the funds raised during the USA partner contributions totalled £18.7 million, enabling a ratio of 2:1 with Europe raising £6.8 million, demonstrating a ratio of 1.2:1.

It is interesting that CTC accepts that in the past industry lobby/representation at regional/provincial level has led to strong marketing concentration on provincial identity.

Table 6.9: Industry partners per programme.

Area	1999	2000	2001
USA	591	480	558
Europe	369	328	409
Asia/Pacific	199	240	258
MC&IT	150	163	192
Product development	189	174	187
Latin America	158	150	133
Canada	113	151	96
Research	34	44	19

Source: CTC.

As a consequence, much of the advertisement of the mid- to late 1990s abandoned iconic representation of Canada to focus on more esoteric and less identifiable images of provincial destinations. It is now widely accepted within CTC marketing that such thinking was more the result of industry partner pressure rather than good understanding of consumers. Accordingly, more recent marketing now emphasises the brand 'Canada' with iconic representation and less provincial promotion. Industrial partnership, whilst a clear strength, can also impact negatively and therefore must be utilised with caution.

Marketing Strategy

Seasonality and developing four-season tourism has been a major thrust of CTC and provincial tourism organisations. Summer is the main season with almost half (44%) of all tourism occurring from May to September. The month of October, November, March and April still remain 'down time' and are amongst the hardest months to promote. There are four main marketing target areas:

1. Canada
2. USA
3. Europe/Latin America
4. Asia/Pacific.

Working with industry partners is important to CTC and it has therefore built strong relationships with travel agents in the UK (over 400) who now specialise in selling Canada. A sophisticated Training and Resource Manual has been produced which enables UK agents to learn about Canada by distance learning and qualifying as Canada counsellors at the end of the learning process. There are three modules included in the manual which cover: basic information on what Canada has to offer as a destination; seasonal tourism and; planning a trip to Canada focusing on knowledge of the cities and festivals and events. The Canada counsellor programme has been in existence for three years and creates specialists on Canada. Increasingly packages are being offered to 'secondary' destinations such as Calgary, Edmonton and Winnipeg. Toronto, Montreal and Vancouver remain the major gateways although as indicated efforts are being made to promote and develop beyond traditional destinations. In 2002, two new communications products were launched to assist operations in Canada. A monthly tourism intelligence bulletin and quarterly Domestic and International Travel Business 'Outlooks' were produced on the web and in limited print form. CTC also developed further resources for operators in Canada including guides to financial performance measures and a risk-management insurance guide for operators in the adventure sector. This is all part of a sophisticated industry support network building quality via targeted assistance.

Certain themes dominate with the traditional offer of an unspoilt wilderness remaining very strong within national and provincial marketing. Other core themes evident in national marketing include:

– vibrant cities
– adventure
– safety/security
– relaxation/natural environment
– vast contrasts in scenery
– mountains, lakes, forests
– museums, festivals, retail.

Such themes are also evident at a provincial level in communication 'strap' lines such as:

• 'Super, Natural British Columbia'
• 'Escape to Saskatchewan'.

Geographical identification and confusion of provincial and city names are issues, and in recent years CTC has focused on the development of a national brand message built around product rather than geography. The various partnerships and joint funding initiatives serve to keep the NTO involved and consulted in what is occurring at a provincial/local level to minimise duplication and poor use of resources.

A degree of politicisation of marketing and organisation is evident in some of the work undertaken on Nunavut, a new territory created in 1999. This is a homeland for native peoples and is attempting to position itself as an adventure and heritage location although its fierce climate and relative distance from generating markets means that its impact in tourism terms remains marginal to date.

Examples of marketing undertaken by CTC include:

• Targeting morning news and talk shows with aspirational journey and exploration films of Canada. These are broken into the sequence of a Canadian trip and aimed at retaining interest across various 'episodes'. The former TV series titled as 'Canada — The Transcontinental Fantastic Journey' brought the Canadian experience to some 20 million Japanese viewers throughout December 2002. The train-based exploration of Canada included stops in Vancouver, Kelo, Edmonton, Saskatoon, Toronto, Montreal, Quebec City, Mont-Joli and Cavendish;
• Product launch, product placement and innovative strategic alliances have been used very effectively by CTC. In December 2002, a joint CTC and Porsche plan to develop new marketing activities profiling Alberta and a new vehicle were launched. The campaign

was focused around the launch of the new Porsche sports utility vehicle; Cayenne. A film 'Top Speed' was used to profile the Canadian Rockies in a visually stunning backdrop to the vehicle (see www.topspeedproject.com). It was based on a highly productive partnership between CTC, Travel Alberta and Porsche. Additional leverage in marketing terms was achieved through the Porsche magazine, which featured Canadian Travel Highlights;

- In an analysis of the impact of 11 September 2001 on the Canadian accommodation sector, Pannell Kerr Forster calculated a loss of 2 million room nights occupied during the final four months of 2001. A loss close to £149 million in room revenue was also recorded. Prior to 11 September, room occupancy at a national level was scheduled to achieve 64% at an average rate of £49 per room; however, the industry ended the year at 62% at an average rate of £48.50 per room. The greatest downturns were felt in Ontario followed by British Columbia and Quebec. The urban destinations of Toronto, Montreal and Vancouver were particularly badly hit. The national tourism agency; the CTC responded with a marketing campaign based on consumer research that indicated that in troubled times, travellers were looking at destinations closer to home and US visitors were utilising car transportation rather than air. The proximity of Canada to the US actually worked in the country's favour in 2002 with car borne tourism from the US increasing by 7.1% in the first eight months of 2002 even though overall visitor figures have fallen;
- As part of the '9/11 New Reality' campaign, £6.4 million in additional funding was allocated, with £3.8 million devoted to the US market and £2.5 million to the Canadian market. This additional effort generated £168.5 million, which equates to £20 for every £1 spent. The £19.6 million spent in Canada realised £108 million in spending. Combined with the campaign 'There's No Place Like Home,' an additional £60 million was spent by US visitors.
- Partnership marketing of £48.5 million was achieved in 2002 (up from £35.3 million in 2001). There are three types of partnership marketing:
  ○ CTC takes the lead role with the partner contributing funds (£5.9 million in 2002)
  ○ Third parties manage the project and CTC contributes a share (£32.7 million in 2002)
  ○ Contribution in kind from third parties (£9.8 million in 2002)
  ○ Partnerships include
    – FNAC Photo in France
    – Fat Face clothing retailer in UK
    – Caldo-Caldo in Italy
    – Amex in Taiwan
    – Scotia Bank in Mexico.
  ○ Non-traditional partnerships include
    – Samsonite
    – Porsche as referred to above
    – Baskin-Robbins.
- An enhanced and extended web presence including an e-marketing strategy, which involved collaboration with Air Canada and Hilton. Meeting a planner was developed. A 5.5% response rate was attracted to the campaign which created 600 business leads;
- 'FeelCanada' campaign in response to SARS;

- In 2004, campaigns focused on
  - Active Travellers
  - Western Urbanites
  - Meetings and Incentives.
- In 2002, a German focused ski co-op was targeted by direct mail including joint adverts with local partners, and a poster campaign. This resulted in an increase of 70% in bookings.
- The production of printed and written promotional material is also considered important with examples such as:
  - The spirit of Canada campaign in the UK
  - A vacation guide for Japan
  - CD-ROM for Taiwan
  - A gay and lesbian guide for the Australian market.

Canada has also demonstrated that it will change marketing agents if necessary to improve overall performance. For example, a new advertising agency, Palmer Jarvis DDB was appointed in recognition of its international reach. A new public relations firm, Weber Shandwick, has been appointed for the US market and new firms have also been appointed in Germany, the Netherlands and Brazil.

Specialist Market 'Niche' Performance

Eco-tourism   Eco-tourism is seen as a rapidly increasing segment of Canada's tourism economy. In 2002, the World Eco-Tourism Summit was organised by the World Tourism Organization and the United Nations Environment Programme (UNEP). It was hosted by CTC and Tourism Quebec, and attracted 3600 delegates. Canada also possesses a range of eco-tourism products and attractions, including:

- Nature/Culture observation (e.g. iceberg, northern lights viewing, aboriginal nature, plant life, cultural landscapes);
- Land-based eco-tourism (e.g. hiking, backpacking, rock climbing, interpretative walks, overland safaris);
- Water-based eco-tourism (e.g. canoeing, sea/river kayaking, river rafting, sailing, scuba diving, cruises, catch and release fishing);
- Wildlife viewing (e.g. birds, whales, polar bears, seals, bears, mousse, etc.);
- Winter activities (e.g. cross-country skiing, dog-sledding, ice climbing, winter camping);
- The Whale and Dolphin Society was allocated a budget of £8500 for marketing such tourism and the Return on Investment (ROI) reached £583,000 in 2002.

National park-based tourism   Closely allied to Eco-tourism are those activities related to and located in the National Park Network in Canada, Canada's natural regions are protected under legislation that ensures their value is communicated to the public and the services and facilities are provided for people to use them.

In 1993 a commitment was made to the System of National Parks. This required the creation of 17 new National Parks by 2000 to represent each of Canada's 39 natural regions. This has been partially achieved in Canada's 39 National Parks and Reserves. There is also a system for National Marine Conservation, which has divided Canada into 29 marine regions. This provides the tourism industry with a vital natural resource protected within federal legislation to ensure sustainable use and development. The key challenge here is to integrate the perspectives of biodiversity, conservation and tourism.

Horticultural Tourism   This is seen as a major tourist activity, which has been targeted for development from 2002 onwards in Quebec. According to CTC, gardens and green spaces are amongst the most visited attractions in Canada. The Quebec infrastructure being developed by the Green Spaces Product Club is a good example of how provincial and local tourism development funding (in partnership with the NTO) target specific aspects of product for improvement. In this case CTC has put in initial funding of £64,000, which is matched by public and private sector partners to achieve £128,000 for the upgrade and development of the new green space products in Quebec.

Other niche markets   Heritage Tourism has been targeted through the campaign, 'Packaging the Potential'. A niche product marketing task force has been set up which includes 23 product clubs and 28 new proposals including activity holidays. A brochure has been produced promoting heritage tourism with 8000 copies in English and 3000 in French. Strong growth is predicted in this market over the next 25 years. The US market is particularly important for Canada, with the market size estimated at 34.5 million and with Canada's potential market being in the region of 2.6 million.

Launch of New Website

CTC launched its updated website www.canadatourism.com during 2004.

There are currently around 1 billion users on the canadatourism website, with 10,000 registered users. The site provides a comprehensive guide to tourism in Canada and allows users to become members of the 'Canadian Tourism Exchange' for no fee. The site provides easy access to annual reports, detailed statistics (annual and quarterly), organisations charts, strategic plans, marketing information, access to publications and CTC's monthly magazine 'Tourism'. This magazine provides valuable information on research and marketing as well as updated statistics and information on product development. The user can also subscribe to a daily update by e-mail which provides a summary of the most recent developments in Canadian tourism. It is a key information resource for stakeholders, delivering news, business strategies, press releases and other material relevant to industry stakeholders, Canadatourism.com also houses important research, marketing programme information and product development data, developed by the CTC and targeted at the tourism industry.

According to the CTC, the website has been updated to include enhanced technology and content. Users will have access to an environment that is easy to use and navigate, and information that is organised in a more intuitive and logical manner. In addition, in an effort to streamline and integrate its communications vehicles, the CTC will bring together *TOURISM Online* and its *Daily Tourism News* e-mail (familiarly known as *CTX News*) via Canadatourism.com.

Current subscribers to Canadatourism.com will notice a new look to their *Daily Tourism News* e-mail, but the content will remain the same. As an added feature, the e-mail will contain links to new reports and publications available on Canadatourism.com, as well as links to the CTC's monthly magazine *TOURISM Online*.

According to former CTC acting President, the CTC has been spending around £851,000 a year on its website, e-marketing, etc. Since costs were escalating and the organisation did not have the right manpower resources to continue managing the site alone, the decision was taken to outsource everything to do with the website and IT from 2004. The cost will actually be lower — £766,000 a year.

Impact Assessment

Wherever respondent information is available to CTC, surveys will be carried out on major promotional activities undertaken to determine the incremental impact of those activities in terms of visits and revenue generated for Canada. A range of performance indicators have also been developed that are used internally to monitor performance, as follows (Table 6.10):

Case Study — The UK market for Canada

The UK, which is the major international source of visitors, has traditionally been a major VFR motivated market, but the last five years have seen increased inbound tourism from the UK. Increasingly the destination is being seen as a holiday option that is feasible and economic to visit.

However, latest figures indicate that visits from the UK are lower (-4.8%) than 2002. Very aggressive pricing is a factor as well as late offers from competitors such as Australia.

Table 6.11 indicates the UK market for Canada between 1995 and 2002.

The distribution between the purpose of travel has also changes as shown in Table 6.12.

A SWOT analysis reveals that from the UK market perspective, Canada has strengths in that it is considered value for money, has friendly people, good infrastructure and is considered a safe destination. Its cities offer easy access to nature and it has a variety of winter

Table 6.10: Performance indicators.

Industry measurables	CTC measurables
Return on investment	ROI
Share of new market share	Industry partnership participation
Average spend	Industry support for programmes
Growth in tourism	Partnership satisfaction
Revenue forecast	Employee satisfaction
Capacity utilisation	Overhead costs
Market penetration for selected products/niches	

Source: CTC and Authors.

Table 6.11: The UK market 1995–2002.

Market information	1995	2000	2001	2002
Visitor numbers ('000s)	641	862	826	721
Spending £ mn	241	457	437	422
Market share(%)	9.1	7.5	8.8	7.8

Source: CTC.

Table 6.12: Purpose of travel to Canada from UK.

Purpose	1995 (%)	1998 (%)	2002 (%)
Holiday	50	57	58
Business	10	9	9
VFR	36	29	28

Source: CTC.

activities. It is weak as a destination due to the initial high cost of travel. There is a lack of 'aspiration' to visit Canada with a perception that it lacks cultural attractions and that there are long distances between destinations within the country.

There are opportunities for Canada to expand in the UK market due to the ageing population with more time and money for travel together with an increasing short break market. The repeat visitor market is strong and there is easy access to the Internet. Threats due to the reduction in short-haul travel costs affect Canada and its major competitors are out-spending Canada in brand-building campaigns.

In order to succeed in the UK market, CTC intends to create 'aspirational' campaigns using Canada's iconic imagery to build a Canada brand. Increased use of new media will help target customers. The provision of financial support to partners is as always deemed important to success.

Canadian Tourism Commission also recognises a need to develop a key understanding of the motivational factors for UK travel, and to this end, investment in further research is essential. Comprehensive consumer research with UK industry partners will be undertaken, and the findings will be shared to ensure that CTC's industry contacts are provided with appropriate knowledge.

To attempt to increase UK visitor spending in Canada, the resources allocated will be divided between the need to increase awareness of Canada (70% of budget) and the remaining 30% on activities to increase short-term sales and impact. Once again a heavy focus is placed on partnerships with industry and the exploration of non-traditional strategic working alliances. Continued expansion of the Canada counsellor (Travel Trade Training) distance-learning programme referred to earlier is also essential together with the use of public relations wherever possible.

All of this must also focus on one of the main aims to make Canada a four-season destination.

Table 6.13: Targeted ratio for CTC partners.

Activity	CTC	Partner	Total
Brand building	1.950	0.720	2.670
Support for campaign partner activities	0.240	0.960	1.200
Other CTC activities	1.448	1.991	3.439
Total	3.638	3.671	7.309

Source: CTC.

It is considered that the partnership programme should work as to attempt to achieve a 1:1 ratio between CTC and the industry partner. The targeted ratio for partners and the CTC expenditure is detailed in Table 6.13.

Demand for North America appears to be positive from the UK market although at the time of the research (early 2004) this was more focused on the USA. Perhaps the US decision to implement more detailed passport requirements and visas will alter the market slightly in favour of Canada. There are positive aspects from the Canadian viewpoint in respect of city breaks and small meetings markets.

Marketing was considered fragmented and there is a need to focus on National branding.

In 2004 it is anticipated that additional funding of £425,000 should be directed towards branding with a main focus on

- overcoming the negative perception of Canada;
- increasing awareness of the brand;
- stimulating visitation in the shoulder months.

Following research of the UK long-haul travel market, three main characteristics have been identified: adventurers, culture vultures and wide open spaces. For 2004, targets have been set for a focus on Active Travellers and Western Urbanites which together make up 54% of the market.

Understanding the NTO Presence — The Canadian Tourism Commission in London

The London office of CTC is considered of significant importance, since the UK represents the third most important market for Canada.

The core departments rely heavily on recruitment of UK staff with market knowledge and the current office has no Canadian nationals working in London. The issue of loss of authenticity is far outweighed by the knowledge of UK staff in CTC's view. The knowledge base is supplemented by the UK advisory board, which is chaired and composed of industry personnel who are responsible for elements of Canadian inbound sales and marketing from the UK. Currently representatives include senior management from e-bookers, the On-line Travel Company, Cosmos, Thompson and a range of other tour operators. This advisory board guides the following activities:

– UK marketing and consumer research;
– UK and European marketing;
– Integrated travel offers;
– Development of inbound UK marketing strategy.

The advisory board meets up to four times per year and its Chair brings forward the UK Marketing Strategy to the European Marketing Strategy Group, which incorporates representatives from the primary generating markets namely:

– UK;
– Italy;
– France;
– Germany/Switzerland/Netherlands.

Current Focus of Activities within the UK Office of CTC

The reduction in demand for long-haul travel from the UK has decreased significantly since 2000. This has been countered by the rise and rise of low-cost carriers opening more routes to Europe and taking advantage of the trend towards shorter/urban breaks. As a consequence Canada has lost market share and the increase in number of visitors to Canada over the period 1995–2002 has fallen substantially behind the general increase in numbers travelling to long-haul destinations, and as a result Canada's market share has declined from its peak in the mid-90s from 9.1% to 7.8%.

The CTC London office records primary market movements as shown in Table 6.14.

Concern is also registered within CTC about changes in the profile of visitors, for example, the proportion of VFR visits has decreased significantly from 36% to 28%. Pure holiday visits are therefore a more important sector of the market whilst business visits remain stable.

Seasonality of visits has also changed with a major shift from the main season 3rd quarter to the 1st quarter, primarily due to the growth of the winter activities market, predominantly downhill skiing.

Against such macro travel indicators, CTC also commission research on trends in the UK market in order to better understand demand and the consumer.

Table 6.14: London office primary markets.

	1995	2000	2001	2002
Visits ('000)	641	862	826	721
Spend (£ mn)	241	457	437	423
Market Share (%)	9.1	7.5	8.8	7.8

Source: CTC.

Table 6.15: Trends in UK consumer holiday preferences.

From	To
Rigidly packaged	Independent
Long-haul	Short-haul
Long holidays	Short breaks
Sand and sea	Exotic, green
Do nothing	Experiences and activities
Down market	Quality

Major trends in UK consumer holiday preferences (according to CTC market intelligence) are summarised in Table 6.15.

From such analysis, attempts are then made to attempt to forecast demand. Key areas of interest for CTC include:

– Growth in pacific region destinations;
– Growth in the Middle East as a destination;
– Short break growth in Eastern and Central Europe;
– The increasing demand for modular/partly packaged holidays/customised holidays and dynamic packaging at the expense of traditional package holidays;
– Trends evidencing decreases in travel elements and increase in expenditure on activities at the destination;
– Demand for 'experience' rather than 'destination';
– Demand for 'authenticity, closeness to nature and local culture';
– The older population, increase in singles, later marriage patterns and declining birth rate and the impact of these trends on tourism patterns.

Basic analytical techniques such as SWOT and PEST analysis are used to drive understanding of the Canadian product from a UK perspective. From this a range of customer types are created which forms the basis of targeted marketing.

From identification, the strategic direction of marketing is developed around a scale as follows:

Unawareness	No knowledge of the destination
Awareness	Basic knowledge of the destination
Understanding	Knowledge of main types of product available within destination
Conviction	Convinced to visit because of appeal of destination
Response	Arrangements made to visit destination.

Building Industry Partnership through Directed Marketing

Following development of marketing activities around key objectives, CTC resources will be allocated to allow the achievement of brand building and tactical sales generation.

The aim is to lever 50% of marketing income from industry partners to meet an operational requirement of a 1:1 ratio. The appropriate campaign package is then created (with

CTC funds and investment by partners) in order to stimulate interest and demand for the destination. CTC also agrees financial support for a programme of tactical activities with those partners so that a fully integrated and complementary planning process is established.

Lessons from Canada

Canada can provide many examples of good working practice as evidenced by the following:

- Structure
  - clear vision and leadership;
  - crucial involvement of the private sector (partnership schemes);
  - strong research base to inform decision-making;
  - use of Tourism Satellite Accounting.
- Products and Services
  - the 'Product Club' approach;
  - importance of integrated transport;
  - commitment to environmental initiatives;
  - importance of air transport and provincial/regional airports accessing international markets;
  - product innovation initiatives.
- Enterprise
  - geographic partnerships that deliver market needs;
  - commitment to e-commerce and internet marketing;
  - strong service ethic and quality commitment;
  - travel trade training.

Factors which have contributed to successful performance include:

- a good record of economic growth;
- positive exchange rates;
- lower tax burdens in certain areas has also helped;
- the structure of tourism organisation enjoys a prominent role in government with significant intervention by the public sector to catalyse funding from the private sector;
- the representation of the private sector at all levels in organisations like CTC and provincial tourism organisations;
- the strong environmental commitment recognises the importance of the natural environment for tourism and acknowledges the significance and vulnerability of the natural elements to negative impact;
- a tax regime which allows overseas visitor to reclaim government/provincial sales tax (amounts vary from province to province); and
- a tax credit/incentive package for the film, TV and computer animation industry.

There are, however, some potentially negative factors that have to be taken into account:

- Too many partnership, provincial and regional organisations;
- Significant variations in provincial marketing and destination awareness where honey-pot areas thrive whereas more remote regions (e.g. Nunavut) struggle;

- There is a high dependency on Canadians and visitors from the US;
- The share of the outbound market is declining;
- Marketing investment is falling behind that of competitors;
- The balance of trade deficit is expected to increase;
- A cold and boring image counteracted by large funding investment to attract visitors.

CTC recognises that, despite the perceived success of its organisation, it has made a lot of mistakes since the CTC was first set up, and the original model has now changed quite a bit — hopefully, for the better. One of the main problems is that CTC management and its Board of Directors have been too reactive until now — rather than being proactive. And their passivity has allowed programmes to develop from the bottom-up rather than being CTC-led.

Office Rationalisation

All the CTC's offices used to be in Canadian Embassies. This was initially considered to be a good way of keeping costs down but, with time, the CTC has come to realise that it can find better real estate in different countries at the same or even a lower price. Hence the decision to exit from all embassies by end March 2004.

Although it is opening at least one new office in 2004 — in Beijing — its number of offices abroad has fallen in recent months/years. The prior Chief Executive, Doug Fyfe says that the CTC was simply in too many markets and could not afford the associated annual costs of some £128 — 170,000 a year.

Among the closures highlighted there have been big staff reductions in the USA — there used to be 26 staff employed in the country — and the trend of office and staff reductions in favour of employing General Sales Agents (GSAs) is expected to continue.

At the same time, a new structure is being tested in India, where the CTC's private sector partners/stakeholders are pooling resources to open an office, which will operate on a commercial basis. The first mission to India to scope out opportunities was in November 2003 and there was very good buy-in from potential investors/office partners. Fairmont Hotels was one of the participants. Fyfe expects this to be a model for the future.

Funding and Resources

In terms of funding and resources, the CTC expects that Parliamentary appropriations will be constant over the next five or so years, and will largely cover operational and project overhead costs. But this will leave very few dollars for programmes and, although the CTC's calls for matching funds from partners have always been highly successful — with partner funds exceeding expectations — the marketing budget is still considered inadequate. So the CTC has to find new ways of cutting costs and being more cost-effective.

Product Clubs

Another weakness of the CTC's organisation and structure is that it has too many product clubs. There are far more requests to create/join clubs than funds permit and, until now, the mistake has been to allow the development of the product clubs to be applicant driven — i.e. those who pay most, or shout the most loudly, get in. The success of the product club concept has become a major problem, in fact. In addition, the person responsible for managing the clubs left the CTC and was never replaced, so the CTC lost its control to some degree.

From now on it is adopting a new approach. The CTC and/or the committee responsible for the specific product club will take the relevant decisions — albeit in consultation with other stakeholders. So the process will be driven from the top downwards and will better respond to industry needs. Clubs will no longer be set up on the whim of a small group of people.

The CTC is currently inviting proposals for the creation of new or enhanced market-ready tourism products in Canada under the Product Club Programme. The new process involves that an executive summary has to be submitted as a first level of screening. Successful candidates at this stage will then be asked to submit the five-year business plan from which new product clubs will be selected.

The current invitation for proposals will emphasise market trends, trade, and marketing and sales linkages. The entire programme is being examined to determine the return on investment (value for dollar) over the last seven years, as well as a review of some programme features and processes. There have been 44 CTC product clubs created (as of January 2004), of which 33 have 'graduated' from the programme. Some 28 of these continue to operate.

Despite a number of weaknesses, the strength of the product club programme is its capacity to bring stakeholders together to accomplish activities and strategies that would likely not be achieved alone. This occurs through the creation of new partnerships and tourism product packages, as well as research to identify products and markets with high potential.

Adopting a More Proactive Approach to Delivering Market Intelligence

The CTC says it has learnt many lessons from 11 September 2001, SARS and the other negative events of the past couple of years — all of which have had a significant impact on demand for Canada's tourism product and services, and which have resulted in a loss of market share vis-à-vis its main competitors.

Over the past 18 months or so, a new process for market monitoring and market intelligence gathering has been put in place. It is much more proactive — trying to anticipate events and developments — but the CTC has also become much faster in terms of reacting to events/developments and providing useful intelligence for its partners. Ways of speeding up its response rate include the switch of its monthly magazine to an electronic-only version — which also saves costs — and simpler communication on a more frequent basis.

The CTC recognises that its market research — it spends some £6.38 million a year on this — needs to change radically and move towards more predictive modelling.

CRM/ERM

Customer relation management (CRM) and enterprise resource management (ERM) are the keys to the CTC's (and any NTO's) future success, Fyfe believes. If NTOs do not change their way of doing business and serving their partners/stakeholders, they will end up as 'merely instruments of advertising agencies'.

Tourism marketing is a business, not a political, decision and the CTC will, in future, focus on providing value for money for its partners — stakeholders in Canada's tourism industry.

In addition to outsourcing its IT/website, etc, it will focus heavily on CRM and ERM. When most NTOs, or DMOs think of e-marketing nowadays, says Fyfe, they think of sending out a few e-mails and just asking people if they want more. E-marketing is rarely linked to management of the process. And NTOs do not know what to do with the data they collect.

The NTO needs to own the data and manage it intelligently so as to make useful information available to its partners and staff — so that they in turn can make better business decisions.

This will be one of the key investment areas for the CTC over the foreseeable future.

Chapter 7

France

France's Recent Tourism Performance

If numbers of arrivals are the prime indicator of a destination's success, France is the undisputed world leader. The country generated some 77 million international tourist arrivals in 2002 — around 50% more than its closest contender Spain. And if same-day travellers are included in the count, the total was well over 160 million (Table 7.1).

France has enjoyed its number one position for over 14 years. Since 1980, it has averaged 4.4% growth a year in international arrivals and 4% in tourist overnights (Table 7.2). Growth has slowed slightly in more recent years — it fell from an annual 5.5% in arrivals and 4.1% in nights in the 1980s to 3.2% and 3.9%, respectively in the 1990s. But these averages have nonetheless been consistently above the growth for Europe and even Western countries overall.

In terms of international tourism receipts, France currently ranks third in the world behind the USA and Spain, recording £21.8 billion in 2002 (up from £21.2 billion the previous year) — having been ousted from second position in the ranking by Spain a few years ago. It remains well behind the USA as leader, primarily because average length of stay in France is comparatively low.

Some 53% of arrivals are for three nights or less, with a further 17% averaging 4–6 nights' stay. This is partly attributed to the fact that France is a leading short-break destination, but there is also a high share of transit travellers in the total count — mainly car-based travellers stopping in France on their way through to Spain, Italy and other Mediterranean destinations (Table 7.3).

Nevertheless, the country's historical performance has been impressive. Receipts have risen 25-fold in the past 30 years (in local currency) and increased by an average 9% a year from 1981 to 2001. Over the same period, France's surplus on its balance of tourism account increased annually by 7% — no mean achievement for a mature tourism destination.

Total tourism demand in France in 2002, according to the country's Tourism Satellite Account (TSA), was £64.0 billion — of which 54.7% from inbound tourism, 36.0% from domestic tourism, and 9.3% from outbound tourism.

France, with Canada, was one of the first countries in the world to develop a TSA and has been a major contributor to the efforts of the WTO, OECD and other international bodies in defining the definitive standard (i.e. *The TSA: Recommended Methodological Framework*) adopted by the United Nations Statistical Commission. According to the latest TSA, around 180,000 companies work directly in the tourism sector in France generating 772,000 jobs directly in tourism. More than 44,000 new jobs were created in the sector between 2000 and 2002. There has been no reliable breakdown of arrivals or nights

Table 7.1: France: Key facts — 2002.

Population	59.7 mn
GDP	£954.3 bn
International arrivals (TF)	77.0 mn
International overnights (TCE)	586.9 mn
Average length of stay (approx)	7.6 nights
International arrivals per inhabitant	1.3
Domestic arrivals	150.6 mn
Domestic overnights	806.5 mn
Average length of trip	5.4 nights
Domestic receipts	£35.0 bn
International receipts	£21.8 bn
as a % of GDP	2.3%
per tourist arrival	£283
per overnight	£37
per inhabitant	£365
Tourism's total contribution to GDP	6.7%
WTTC estimate for T&T industry GDP	*4.7%*
NTO's total tourism budget (% annual change)	£36.2 mn (NA)
State contribution (% share)	£16.3 mn (45.0%)
Marketing budget (% share of total budget)	£26.4 mn (73.0%)
Rate of Exchange	£1 = €1.58

NA, not available.

for France since 1996, the last year that the *Enquête aux Frontières* was undertaken. All annual data between 1997 and 2003 has been extrapolations based on the 1996 survey. The following are the official estimates for market breakdown in 2002 (Table 7.4).

The MICE Market

Estimates based on the latest available data from the 1996 *Enquête aux Frontières* suggest that business tourism generates some 14% of arrivals. However, according to France Congrès, a grouping of 47 conference towns in France, business tourism overall accounted for just 10% of total arrivals and 35% of tourism receipts in 2000. These shares are corroborated by a recent press release from Maison de la France's Conference/MICE Club.

In fact, the share could also have fallen, as international business travel to France has been the sector most adversely affected by the events of the past couple of years.

Table 7.2: International tourist arrivals and overnights in France, 1982, 1992, and 1996–2002.

Year	Arrivals (mn)	% Annual change	Nights (mn)	% Annual change
1982	33.5	9.8	298.9	13.6
1992	59.4	8.0	428.4	8.2
1996	62.4	4.2	459.5	8.1
1997	67.3	7.9	468.0	1.8
1998	70.0	4.0	490.9	4.9
1999	73.0	4.3	538.7	9.7
2000	75.6	3.5	559.2	3.8
2001	75.2	−0.5	580.9	3.9
2002	77.0	2.4	588.4	1.3

Note: Figures for 1982 and 1996 are the results of the Direction du Tourisme's frontier survey, the *Enquête aux Frontières*; other years are estimated based on these and other survey results.
Sources: Direction du Tourisme; World Tourism Organization (WTO).

Table 7.3: Breakdown of foreign arrivals in France by length of stay, 2002.

Length of stay (nights)	% Share of trips
1	21.5
2	17.5
3	14.0
4–6	17.4
7–13	17.5
14–27	9.4
28–120	2.5
121–365	0.2
Total	100.0

Source: Direction du Tourisme.

It is important to note, however, that a significant share of business tourism that used to involve overnight travel to France — from the UK, Belgium and the Netherlands, in particular — is now transacted within a day, thereby not appearing in official tourism statistics. Same-day travel to/from France has been stimulated by the Eurostar and Thalys high-speed rail services.

France's Main Strengths as a Tourism Destination…

France's prominent position in world tourism today is due in no small part to the fact that the country is blessed by an enormous number and range of attractions and, therefore, holiday options for tourists. From its 5000 km of varied coastline to its high mountains, spectacular gorges, and vast rural areas — not to mention its overseas dominions and territories

Table 7.4: Breakdown of arrivals, overnights and tourism receipts by key source regions and individual markets, 2002.

	% of arrivals	% of overnights	% of receipts
Source region			
Europe	89.7	85.3	68.7
America	6.0	8.5	17.5
Africa	1.2	2.6	5.8
Asia Pacific	3.0	3.4	6.0
Other	0.1	0.2	2.0
Market			
UK/Ireland	19.4	18.6	15.0
Germany	18.6	18.6	11.5
Netherlands	16.4	13.9	5.6
Belgium/Luxembourg	11.0	10.9	9.1
Italy	10.0	9.1	7.9
Switzerland	4.0	3.5	9.1
USA	3.9	5.2	15.2
Spain	3.9	3.4	4.1
Japan	0.9	0.8	2.6

Source: Direction du Tourisme.

(DOM-TOM) — France caters for all types of sporting and other leisure activities. But it is equally renowned for its vibrant cities, rich cultural heritage and outstanding cuisine and wines.

During the past 10 years or so, the country's inbound tourism performance has also been boosted by a number of different events and developments. Most significant was the opening of Disneyland Paris in April 1992. Despite the American theme park's disappointing financial performance, visitor attendance at what is Europe's leading attraction averages well over 12 million a year, and it generates more tourist nights than most European cities.

...and its Weaknesses

However, despite France's great diversity in terms of its tourism offer, its modest share of demand in some sectors of the market demonstrates clearly that there are still a number of weaknesses to be overcome. European Travel Monitor (ETM) data suggest that France attracts an 11% share of all European outbound trips. However, the respective share varies sharply from sector to sector.

Thanks largely to Disneyland Paris, the country boasts a 48% share of all visits to theme parks by Europeans. It is also a leader in terms of rural tourism, accounting for 20% of trips involving holidays in the countryside. Other sectors generating higher

Table 7.5: France's share of European international trips by selected holiday sectors, 2000.

Sector	% Share
Theme parks	48
Rural tourism	20
Touring holidays	15
City trips	14
Summer mountain holidays	12
Winter sports	9
Beach holidays	7
Overall	11

Source: European Travel Monitor, IPK International.

shares than average for France are touring holidays, urban tourism and summer mountains holidays.

In contrast, France is surprisingly poor at attracting foreign winter sports tourism, despite having an extensive range of ski stations and mountain resorts. After gaining share in the early 1990s at the expense of competitive destinations in Europe, it seems to have lost its competitive edge and suffered a declining foreign market share once again.

France's modest 7% share of European beach holidays is much easier to explain. Since it has never been developed as a sun and beach package holiday destination — like Spain and most of the other Mediterranean-bordering countries — it has happily avoided being overwhelmed by mass-market tourists in search of cheap sun and fun (Table 7.5).

2003 Trends

Despite mid-year concerns that some key markets would record double-digit declines in tourist arrivals in France in 2003, preliminary results point to a relatively modest downturn of some 2.6% in frontier arrivals (TF). After an increase of over 10% in Q1, Q2 and Q3 suffered decreases of 6% and 7% respectively. Tourism reportedly picked up quite strongly in Q4, although there were still expected to be declines from the USA, Japan and UK.

Tourist arrivals in hotels (THS) fell by an estimated 9.6% in 2003, based on actual data for the first 11 months, and international tourism receipts were down 2% at end-October.

Organisation of Tourism in France

France's National Tourism Organisation (NTO) is Maison de la France, which reports directly to the Secretary of State for Tourism within the Ministère de l'Equipement, des Transports, du Logement, du Tourisme et de la Mer. It co-operates closely with the

Direction du Tourisme, the executive arm of the ministry, and with the Agence Française de l'Ingénierie Touristique (AFIT).

Ministère de l'Equipement, des Transports, du Logement, du Tourisme et de la Mer

The ministry ultimately responsible for tourism management and development in France is le Ministère de l'Equipement, des Transports, du Logement, du Tourisme et de la Mer (roughly translated as the Ministry of Amenities, Transport, Housing, Tourism and the Sea). Although the Secretary of State for Tourism within the ministry is a relatively junior post, the French Government (notably under right-wing governments) has always recognised the importance of tourism to the national economy. This lends a certain level of authority to the post.

Moreover, through the Inter-Ministerial Committee for Tourism (which met for the first time in 20 years in September 2003!), tourism has formal direct access to all the major ministries — finance, the economy, foreign affairs, education, culture and sustainable development — as well as to the prime minister (Figure 7.1).

The significance of tourism in France is also reflected in the overall central government budget allocated to tourism — £54.0 million in 2003, albeit down 4.3% (in euro) in 2002s £51.7 million. The decline can be partly explained by the fact that, before the present government came to power, a much larger share of the budget was allocated to social tourism — e.g. encouraging and financially supporting domestic holidays for the French lower socio-economic classes — and this has been progressively reduced.

The 2004s total state allocation for tourism is expected to fall by a further 4.2%, to £51.8 million, although the total amount is being boosted by an additional £1.6 million (2003 exchange rate) for marketing and promotions — split equally between 2003 and 2004 (the publicly announced £4.6 million includes VAT). This is aimed at strengthening France's 'Recovery Plan' — reinforcing action plans in target markets, enhancing France's image in the USA, increasing e-marketing and improving marketing through the website www.franceguide.com.

The overall budget covers the total budget of the Direction du Tourisme, plus central government allocations to Maison de la France, l'AFIT, the Observatoire National du Tourisme (ONT), and the Conseil National du Tourisme (CNT). Some £1.6 million has

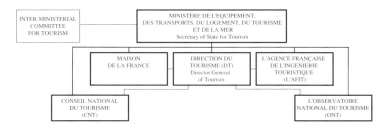

Figure 7.1: Structure of the French tourism support system. Note: Excludes the regional and departmental tourism committees (CRTs and CDTs), which are elected or appointed locally and work largely independently. Source: The Travel Business Partnership.

also been allocated to carry out a new Frontier Survey (*l'Enquête aux Frontières*) — France's main source of data on inbound tourism — and around £2.8 million has been set aside for meetings and related expenses of the reactivated Inter-Ministerial Committee for Tourism.

The Secretary of State's budget does not, however, include all additional funding earmarked for special campaigns, which are usually decided after the provisional budget has been drawn up for the year. Examples of these are campaigns to revive tourism after disasters such as the Erika oil tanker sinking and oil spillage off the southwest coast of France in 2002 (£42.3 million over two years), or to support rural regions after devastating storms (1999), or mountain regions when snow conditions are particularly poor.

The Secretary of State — sometimes in partnership with other ministries, and usually through the Direction du Tourisme — is responsible for tourism policy, planning, tourism investment facilitation, fiscal and other incentives, education and training, development of the brand 'France', the use of new technology, overall management of tourism research, etc. However, responsibility for promoting the France brand — a decision emanating from the Inter-Ministerial Committee for Tourism — is also shared with Maison de la France — and the NTO is also very active in market research and the harnessing of technology for improved communication and e-commerce/distribution.

Direction du Tourisme (DT)

The Direction du Tourisme (DT) is the central government body responsible for national tourism administration — acting as the executive arm of the Secretary of State, supporting him and his cabinet in all the areas cited above, as well as providing industry support, assuming much of the responsibility for international relations, European Union affairs, etc.

It carries out its own economic analyses and research and co-ordinates public sector research activities concerned with tourism in or to France, including the *Enquête aux Frontières* and the monthly French travel survey. The latter, which covers domestic and outbound trips, is a panel survey conducted on the DT's behalf by TNS Sofres. (Maison de la France carries out research in foreign markets.)

The DT has around 230 staff, including those employed in its 27 regional offices — representatives of the state (préfets) who oversee tourism in the regions on behalf of the state as part of their overall activities, plus support staff. Following the Decentralisation Law in France in 1992, competence for tourism has been split between the state and the regional tourism authorities (the Comités Régionaux du Tourisme). But there is (supposed to be) close co-ordination between the two — in all areas, but especially in the context of the European Union's regional Structural Funds Programmes.

There are some 120–130 staff at the DT's Paris HQ, split between two 'sous-directions' (sub-directions/divisions), one department, two 'missions' and the Service d'Etude et d'Aménagement Touristique de la Montagne, or SEATM (which looks after the needs/concerns of mountain resorts etc. in conjunction with l'AFIT). The 'sub-directions' account for at least two-thirds of the HQ staff between them, looking after general administration (including HR, legal and fiscal matters, etc.) and tourism policy (including education and training, tourism employment, social tourism, etc.).

This one 'department' focuses on strategy, tourism satellite accounting, market intelligence, research and forecasting and employs some 15 staff. The 'mission' responsible for new technology and communications has around 10 staff, as does the 'mission' for international affairs, which handles bilateral and multilateral negotiations with other countries and is responsible for promoting French know-how abroad in conjunction with l'AFIT.

Significant investment is currently being made (estimated at hundreds of thousands of pounds sterling) to upgrade the DT's website www.tourisme.gouv.fr, and the new site should be up and running sometime this year. The current site, aimed at informing the industry and the public sector about the DT's and Secretary of State's activities and achievements, is already considered one of the better sites of this kind — in terms of the provision of useful information — operated at central government level.

Association Française de l'Ingénierie Touristique (AFIT)

L'AFIT, first established in 1993, is the French agency for expertise and know-how in tourism. It is 95% funded by the state and its role is twofold. In France, it attempts to stimulate private sector investment in tourism and, in foreign markets its role is to assess business development opportunities for French companies. This reflects the ministry's efforts to stimulate all export sectors, not just tourism.

Observatoire National du Tourisme (ONT)

A mixed public–private sector body with around 200 members — representatives of all the industry associations and federations, private sector companies such as airlines, hotels and tour operators, research institutes, and regional and municipal tourism bodies — the ONT provides regular monitoring and tracking of the travel and tourism market on the demand as well as the supply side.

The ONT commissions about 20 studies/projects a year, and also addresses key issues affecting the industry through different commissions and regular working groups.

Inter-Ministerial Committee for Tourism

The committee, which met for the first time in 20 years in September 2003, includes either the ministers or secretaries of state — or both — of 23 key ministries. It is the 'vehicle' set up to address issues involving tourism but which involve more than one ministry — such as the staggering of school holidays, education and training, quality control, development and management of the France brand.

Rencontres Parlementaires sur le Tourisme

One of the initiatives of the current Raffarin government was the (revived) Inter-Ministerial Committee for Tourism. At the same time, a number of very high-level meetings — the Rencontres Parlementaires sur le Tourisme — involving all stakeholders in France's tourism, have been organised over the past 12–18 months.

The third such meeting, organised by Paul Dubrule (Co-chairman of the Accor Group and a mayor of a medium-sized town in France), is being promoted under the title 'Quel tourisme pour la France en 2020?' (What kind of tourism should we be targeting for France in 2020?). The meeting will be held in April and will be hosted by the Prime Minister and the Secretary of State for tourism.

Participants will include heads of the different CRTs and CDTs, mayors of key cities, leading tourism players (Club Méditerranée, Disneyland Paris, etc.) and other invited guests. From the draft programme, the main themes appear to be local development, infrastructure needs, investment facilitation and incentives, plus different sectors of tourism earmarked for investment or support over the foreseeable future. These include rural tourism, 'workers tourism' (factory visits, etc.), health and wellness ('thermalisme et thalassothérapie') and cultural tourism.

Consultative and Other Related Bodies/Organisations

Conseil National du Tourisme (CNT)   The CNT is an advisory body to the Secretary of State, comprising around 300 high-level public and private sector representatives involved in tourism and related fields, including the heads of all the tourism industry associations and federations. It holds an annual general assembly and convenes special committees as needed.

Bourse Solidarité Vacances   This is a public–private fund — officially termed a 'grouping of public interests' — to help stimulate holiday-taking by the lower economic classes of France, who would not normally be able to afford to take holidays. Contributions to the fund come from government and major public and private sector employers.

Association Nationale pour les Chèques Vacances (ANCV)   This association is responsible for managing the vouchers used in the above-mentioned scheme. Employees from a growing number of public and private sector companies and organisations are encouraged to save money from their salaries every month, and the resulting savings are matched by employers through the above-mentioned fund. Savings by employees are matched in terms of value with vouchers that can then be used to purchase transport, accommodation or full packages for holiday travel.

Conseil National des Villes et des Villages Fleuris   This is a committee responsible for organising the annual competition for the best village/town in France in terms of flower displays.

Maison de la France

Structure

Founded in 1987, Maison de la France is what is called — roughly translated from the French — a 'grouping of economic interests' (GIE). It is the official NTO responsible for the promotion and marketing of France and French products and services abroad, and it also co-ordinates promotions abroad on behalf of France's 22 regions (see below), although the regions are also free to handle their own promotions in foreign markets. It has no other areas of responsibility.

Education and training, sector skills, environmental concerns, hotel classification, etc. are the areas of responsibility of the Secretary of State and/or the Direction du Tourisme.

Membership

Maison de la France is a membership organisation, with members contributing over €9 million to its annual budget. Membership now totals around 1300 (up from 70 in 1987) comprising the following different categories:

- some 200 regional and local tourism authorities (the Comités Régionaux du Tourisme (CRTs) and the Comités Départementaux du Tourisme (CDTs)) (34%);
- industry associations, including local chambers of commerce and the operating sector (40%); and
- companies/organisations indirectly linked to tourism and leisure activities (26%).

The operating sector comprises hotels, resorts and leisure parks, transport companies, reservation services, travel agents, inbound tour operators, etc. Companies/organisations not directly involved in tourism include high fashion goods and automobile manufacturers.

Board of Directors

Maison de la France's Board comprises 27 members, of whom seven come from central government — four from Tourism, one from Culture and one from the ministry responsible for the Budget. The remaining 20 are heads of the CRTs, CDTs and industry associations, and the membership also includes tourism specialists directly appointed by the minister and representatives of the private sector. The chairman (currently Gérard Brémond from Pierre & Vacances) is elected by the membership for a three-year renewable term.

The Board meets a minimum of four times a year, but can be convened at any time on the request of its chairman or eight members of the Board. Each member has one vote.

Staff and Offices

The NTO has 285 staff, of whom 83 work at its headquarters in Paris and 202 (71%) are spread through 33 offices and representative offices in 29 countries around the world. Of these offices, 17 are outside Europe. However, Miami is due to close at the end of March 2004. A Chicago office was closed in January, although one person continues to represent Maison de la France on a retainer basis.

Offices Abroad

Of the total offices abroad, some are 100% operated by Maison de la France, some are housed in Air France offices or the local French Chambers of Commerce — often with shared staff — and one, in Beijing, is a joint operation with Air France. Offices — which are fully operated by Maison de la France unless otherwise indicated — are located in:

Europe

- Austria — Vienna (also responsible for Central Europe);
- Belgium/Luxembourg — Brussels;
- Germany — Frankfurt and Berlin;
- Hungary — Budapest (c/o Air France);
- Ireland — Dublin;
- Italy — Milan;
- Netherlands — Amsterdam;
- Poland — Warsaw (c/o French Chamber of Commerce);
- Russia — Moscow);
- Scandinavia — Copenhagen and Stockholm);
- Spain/Portugal — Madrid, Barcelona and Lisbon (Lisbon c/o Air France);
- Switzerland — Zurich and Geneva;
- UK — London.

Outside Europe

- Australia — Sydney;
- Brazil/Latin America — Brazil and Buenos Aires (BA c/o French Chamber of Commerce);
- Mexico — Mexico City (c/o Air France);
- Canada — Montreal;
- Greater China — Beijing (joint operation with Air France), Hong Kong, Taipei and Seoul (all c/o Air France);
- Japan — Tokyo;
- South Africa — Johannesburg/Craig hall (c/o Air France);
- Southeast Asia/India — Singapore and Delhi;
- USA — New York, Los Angeles.

As already indicated, one person represents Maison de la France in Chicago on a retainer basis following the closing of its former office in January 2004. The trend towards appointing GSAs or sharing of offices appears to be growing as a means of cutting costs.

A significant share of the offices abroad (no details as the exact number changes too frequently) has walk-in offices serving the public, but these are declining. This is both due to the high associated costs and to the fact that, with increased internet usage, enquiries from walk-in visitors have fallen quite significantly in recent years. In 2003 some 900,000 walk-in visitors were recorded by Maison de la France's offices, and 700,000 requests for information were received by email. Postal enquiries totalled approximately 500,000.

Of the 202 staff employed in Maison de la France's offices abroad, 132 (65%) are locally employed — a share that is rising annually. Most of these are support staff.

Table 7.6: Staff responsibilities in Paris headquarters.

General management	5
Finance	9
HR, secretariat, other support staff	13
Marketing	33
Communications, partnerships	14
New technology	9

Source: Maison de la France.

Headquarters

Maison de la France's staff at its Paris headquarters work in the following areas (staff numbers per activity/area of responsibility) (Table 7.6).

The salaries of six members of staff — from across all areas of activity/responsibility — are paid by the Secretary of State. This situation apparently goes back to the early days of Maison de la France, when the newly established NTO had insufficient funds to cover fixed costs, and the Secretary of State agreed to fund certain posts. There does not appear to be any rhyme or reason as to why the particular posts were selected.

Resources and Funding

Maison de la France had an official budget of £36.2 million in 2002, and this declined by 5% (in euro) to £37.5 million in 2003 — despite additional funding of £2.3 million made by the government in the last couple of months of the year for the post-Iraq war recovery campaign (Table 7.7).

Year-on-year comparisons are misleading because of exchange rate fluctuations and variations in accounting procedures. It is also very difficult to provide clear details of the government share of Maison de la France's budget, which appears to have been 45% for 2002 and 46% for 2003. In fact, these shares are based on the annual budgets excluding contributions by third parties to advertising and promotional campaigns and other activities. Since these contributions usually go direct to advertising and PR agencies, they are not included in the official, published budget. The consolidated budget in 2002 was £42.3 million. This included £20.2 million from the state/central government (48%).

Some £22.2 million (52%) came from its various partners (partners of course include provincial/regional governments/tourism authorities) membership fees of some £5.7 million, as well as contributions to marketing and promotional campaigns, commercial activities in some markets, and an estimation of contributions in kind — e.g. complementary hotel accommodation for journalists and tour operators on familiarisation trips. Commercial activities — undertaken at only some offices, e.g. Madrid — include sales of entrance tickets to museums, city cards, etc.

Marketing and promotions (variable costs) accounted for 73.8% of Maison de la France's non-consolidated budget in 2002, or £26.7 million. (An additional £6.3 million or so in partner funding (which went directly to advertising and PR agencies) can be added

Table 7.7: Maison de la France's budget, 2002–2004.

Year	Total budget (£ mn[a])	% Annual change (in euro[a])	State's contribution (%)[b]	% Share to marketing & promotion[c]	Actual M&P (£ mn)
2002	36.2	NA	45	73	26.4
2003	37.5	−5.1	46	71	26.6
2004[d]	40.2	7.2	NA	72	28.9

NB: It should be noted that budget data provided by Maison de la France is exclusive of VAT. However, the total budget calculated annually includes VAT payable at 19.6%. The NTO was first required to pay VAT 2–3 years ago. NA, not available.
[a]€1 = £0.632 in 2002, £0.690 in 2003 and 2004 (estimated).
[b]The state is the central government — the balance of funding includes contributions from provincial and local/municipal governments/tourism authorities.
[c]The % share allocated to marketing and promotions excludes money paid directly to advertising and PR agencies by partners and third parties.
[d]Provisional.
Source: Maison de la France.

to that to make a total of £33.0 million for marketing and promotions overall.) The respective figures were 71.2%, or £24.8 million for 2003.

Current estimates point to a 7.2% increase in Maison de la France's total budget for 2004, excluding the £2.3 million expected as additional special funding to compensate for losses in 2003. If this is confirmed, the total budget would be £42.4 million, up 13.3%.

The state's share is not yet determined but will certainly increase by more than the overall budget, and the contributions targeted from partners and membership dues are forecasted to remain at around 2003's level. Current estimates also suggest that the marketing share of the budget (variable costs) will be about 72%, with 28% allocated to fixed costs/administration.

Role and Activities

As already indicated, Maison de la France's role is to promote and market France and French products and services abroad, with partnership the core of its activities.

Specifically, its remit is to:

- promote France as a tourism destination in partnership with the CRTs and CDTs;
- Develop a strong partnership between the state, the regional/local authorities, the travel trade and other important sectors of the economy;
- Provide support to members in the area of international marketing, so as to help them develop their business; and
- Represent the Secretary of State, when required to do so, in dealings with international organisations (such as the World Tourism Organisation), as well as in bilateral and multilateral negotiations.

Mission

The prime goal, established by the Secretary of State, is to increase average length of stay, increase average spend per person per day and per trip, and improve the seasonal and geographic spread of tourist arrivals and overnight volume in France.

The arrival of Europe's major tour operators and low-cost airlines in France (TUI, Thomas Cook, etc.) over the past year or two has been of increasing concern to Maison de la France and the government generally because they have significantly reduced the price of holidays abroad. As a result, extra effort is deemed necessary to attract more, higher-yield foreign tourists staying for longer periods in France, so as to ensure that the country's positive balance on its travel and tourism account is not reduced.

Controls/Audits

Like all public sector and part-public sector enterprises, Maison de la France undergoes frequent controls and audits by the Inspection Générale du Tourism. In addition, its activities are monitored by its Board of Directors and the Secretary of State for tourism. Evaluation criteria are based on the four performance indicators identified by the new Loi des Finances. These include success of its programmes and activities, the visibility of its marketing and its share/number of partners.

There are also plans to introduce more sophisticated indicators to evaluate the performance of offices abroad, notably to try to assess return on promotional spending.

Marketing Strategy, 2005–2010

Maison de la France's existing Marketing Strategy applies to the three-year period 2002–2004. It is currently being revised — in part because of the above-mentioned trends, but also because of the need to focus more on harnessing new technology to improve marketing and distribution — and the whole of the NTO's activities are being reviewed. It is too early to give any indication as to the direction the new strategy is likely to take, since preliminary feedback from the different surveys/reviews being carried out has not yet been received by Maison de la France's HQ.

As an example, surveys are being conducted in different key markets to assess France's image – as well as its strengths and weaknesses as a tourism destination — among consumers and the travel trade. Preliminary feedback is due by the beginning of March.

On the initiative of the Secretary of State for Tourism, Maison de la France has set up two committees over the last few years to facilitate the development of its longer-term marketing strategy — expected to cover 2005–2010 (i.e. six years instead of the normal three years). Once this has been decided, annual strategies/plans will be drawn up according to the long-term strategy, updating it when necessary.

The two committees are the:

International Consultative Committee (ICC) Established in January 2003, the ICC currently comprises 250 tourism professionals from all over the world who are active in the marketing of France as a tourism destination. By way of example, current committee members include representatives of all sectors of the industry from countries such as the UK (17), Germany (14), Italy (11), Brazil (9), Austria (8), Canada (6), Russia (5), South Korea (4) and China (3).

Committee members act both as advisers to Maison de la France and as ambassadors for France in their local markets. Their prime role is to enhance the brand 'France' and to contribute to the thinking with regard to Maison de la France's long-term marketing strategy.

Marketing Commission (Committee) The Marketing Commission, which includes 25 paid-up members of Maison de la France, has actually existed since 1998, but it was recently called on to play a greater role in helping the NTO define its longer-term strategy. The Commission meets on a regular basis, providing feedback from the individual members' key markets/clientele as to the image of France, perception of the destination in terms of quality, diversification of products, etc.

Members are actively involved in trying to reposition France — and, in particular, Paris as the country's main gateway — as an attractive, interesting and affordable tourism destination.

Marketing Strategy/Plan, 2002–2004

According to the 2002–2004 Marketing Strategy/Plan, marketing and promotion is currently divided into four separate areas of activity/responsibility in terms of goals and actions.

Public Information

Goals

- Present the quality and diversity of the French tourism product;
- Maintain the loyalty of those tourists already interested in France and attract new target markets; and
- Promote www.franceguide.com as the gateway to France's tourism offer.

Actions in 2002

- 183 advertising campaigns aimed at all markets, and involving the presence of Maison de la France, reinforced by 43 direct marketing operations;
- 32 online campaigns;
- 70 different types of brochures (total distribution 2 million);
- 6 million website visits; and
- 24 million pages read at www.franceguide.com.

Sales Promotion

Goals

- Increase the presence/programming of France in tour operators' brochures;
- Encourage tour operators to diversify their programmes to France;

- Train foreign tour operators to sell France; and
- Organise joint sales promotions/meetings between French and foreign tour operators and help Maison de la France's members form partnerships abroad (through fairs, conferences, workshops, educational trips, etc.).

Actions

Participation in/organisation of:

- 137 public and/or trade fairs (i.e. 2.5 million visitors);
- 103 trade workshops (i.e. 9000 tourism professionals meeting with Maison de la France's partners); and
- 158 training seminars for tour operators and travel agents (i.e. 11,000 individuals/companies contacted).

Press and PR

Goals

- Enhance France's image as a tourism destination with the international media;
- Keep the trade press and members informed about Maison de la France's marketing activities; and
- Organise press trips, conferences and social evenings.

Actions

- 574 public relations' events with the media;
- 1292 media familiarisation trips to France; and
- 11,000 press articles generated.

Market intelligence and planning

Goal

- Analyse the requirements and expectations of foreign visitors in order to help the trade and suppliers develop suitable products;
- Monitor significant market developments;
- Develop market intelligence and benchmarking in foreign markets; and
- Undertake studies to determine prospects/likely trends in key and emerging markets.

Actions

- a three-year marketing strategy;
- more than 50 market studies;
- quarterly marketing intelligence newsletters for members; and
- collaboration with the European Travel Commission on pan-European marketing studies.

Total spending in 2002 (including funding for campaigns from third parties that does not show up in Maison de la France's official budget) was broken down as follows. For this breakdown — which appears in Maison de la France's consolidated financial statements, staff salaries are split between the different activities/areas of operation.

- Research, studies   £1.8 mn
- Press, PR   4.4 mn
- Consumer campaigns   20.5 mn
- Trade/industry campaigns (including trade shows):   12.1 mn
- Other costs   3.5 mn

Total: £42.3 mn

A Product-Based Marketing Approach

Maison de la France's main activities focus on its 16 clubs. These cover specific sectors of the market and group all interested stakeholders, who pay club membership dues to fund activities, including promotional campaigns. There are special financial packages available for those short of resources — e.g. an 'associate' membership category allows companies to take part in club activities without being full members of Maison de la France.

More than 500 of its members (43%) participate in at least one of the clubs, which focus on themes/sectors such as business travel, health/wellness, wine tourism, youth and senior travel, urban tourism and golf. This club concept has become an envied model the world over and has been copied by many other NTOs, e.g. Canada. Spain also tried to introduce the concept in the mid-1990s, but the local travel industry and tourism authorities of the autonomous regions were not in favour.

Branding France

The Brand France campaign is supported by the Inter-Ministerial Committee for Tourism, i.e. other ministries as well as the ministry responsible for tourism. The aim is to provide a framework for France's image abroad, create synergies between the different famous French brands (high fashion goods, perfumes, automobiles, etc.), and reinforce the visibility of the brand marketing.

New Media and e-Marketing

New media and e-marketing play an important role in Maison de la France's marketing and promotion strategy. An estimated 10% of the NTO's budget is currently spent on IT, for the development and further enhancement of its portal, as well as for research into the potential of new technology such as Wireless Application Protocol (WAP) and digital TV-based applications and customer relationship management (CRM).

This area is projected to develop strongly over the next couple of years, helping Maison de la France introduce cost efficiencies as well as to improve its e-marketing and the e-sales of its members. Once e-marketing is sufficiently improved, the need for telephone and walk-in information services will decrease substantially, it believes. The intention is also to link its portal/website to all members' sites so that consumers can access these sites with three simple clicks, allowing them to make bookings online.

Maison de la France's website development strategy is three-pronged — aimed at consumers, the travel industry and its partners/members. For this last category, it provides a cost-effective and simple-to-access communications channel.

The consumer website www.franceguide.com covers 40 markets in nine languages (with Japanese and Korean only accessible in the respective countries). Chinese is due to be added shortly. In 2002, more than 24 million pages were read during 6.4 million visits to the website. The target is more than 9 million in 2004.

As far as CRM is concerned, the current target is to obtain a total of 5 million qualified addresses from visitors to the site interested in France from all over the world. These will be used for e-marketing from 2005.

In addition to obtaining basic information on France's tourism offer, the travel industry also has access to market research and statistics (on a paying basis), a photo library, a timetable of marketing opportunities, different newsletters, etc.

The site is even more comprehensive for members/partners, providing themed areas that list the activities of different clubs, discussion forums, free (non-paying) access to studies and research, etc. The number of services for members is continually being expanded, and the quality improved.

Individual offices of Maison de la France abroad can personalise their country websites to focus on the needs of their specific markets.

Domestic Tourism Promotion

Although Maison de la France has no official responsibility for domestic tourism promotion — this is assumed by the Secretary of State/Direction du Tourisme — it does carry out ad hoc campaigns on behalf of the DT and Secretary of State to stimulate tourism demand in the French market, particularly at times of crisis.

One example was the special campaign aimed at supporting the southwest coastal region after the tanker disaster and resulting oil slick had a major impact on domestic tourism demand.

Other examples are the Bonjour campaign, initially intended to train tourism professionals to be more welcoming to foreign visitors, but which now also encompasses the domestic market. Maison de la France assumed responsibility for the campaign 10 years ago and it has since been brought up to date and incorporated into a new campaign Bienvenue en France (Welcome to France). In addition, Maison de la France carries out marketing and promotions in the French market on behalf of the country's overseas DOM-TOM.

The cost of the domestic tourism campaigns is not included in Maison de la France's budget. Funds are provided, as and when required, by the Secretary of State.

Market Intelligence and Research

Marketing based on scientific research   Maison de la France's marketing and promotional efforts appear to be based on hard, scientific research. Its 2002–2004, Marketing Plan provides some detail as to how spending is allocated to different markets, and which criteria are used to establish priorities. The criteria for evaluation, which are weighted according to their perceived importance (the higher the number, the more important the weighting) — and which are reviewed on an annual basis — are:

- total arrivals and overnights (3);
- total receipts (4);
- investment by Maison de la France per arrival (1);
- seasonality and geographic spread (3);
- GDP growth (1);
- potential tourism growth (4);
- elasticity of the market (e.g. Is it reaching a ceiling?) (2); and
- interest in the market among partners/members (4).

There are no surprises as to key markets, in terms of marketing spend. They are the major source markets for France deemed to have the greatest growth potential in terms of absolute volume — notably the UK, Germany and the USA. Canada, Japan, Spain and Switzerland are also considered important.

Among the emerging markets, where Maison de la France is increasing marketing spend — as well as undertaking increased market research — Russia, Poland, the Czech Republic, Mexico, Brazil, China, South Korea and India are the priorities.

It should be noted that — as can be seen on the head office organigram — marketing strategy is divided into four separate zones: continental and 'Atlantic' Europe, the Americas and Asia Pacific/Near Middle East.

Interestingly, Maison de la France carries out no research and spends very little on promotion in the main Middle East markets, although it says it already has a captive market in Saudi Arabia (mainly owners of property in the south of France). The lack of recognition of the Middle East's potential would seem to be a big weakness of Maison de la France's marketing plan/strategy, but it says that funds are currently inadequate and that it has had to limit its spend to priority markets.

NB Rumour has it that Maison de la France management is now thinking of opening an office in the Middle East by early 2005.

Competitive analysis   In addition to this evaluation, Maison de la Frances also carries out regular surveys in each market to benchmark France against other destinations, as well as carrying out regular competitor analysis.

Case study — UK office of Maison de la France

Sector research   Most sector research is initiated by Maison de la France's clubs, members of which contribute to the cost of such research. Their contributions are matched by Maison de la France.

Staff and Responsibilities

The UK, or London (Piccadilly), office has 22 staff, headed by Director Christian Lepage. Staff handling walk-in enquiries are based in a ground-floor, street-front office shared with

Rail Europe (Maison de la France pays a lower rent). Most of the staff, however, are in the main third-floor office, which is closed to the public.

The UK team includes two members of staff dealing with telephone calls from the public. One of these also handles market research and compiles a newsletter that goes to all Maison de la France's members. One person looks after publications and the general public database, as well as producing a monthly consumer-oriented newsletter. Three handle public relations (press trips, events, etc.) and six people are involved in travel trade activities and promotions — the most important area of work for the UK office.

They also produce a quarterly newsletter for the travel trade, and organise workshops and trade fairs, such as France's participation in World Travel Market under the Maison de la France umbrella. Three of the staff working with the trade focus on the MICE sector, and one also helps with database management and IT work.

Enquiries

The office receives up to 700 visitors a day, but numbers are a lot lower in the quiet months. Walk-in customers are often just international tourists who come in to buy a train ticket, and take the opportunity to ask about France at the same time. Walk-in enquiries have substantially declined over the past decade.

For consumers, Maison de la France operates a special phone line operated by two members of staff. Calls usually result in the despatch of one or more brochures. This is handled from a mailing centre (fulfilment house) on the French/German border, which distributes brochures on behalf of most of the NTO's European offices. The HQ is responsible for distributing and updating the electronic catalogue of available brochures, reports, etc. for members and the travel trade.

The HQ is heavily used in the UK market. It receives an average of 30,000 visits, and the number sometimes exceeds 50,000. The high usage among consumers is not surprising given the interest among the British for short breaks in France — Maison de la France's UK office claims that the independent short-break market is the largest source of visitors from the UK now.

Brochures

London publishes three brochures (designed and produced by an outside company). The main one is *The Traveller in France*— which this year, is celebrating its 80th anniversary. Advertising comes from Maison de la France's membership clubs — ads are sometimes included as part of their membership package. The circulation of the publication is 150,000. Two other brochures, with a circulation of around 40,000 each, are *The Shortbreak Traveller in France* and *The Winter Traveller in France* (skiing is an increasingly important segment in the UK market).

Three newsletters are produced in London, all delivered by e-mail — a monthly newsletter for the media (the last to stop being published, in 2003), a consumer monthly and a trade quarterly. Again, advertising is largely from product clubs, but can come direct from CRT and CDT members.

Public Relations

Press trips are organised up to twice monthly. They are usually linked to advertising campaigns and organised on the request of French regions/destinations.

A number of different events are organised for the media in the UK. The major event is the Prêt à Partir day-long annual workshop, which involves 145 invited journalists. It is organised with support from the French Embassy and in partnership with the French regions. It involves a lot of work and expense, but is considered worthwhile in terms of return on investment.

Travel Trade Activities

The main job of the travel trade department is to link supply and demand. It maintains a trade database and organises a number of travel workshops — e.g. in March it is holding a workshop in Jersey, with 150 UK tour operators invited to meet French suppliers. Suppliers pay €1600 but UK operators are only charged a small fee. Maison de la France handles organisation of the whole event, including arranging charter flights.

In general, the NTO tries not to put in more than 15–20% of the total costs of promotional events — although it sometimes has to invest higher amounts.

It also organises the French presence at trade shows — the Maison de la France exhibit at WTM included 145 exhibitors last year. One full-time staff member looks after arrangements for trade shows.

Consumer Events

The only consumer show that Maison de la France is involved with in the UK — Vive la France — is in London. The NTO did not initiate the event, but organisers work closely with them and they are the main sponsors and help with planning and organising. Some 38,000 visitors attend the show. It generates a lot of positive press on France.

SNAV, the French national travel agents association, works closely with Maison de la France on this event. The fact that non-tourism companies such as real estate agents and food suppliers exhibit is good news for France's travel sector as it draws on a wider than usual range of visitors.

Advertising

This year major campaigns in the UK market will focus on:

- main holidays — in partnership with Brittany Ferries;
- city breaks; and
- short breaks.

Maison de la France prefers to focus on theme/segment-based advertising, rather than destination ads. It contributes to the latter, but is less likely to put much money into single destination/region promotions. As an example, Alsace has requested a specific campaign in the UK this year, but the NTO has agreed to very modest funding.

Dealing with Negative Publicity

With regard to negative events that impact on the whole travel market (e.g. the oil slick in southwest France, forest fires, etc.) head office tries to secure additional funds from the government and masterminds the response. In such cases, Maison de la France in London works closely with the French Embassy, and London's press department was well briefed on the situation so it could deal with journalists — even non-travel industry media.

The London office was allocated an additional £120,000 for an autumn 2003 campaign to encourage the British back to France (although details are not available, the market is reported to have fallen fairly sharply in 2003). The allocation of funds for specific negative events/developments depends, of course, on how badly other markets have been affected. The Germans, for example, took the oil-slick much more seriously than the British did.

Lessons from France

Niche Segments

In the UK, the main niche markets are skiing and golf, although both are really big — skiing is expected to generate 1.5 million arrivals in 2004 — hardly a niche market. Ski workshops are held every year in the UK for the trade.

Specific campaigns are already planned for these two sectors, and the London office is also considering new niche markets, although no specific campaigns exist for these at present. They include activity holidays, health/wellness and the gay market.

Strong Government Support...

2003 was a difficult year for France's tourism industry. In addition to continued terrorism and health issues — which affected all destinations — the combination of President Chirac's lack of support for the US invasion of Iraq, forest fires and the unbearable heat wave of last summer had a major impact on demand for France. All key source markets were affected, but the UK, the USA and Japan were the hardest hit, according to preliminary indications.

The downturn, accompanied by widespread media publicity, had at least one positive outcome. State support for tourism had become rather half-hearted during the previous Socialist government — especially given the significant presence of Communist party members in tourism who appeared to be more concerned with developing social tourism among the French than high-earning inbound tourism.

The present government recognises the economic value of tourism and its major contribution to the balance of trade and employment. This is reflected in its reactivation of the Inter-Ministerial Committee for Tourism, the creation of the International Consultative

Committee, and the staging of events such as the Rencontres Parlementaires sur le Tourisme, as well as in the provision of additional funding to help kick-start the recovery.

...Despite Continued Criticism

Nevertheless, there is still considerable criticism from stakeholders interviewed for the purpose of this study. But we believe this is simply typical of the French tendency to criticise public institutions, so most comments need to be taken with a pinch of salt.

The main criticisms are in fact directed more at the government and its lack of support for the industry — especially SMEs in the tourism sector — rather than at Maison de la France.

Among the more credible criticisms is the perceived lack of real co-operation between central government and the regions, which seems to be due to the general lack of interest of most 'préfets' in tourism in their respective regions.

Another criticism concerns the overly bureaucratic structure of tourism support — and especially the perceived overlapping of responsibilities between the Direction du Tourisme and Maison de la France. Discussions with former tourism officials — such as Francesco Frangialli, Secretary General of WTO (former head of the DT) — suggest that there may be changes planned in 2004. This was confirmed by Thierry Baudier, Director General of Maison de la France, who indicated in a brief interview at the end of January that there are tentative plans to merge l'AFIT and the Observatoire National du Tourisme.

There is also talk (possibly wishful thinking) of a reduction in some of the DT's responsibilities/activities — in line with moves in Europe generally to reduce government's direct intervention in tourism. Given its 200-plus staff numbers, this would probably be a good (and cost-effective) move.

A Solid Partnership with all Key Stakeholders

Despite the criticisms, Maison de la France is generally perceived as being one of the most successful NTOs in Europe, if not worldwide. Particularly envied is the fact that its remit is to handle marketing and promotions only — it does not have to get bogged down by policy, education and training matters, etc.

Maison de la France's membership structure enables all stakeholders to have a hands-on involvement in the marketing and promotion of France and French tourism products. They are invited to contribute to marketing strategy and receive support in their own activities in foreign markets.

Communication between members/partners is very regular — through the different committees, commissions and electronically. And there appears to be excellent buy-in, on the part of provincial tourism authorities and the private sector, of campaigns such as 'Bonjour'. The logo is very visible in advertising across all types of media in all countries.

The Club Concept is a Winner

Maison de la France's club concept, conceived in 1987 with the launch of the business tourism and youth travel clubs, is respected by everyone who has had any experience of it. Industry players say they have gained enormous amounts of business through these clubs, not to mention guidance on how to enter new markets and research support to help them take marketing decisions. The only weakness is that small companies are sometimes not able to participate in as many club activities as they would like because of the associated costs. But the system is considered fair.

The club concept, conceived by Maison de la France at the end of the 1980s, also responds well to the needs of today's changing market and, therefore, changing marketing strategies. Tourists are increasingly interested in experiences, involving activities, rather than choosing specific destinations.

Partnership with Non-Tourism Companies

Another initiative lauded by many is Maison de la France's innovative use of non-tourism companies and organisations in its promotion of the brand France. It rightly believes that France's fame as a source of high fashion goods and perfumes, for example, plays an important role in attracting tourists, who in turn spend money in France and abroad on these goods, thereby supporting the business interests of French companies.

One important — and unusual — strategy of Maison de la France that later lost steam was its funding of the operations of foreign tourist offices without the support of central government. Its Taiwan office, opened in February 1995, was initially funded by selected members/partners of Maison de la France, including one provincial tourist office, Champagne-Ardennes, the French Railways (SNCF), the department store chain Galleries Lafayette, the inbound operator cum sightseeing company, Paris Vision and the Concord Hotels' group.

Strong Focus on Market Intelligence and Research

Maison de la France relies heavily on market intelligence and research on which to base its marketing strategies. It works closely with the Direction du Tourisme, which looks after major surveys focusing on tourism to/in France and which, with the Central Statistical Office, is responsible for the national Tourism Satellite Account (TSA) in conjunction with the DT.

The TSA has helped raise awareness within government and the travel industry, as well as among the public of the importance of tourism.

Research has helped Maison de la France diversify the destination's markets, both in terms of geography and sectors. However, there is still a long way to go to harness the country's full potential as a tourism destination, not to mention increasing length of stay and yield.

Chapter 8

Ireland

Ireland's Recent Tourism Performance

The growth of tourism in Ireland over the past 10 years has led to the recognition of its important contribution to the success of the Irish economy (Table 8.1). In the Republic of Ireland alone it provides:

- £2.5 billion in foreign earnings;
- Over £0.6 billion in domestic earnings;
- 140,000 jobs (which grew by 70% in the period 1990–2002); and
- £1.4 billion in tax receipts.

International Tourism

Preliminary estimates of visitation during 2003 indicate a return to 2000 levels with a potential 4% increase in international tourist arrivals to the Republic of Ireland to take visitor levels to in excess of six million. Total receipts (domestic and international) are expected to increase by 5%. Arrivals from North America were estimated to be up 6% and from Continental Europe up 8%. The visitation levels up to 2002 are presented in the following Table 8.2.

Much of the growth has been driven by the UK and US markets as highlighted in the following graph (Figure 8.1).

By 2002, the most significant European markets were France (298,000) and Germany (288,000) although the German market is showing some indications of a downturn. There is some evidence that this is due in part to a perception that the peace and charm of Ireland is largely a marketing creation and that poor transport infrastructure, bad traffic management and high prices represent the reality of the Irish experience. The profile of visitors is dominated by holiday/leisure tourists (see Table 8.3) with a significant VFR market from the UK. The business and conference market is growing but remains hampered by the slow development of any significant convention centre within the capital. This leaves Dublin well behind rivals such as Glasgow, Edinburgh, Birmingham and London.

Expenditure levels are shown in the following Table 8.4.

Buoyed by the strong performance in overseas visitor growth in 2003, Tourism Ireland is confident of meeting its ambitious target of increasing overseas visitor numbers by a further 4.4% to over seven million in 2004. It will continue to focus the bulk of its resources on Great Britain, the USA, France and Germany, which together represented 83% of total visitor numbers in 2002, and which performed strongly again in 2003. The British market

Table 8.1: Ireland: key facts — 2002.

	Republic	**Whole of Ireland**
Population	3.9 mn	5.6 mn
GDP	£80 bn	£106 bn
International arrivals (TF)	5.9 mn	7.1 mn
International overnights (TCE)	45.3 mn	46.9 mn
Average length of stay	7.7	6.6
International arrivals per inhabitant	1.5	1.3
Domestic arrivals	5.9 mn	6.5 mn
Domestic overnights (TCE)	17.3 mn	NA
Domestic overnights (THS)	14.6 mn	NA
Domestic receipts	£0.61 bn	NA
International receipts	£2.05 bn	£2.19 bn
• as a % of GDP	2.5	2.1
• per international tourist arrival	£347	£308
• per international overnight	£45	£47
• per inhabitant	£526	£391
Total tourism receipts:	£2.66 bn	
• as a % of GDP	3	
• per total tourist arrival	£2252	
• per total overnight	£42	
• per inhabitant	£682	
Tourism's total contribution to GDP	4.2%	NA
• WTTC estimate (industry GDP)	1.8%	NA
NTO's total tourism budget	£31.6 mn	
State contribution	£30.3 mn (96.0%)	
Marketing budget (% of total budget)	£19.7 mn (62.4)	
Exchange rate	£1 = €1.58	

Table 8.2: Overseas visitors to the Republic of Ireland by source 1990–2002 (000's).

Country/Area	1990	1995	2000	2001	2002
UK	1,785	2,285	3,428	3,340	3,452
North America	443	641	1,056	903	844
Europe	744	1,101	1,435	1,336	1,378
Other overseas	124	204	261	261	245
Total overseas	3,096	4,231	6,181	5,840	5,919

Source: Tourism Ireland.

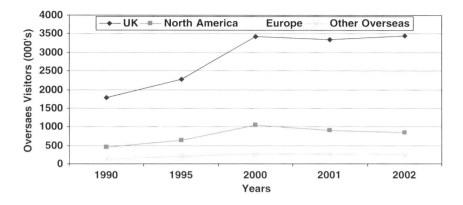

Figure 8.1: Overseas visitors to Ireland 1990–2002.
Data Source: Tourism Ireland.

Table 8.3: Overseas visitors by purpose of visit (percentage of total visitation), 2002.

Purpose	Total	UK	Europe	North America	Others
Holiday	37	28	43	57	48
VFR	24	30	14	19	20
Business	25	29	27	12	19
Other	14	13	16	12	13

Source: Tourism Ireland.

Table 8.4: Tourists' expenditure in Ireland (£ bn).

Expenditure type	2000	2001	2002
Total tourist expenditure	2.46	2.75	2.66
UK visitor expenditure	0.76	0.84	0.91
External tourists expenditure (exc. UK inc. NI)	1.01	1.10	1.14
Internal expenditure	0.69	0.79	0.61

Source: Tourism Ireland.

is targeted to grow by 3.5%, mainland Europe by 5.8% and North America by 6.6% in 2004. The next most important markets for short-term growth include Australia, Italy, the Netherlands and Canada. Additional emphasis will also be given to Spain and Belgium, which have been identified as offering good opportunities in the short term.

In implementing a strategy for the period 2003–2012, Tourism Ireland has a clear role in concentrating overseas expenditure on the British and United States markets, which account for 70% of the total international visitation. Mainland Europe has also been identified as suitable for review in early 2004 to raise the profile of Ireland. Partnerships are encouraged with the airline industry particularly in view of the role and growth of the low-cost airline sector.

For 2004, reviews of marketing expenditure that has been allocated throughout the year together with the results achieved will be published to enable an analysis of the success and failure of various campaigns. Ireland's market share in all overseas markets will also be monitored closely.

MICE Market

As detailed previously, business tourism accounts for 25% of the overseas market. The lack of an international conference and exhibition arena has, however, clearly reduced the appeal for larger elements of the business tourism market. This has made MICE promotion by Tourism Ireland particularly difficult. However, in June 2003, the government agreed in principle to the provision of a National Conference Centre through an open competitive procurement process. A high-level steering group was set up to review the specification, including operational requirements, for the project and to agree to the parameters of a procurement process. A notice inviting expressions of interest in the provision of a National Conference Centre in the Dublin area, with an expected minimum delegate capacity of the order of 2000, was issued by the Office of Public Works and published in the Official Journal of the European Union in November. The deadline set for the receipt of requests to participate was 21 January 2004.

Meantime, Dublin Convention Bureau was set up in 2003 as a non-profit destination-marketing organisation supported by members and the Association of Irish Professional Conference Organisers, Dublin City Council, Dublin Tourism and the Irish Hotels Federation. Services are offered to any national or international organisers free of charge. The Republic of Ireland's European Union presidency from January to June 2004 is also recognised as a source of potential benefits with 25 Ministerial meetings and 160 meetings/conferences throughout the country providing associated publicity.

Domestic Tourism

Until 2002, domestic tourism in Ireland had shown itself to be surprisingly resilient to the increasing availability of cheap flights to Europe offered by Ryanair and other budget carriers. Interestingly, although visitors from Northern Ireland have increased, the number of Republic of Ireland domestic tourists have reduced (Table 8.5).

Tourism Ireland is *not* responsible for domestic tourism promotion. However, some £8.4 million seems to have been spent last year in domestic tourism marketing and promotions on behalf of Fáilte Ireland and the NITB. The importance of the home market has been emphasised by the 2003 figures, which indicate that almost three in every four-hotel bookings are generated by the domestic market. Total expenditure has increased by 12%

Table 8.5: Northern Ireland and domestic tourism in Ireland (1997–2002).

Date	Northern Ireland visitors ('000)	Northern Ireland expenditure (£ mn)	Domestic visitors ('000)	Domestic expenditure (£ mn)
1998	530	78	6,934	602
1999	460	73	7,285	706
2000	471	78	6,556	690
2001	518	90	7,488	798
2002	557	102	5,891	607

Source: Tourism Ireland.

to £0.7 billion and the number of holiday trips has increased by 5% in the first eight months of 2003. This suggests a buoyant domestic short-breaks leisure and tourism market reinforced by growth in the economy.

The Importance of Dublin

Dublin as the capital of Ireland, accounts for approximately 30% of the population. It is nearly twice as large as the combined total of the next four largest cities in Ireland and constitutes the economic, political and industrial heart of the country. It is also the major tourist attraction in Ireland with a buoyant retail, hotel, restaurant, bar, arts, theatre and music scene. It is the home of three Universities and it has seen a massive shift in employment from manufacturing to services with tourism becoming an increasingly important element of the city economy. For example, there are proportionately more people employed in the licensed premises sector in Ireland than in the UK and more males have been attracted to the industry over the past 10 years growth period. In tourism terms, Dublin accounts for between 25% of all domestic tourism and 30% of all overseas tourism and has experienced real growth of 151% over the period from 1990 to 2002.

A crucial aspect of the Dublin (and indeed Irish) tourism success story has been the key role played by the budget airline sector and the subsequent development of Dublin Airport. In Dublin airport passenger traffic has increased from 2.6 million in 1986 to over 13 million in 2003.

Organisation of Tourism in Ireland

In the past the structure of tourism organisation appeared simple, coherent and focused with Bord Fáilte having responsibility for marketing and development of tourism in the Republic of Ireland (Deegan and Dineen, 1997). This ensured a degree of continuity in policy development and high visibility in the government administration (notably at Ministerial level for a number of years). The situation has now become more complex by the politicisation and development of marketing of the island of Ireland (North and the

Republic). In the past, Bord Fáilte had responsibility for Marketing (domestic and overseas), quality and product development. It was financed by an annual government grant and supplemented by additional monies from partners and industry. In addition there were seven Regional Tourist Authorities overseeing development and at a county level there are also tourism offices providing information services and local marketing. National tourism training was led by CERT, the state training authority responsible for education, recruitment and training. The current structure of tourism for the island of Ireland is as follows.

Responsibility for promoting tourism to Ireland (including Northern Ireland) from overseas markets now lies with Tourism Ireland Limited (Tourism Ireland) established under the framework of the Belfast Agreement of Good Friday 1998 to promote increased tourism to the island of Ireland. A company limited by guarantee, Tourism Ireland is jointly funded by the Governments of Great Britain (Northern Ireland Office) and Ireland, with the marketing based on a 2:1 expenditure ratio South:North. Tourism Ireland has been fully operational since January 2002 and is responsible for the overseas marketing of Ireland, brand review, and related market research. Its role is discussed in more detail below.

The current structure of tourism in Ireland is illustrated in Figure 8.2.

The first major review of tourism policy and performance in 10 years in the Republic of Ireland was completed in 2003 and a new policy document has been drawn up following this review — *New Horizons for Irish Tourism: An Agenda for Action* (www.tourism-review.ie). The review provides a framework for policy development over the next decade and over 70 recommendations have been selected for progress in the first two years of implementation. Further information is contained later in this section. A review of strategy for Northern Ireland is also currently underway.

Ministries Responsible

Ministries responsible for national tourism administration in Ireland are the Department of Arts, Sports and Tourism (Republic of Ireland) and the Department of Enterprise, Trade

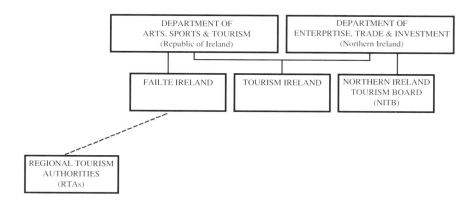

Figure 8.2: Structure of tourism support system in Ireland (including Northern Ireland). Source: The Travel Business Partnership.

and Investment (Northern Ireland). The Department of Arts, Sports and Tourism was established in June 2002 and the responsibilities of the former Department of Tourism Sport and Recreation have been transferred to this new Department. It has responsibility for the formulation, development and evaluation of policy for the tourism sector including:

*   Human Resource Development and training;
*   Marketing and promotion;
*   Product development;
*   Structure;
*   Funding;
*   North and South co-operation.

For example, the Tourism Marketing and Impact Assessment Unit develops, monitors and reviews the policy and arrangements for tourism marketing and promotion. It also prepares and administers the annual/multi-annual budgets for tourism marketing based on the plans developed by Tourism Ireland and Fáilte Ireland. In addition, the Tourism Development Policy Unit is responsible for policy issues relating to the regional tourism authorities.

Fáilte Ireland

Fáilte Ireland, the new National Tourism Development Authority for the Republic of Ireland, was set up in May 2003, and is the result of a merger between Bord Fáilte (the former National Tourism Organisation) and CERT, the national body formerly responsible for training and development. Fáilte Ireland has taken over the complete range of tourism support and development functions previously carried out by Bord Fáilte and CERT. But this is expected to change over time.

By working with industry groups, Fáilte Ireland's role is to promote and support the development of Irish Tourism through, for example, sustainable growth in visitor expenditure with an emphasis on a wider regional and seasonal spread of business. It provides the Irish tourism industry with a one-stop shop for a range of support services including enterprise relevant research, support for enterprise and product development, promotion of domestic tourism, and the packaging and promotion of specific product offerings to the international markets. Its role also includes benchmarking competitors in other destinations and identifying and applying best practice.

The Tourism Product Development Scheme is administered by Fáilte Ireland and is co-funded under two regional operational programmes. The first three grants in the scheme were provided during 2003 and around £0.7 million has now been allocated towards tourism businesses operating within the cruising, watersports and equestrian sectors. They reaffirm the commitment to key niche sectors seen as appropriate for diversification away from Dublin based growth. Product development has also been actioned through the use of EU-funded tourism and selected fiscal incentives for investment. Other responsibilities/areas of activity include:

*   stimulating investment — through selected fiscal incentives;
*   education and training — primarily focused on the provision of educational, basic training and recruitment services;

- setting quality standards — maintenance of top-class standards and services regarded as imperative for the continued success of the tourism industry; and
- marketing and promotion — domestic marketing to the people of Ireland.

Like the NITB, Fáilte Ireland works closely with Tourism Ireland in promoting the destination internationally, and with the Regional Tourist Authorities and Shannon Development in promoting, developing and servicing Ireland's tourism industry at regional and local level. It promotes seasonal extension and the balanced distribution of tourism activity and conducts promotional campaigns to consumers and the travel trade in the overseas and domestic markets, as well as providing a range of support services to incoming tour operators, the travel trade and publicists. Finally, it supports tourism planning and co-ordination for potential investment in tourism enterprises and operations.

Fáilte Ireland is a 100% public body, with 93% of its 2003 budget of £56.7 million funded by government. The balance of 7% is self-generated from its commercial activities. Marketing and promotion was expected to account for 32% of its budget in 2003 (£17.9 million), with a modest £1.7 million allocated to the domestic market. Fáilte Ireland has a staff of 224.

Northern Ireland Tourist Board (NITB)

The NITB is a non-departmental public body within the Department of Enterprise, Trade and Investment (DETI) with responsibility for the development, promotion and marketing of Northern Ireland to the host population, provision of information services, research, product development, festivals and events and quality assurance. It also advises DETI on the formulation of policy in relation to the development of tourism and is constituted under the Tourism (Northern Ireland) Order 1992.

The NITB is also responsible for co-ordinating the activities of regional tourism organisations in Northern Ireland.

Regional Tourism Bodies

In the Republic of Ireland, there are seven tourism regions — six administered by Regional Tourism Authorities (RTAs) and Shannon, which is administered by the Traffic & Tourism Division of Shannon Development.

The regional tourism bodies are funded through, and report to, Fáilte Ireland. Fáilte Ireland, in turn, liaises with Tourism Ireland over regional strategy. Like the private sector, the regional tourism bodies contribute funding to tourism campaigns developed and carried out by Tourism Ireland.

There are also county and city/municipal tourism organisations providing local information services and some domestic and international marketing.

Industry Advisory Bodies

The Irish Tourist Industry Confederation is the representative body of the Irish tourist industry and works in partnership with government agencies, tourist boards North and

South, Tourism Ireland, Fáilte Ireland, European Union and other agencies that can impact on tourism. Its main focus is on researching and producing data, trends and reports that can influence policies and planning. The council members comprise the private and public sectors. The Tourism Marketing Partnership is a formal industry consultation group. A very low level of private sector leverage is evident in Irish tourism marketing.

In the *Tourism Strategy Review* (www.tourismreview.ie), it was highlighted as essential that an ongoing review of the functions, activities and interactions of all involved in tourism promotion and development take place to identify the clear definitions between the roles and functions of all and to be aware of any overlaps or duplication of work/responsibilities.

A *Research, Advisory and Co-ordination Group* is to be set up with representatives from Industry, the public sector and the research community to identify information and research gaps. In addition, a research register database is to be created in 2004 to collate data already in existence. In 2002, research by Bord Fáilte included a 10,000 interview survey with overseas travellers, and a visitor attitudes survey with 1000 visitors. Gaps exist in key areas such as visitor attractions, activities and environmental impact analysis. A tourism barometer was however produced three times per year between June and October for all accommodation sectors including golf and equestrian focused operators.

Recognising the benefits it can bring in determining the economic value of tourism, a Tourism Satellite Account is to be put in place following the WTO model. The feasibility study and action plan is to be completed in mid-2004.

Tourism Ireland

Structure

Tourism Ireland is a 100% publicly funded body, owned 50% by each of the governments of the Republic of Ireland and Northern Ireland. It reports to the North-South Ministerial Council, where the Northern Ireland Executive and the Government of the Republic of Ireland make joint decisions about cross-border issues.

The Board of Directors of Tourism Ireland comprises 12 members from the public and private sectors representing leading tourism industry interests North and South, Fáilte Ireland and the Northern Ireland Tourist Board.

Details of the Structure of Senior Management in Tourism Ireland is detailed in the following chart (Figure 8.3).

Staff and Offices

Tourism Ireland has two offices in Ireland (in Dublin and Coleraine) and 13 fully staffed (by Tourism employees) offices abroad. In addition, it has general sales agents in five other markets. The 13 fully staffed offices operate in the following locations:

Europe

- United Kingdom — London (plus a sub-office in Glasgow);
- Belgium/Luxembourg — Brussels;

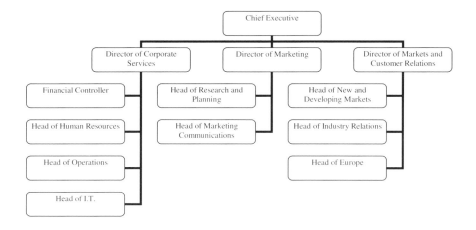

Figure 8.3: Tourism Ireland — senior management.
Source: Adapted from Tourism Ireland Information.

- Denmark — Copenhagen (plus an office in Oslo);
- Finland — Helsinki;
- France — Paris;
- Germany — Frankfurt;
- Italy — Milan;
- Netherlands — Amsterdam;
- Spain — Madrid;
- Sweden — Stockholm.

Outside Europe

USA — New York
Canada — Toronto
Australia — Sydney

Some of the offices, for example, New York and Helsinki are shared with the Embassy while others, for example, Milan share with Enterprise Ireland. The current offices are in the majority of cases the offices that were used by Bord Fáilte, with the exception of London, which has moved to a new office.

The general sales agents are local businesses in Austria (Vienna), Switzerland (Uitikan), Japan (Tokyo), New Zealand (Auckland) and South Africa (Gauteng) that operate on either a full-time or part-time basis and provide Ireland with a measure of representation in these countries.

Most offices overseas provide a walk-in enquiry service. However, smaller offices are moving away from providing this service due to human resource limitations.

Staff total 52 in Ireland (15 in Coleraine and 37 in Dublin) and 95 abroad (65%). Staff employed overseas are a combination of local hires and Irish expatriates, all working in marketing and promotions. The main activities/areas of responsibility of staff include the following, with a total of 20 staff working in the first two areas (marketing communications and research and planning):

- Marketing Mommunications;
- Research and Planning;
- Human Resources;
- Finance;
- Information Technology;
- Print & distribution;
- Industry relations;
- Customer enquiries. The call centre operation was transferred to Tourism Ireland in July 2002 and handled 100,000 calls in 2002.

Tourism Ireland has closed no offices in the past year, although the area remains under review. There are also no new openings under consideration, although this does not preclude hiring local representatives in emerging markets such as China.

Resources and Funding

Ireland and its capital have had at its disposal a comprehensive level of European funds available for investment in key aspects of the product. However, it is interesting to note that in the case of accommodation (which is the tourism industry's largest investment category) in excess of £400 million worth of non-grant assisted projects occurred over the time frame 1994–1999. The concentration was notably on the capital, Dublin. However, as identified in the recent strategy review document Ireland may not be able to rely on such assistance in the future.

Tourism Ireland had a budget from government of £37.9 million in 2003, up 10% (in Euros) on 2002's level (Table 8.6). Some 70% of it came from the Government of the Republic of Ireland and just under 30% came from Northern Ireland. A very small share (around 4%) comprised industry contributions to marketing/promotional campaigns.

Total government investment in support of tourism in Ireland in 2004 is projected to be almost £80 million. Of this, almost £50 million will be spent in general support for the marketing and promotion activities of the tourism state agencies, including the largest ever provision for the Tourism Marketing Fund of around £22 million.

Role and Activities

The role of Tourism Ireland is to:

- carry out strategic all-Ireland destination marketing in all markets outside the island of Ireland;
- to undertake regional/product marketing and promotional activities on behalf of Fáilte Ireland and the NITB overseas;

Table 8.6: NTO budget.

Year	Total budget (£ mn)	Government share (%)
2002	31.6	96
2003	37.9	96
2004	37.9	96

Source: Tourism Ireland.

- to operate the overseas marketing office network; and
- to own and manage the Tourism Brand Ireland and its associated communications materials.

Tourism Ireland's main goal is to grow the number of tourists to the whole island of Ireland and to assist Northern Ireland in achieving its potential through above average growth in tourism.

Most of Tourism Ireland's marketing and promotion is carried out in co-operation with the regional tourism boards and the private sector. For example, there is a formal industry consultation group, the 'Tourism Marketing Partnership'. In addition, Tourism Ireland engages in marketing activity in the form of co-operative advertising or attendance at market promotions. Fáilte Ireland (and Northern Ireland Tourist Board) provides Tourism Ireland with additional funding for niche product marketing overseas. Fáilte Ireland also works with Tourism Ireland to educate the Irish tourism trade on overseas marketing opportunities.

Marketing

Marketing strategy   During the period 2002–2004, the spend and projected spend on marketing (Table 8.7) is as follows.

Direct comparison of figures is difficult because of the inclusion of Ireland's spend on marketing to the UK. Furthermore, three other issues further complicate the situation:

- The Irish figure now includes an element of the former NITB budget;
- Some elements of the Irish budget allocation are for 3–5 years duration, thus only a portion is likely to be spent in the next year;
- The Irish expenditure includes the cost of operating overseas offices in addition to core marketing activities.

Historical analysis of marketing spend and growth of visitors to Ireland evidenced some interesting correlation. Notably, the most rapid rise in visitor numbers was in the late 1980s (particularly 1988–1989) a period when the allocation of funds for tourist marketing was greatly reduced by the Irish government. Suggesting perhaps that other factors such as low-cost carrier access to the country were more significant in stimulating tourism growth.

Table 8.7: NTO marketing budget.

Year	Total budget (£ mn)	Marketing share of total budget (%)
2002	19.7	62.4
2003	23.0	66.2
2004	24.3	62.0

Source: Tourism Ireland.

Dublin, possesses a range of clear advantages as the national capital, with an international history of literature and culture which has been further enhanced by the government's decision to reduce taxation on artists, musicians and those in the creative industries. Such a policy was intended to reinforce the reputation of both the city and the nation as contemporary and culturally aware.

Image and reputation are intangible elements of any national tourism product and though extremely popular in marketing strategies and plans they are rarely founded on detailed effect analysis. The international growth in Irish pubs has undoubtedly acted as a very effective 'soft sell' for the whole country as have the catalogue of films produced in Ireland because of financial incentives offered. Other factors influencing tourist demand such as the 'peace dividend', which though somewhat erratic, appears (at least in the Republic) to have quelled the misrepresentation of the destination as being 'unsafe'.

As examples of marketing undertaken:

Niche marketing and the Irish product
Niche markets as follows are being targeted:

- Golf;
- Angling;
- Inland cruising;
- Sailing;
- Water sports;
- Walking;
- Cycling;
- English as a foreign language.

In addition an International Sports Initiative has been implemented and will operate until 2007 aimed at catalysing sports tourism. There were 17 international events in 2002 and included in the 13 already established for 2004 is the American Express World Golf Championships. A festival initiative has also been implemented with 188 applications having been received for the development of future events. Events such as the Special Olympics World Summer Games (for the first time outside the USA), were regarded as highly successful and a valuable platform for Ireland. The Irish Government provided around £10 million for the operating costs of the games. Tourism Ireland is seeking to expand trade involvement in overseas marketing, activities which are considered essential in the highly competitive global environment.

As an example of further marketing, in Canada, Tourism Ireland are holding Best of Ireland seminars in nine cities with two teams of Irish and Canadian partners. Such seminars provide Canadian travel agents the opportunities to meet 25 suppliers to find out more about selling the Irish tourism product.

In recognition of the positive prospects for 2003 and 2004, Tourism Ireland invested a further £5.5 million in marketing, considered to be the largest ever programme of investment, towards an extensive autumn/winter campaign. The campaign was directed at all major overseas markets to assist and capitalise on late booking trends.

Potential Impacts of the Tourism Policy Review Group

The mandate of the Tourism Policy Review Group 2003 was to identify the key elements of a strategy for the sustainable development of tourism in Ireland within which the industry and government sectors could work together in an effective and beneficial partnership in the years ahead. Included were targets to double visitor spend from £3.8 billion and to increase overseas visitation from 6 million to 10 million. It identified around 70 recommended actions to be pursued within the first two-year rolling plan. The group commented that the economic and social contribution of the Irish tourism industry was seriously undervalued, both nationally and at government level.

The tourism industry in Ireland is now at a crossroads. Although Ireland performed much better than the European average in 2003 in terms of international tourist arrivals, there have been indications of deterioration in the destination's competitiveness in the international tourism market since the beginning of the decade — and this, after a very successful decade in the 1990s. A reduction in financial support will also occur as the high levels of European Funding that characterised the 1990s will reduce or disappear. Moreover, the destination has perhaps not adequately recognised that the nature and structure of the industry is changing in response to changes in customer demands, information technology.

The review concluded that, despite recent external shocks, the prospects for the international travel and tourism sector remained positive in the medium and longer term. The report concluded that the key to future success for Ireland is for the industry to focus on the quality of the holiday experience. A relentless emphasis on value for money, encompassing high quality and service standards combined with product innovation was essential.

Key recommendations of the review include the following.

Influencing the wider government agenda. The tourism industry is, arguably, the most important sector of enterprise, national and regional wealth creation and employment generation. It has major potential to contribute more to national and regional development. These realities do not appear to be sufficiently understood and reflected in the recent development of organisational structures and prioritisation of work.

The Department of Arts, Sport and Tourism needs, in consultation with the Tourism State Agencies, to play a more dynamic and effective role in shaping the range of government policies that impact upon the development of tourism in a significant way. These policies include, in particular, those that relate to competitiveness, taxation, heritage and environmental conservation, and internal and external access transport. This role should be complemented by strengthened industry representation structures to champion industry interests.

Most importantly, there should be greater co-operation — more of a real partnership — between the key stakeholders, and there should be no overlapping of responsibilities and duplication of efforts.

Access and transport. An early renegotiation of the Ireland/US Bilateral Air Agreement is necessary to achieve additional air services and enhanced visitor flows from North America, to the ultimate benefit of all regions, including the mid-West.

The provision, at the earliest possible date, of additional, competitive fast turnaround terminal facilities at Dublin Airport (plus improving the Dublin Airport Metro link) is required, in particular to help develop additional air services from continental European and UK markets with strong inward tourism potential. The benefits of additional air routes and seaports enhancement must also be recognised.

Competitiveness/value for money. The full implementation by all the social partners of the anti-inflation and competitiveness-enhancing provisions of the Social Partnership Agreement (2003–2005 — Sustaining Progress) is essential, particularly those relating to pay, productivity and the facilitation of change in the workplace. Increased salary levels will create a need to focus on productivity and the notoriously lax aspect of tourism product and service quality.

In order to prevent the embedding of high-inflation expectations, which would damage the competitiveness of traded sectors, including tourism, the government should commit itself to an inflation target for prices within domestic control, including charges for government services, excise duties and indirect taxation. Other actions such as benchmarking the competition, enhancing customer relationship management and general management skills and forging a stronger role for tourism industry representative bodies are also stressed.

Exploiting information technology. The better exploitation of new e-commerce technologies, such as the Internet, by the industry and tourism state agencies, is necessary to improve marketing and customer relations management. In the past Bord Fáilte has invested major funds in web-enabled reservations and interactive systems with some inspired marketing alliances with organizations such as Microsoft. However, the investment in site development has been substantial and if anything there would now appear to be a withdrawal from the role of NTO in a central reservations portal towards a position on 'signposting' to hospitality and tourism sites with a conduit for reservations and sales. This is an interesting and expensive volte-face in response to a sector that progresses more rapidly at a private level than at a state level.

Product development and innovation. The current under-utilisation of accommodation and visitor attractions should be addressed by better presentation, more integrated packaging, co-operative marketing and targeted public sector incentives to encourage innovation and re-investment by the private sector. The product cluster approach is recommended (for example, golf tourism or a multi-product such as golf and health) plus an innovation fund to encourage fresh ideas.

As a priority, there is a need to fill significant gaps in tourism product stock, including establishing a dedicated national conference centre and a new world-class sports stadium in Dublin.

The fundamental principles of the review provide indicators of the way forward. These comprise:

- tourism growth driven by private sector enterprise, innovation and investment;
- a need for a consistent framework of well chosen actions across all areas of government activity; and

- targeted public sector interventions to be confined to market failure in close partnership with industry.

Although visitation levels for 2003 appear positive, Ireland is a country where its best tourism success may now be behind it. Image and brand marketing is now undermined by competing agencies, the private sector is dependent upon the NTO (public sector funded marketing) and the role of low-cost airlines is crucial to sustaining the short-break market.

Lessons from Ireland

Due to the fact that Tourism Ireland is a new organisation it is difficult to identify best practice at this early stage in its life. However, there are lessons to be learned from the performance of Ireland over the past few years and these are reflected in the following discussion. The success and growth of tourism to Ireland may be attributed to a number of possible causes:

- Ireland up to 2001 evidenced constructive and joined up thinking in policy, marketing and some elements of development in tourism. The government presided over long-term investment in the industry primarily through the Operational Programmes for Development (planned EU and Irish government funded expenditure). Tourism was taken seriously and seen as an industry that required long-term investment. It was no doubt helped by having a designated Minister in government with responsibility for this industry;
- The brand development and brand marketing work carried out by Bord Fáilte in the 1990s was exemplary and undoubtedly contributed to awareness of the country and heightened its appeal. In advertising terms it was seen as ground breaking and won a number of awards and plaudits. However, isolating the direct impact of the marketing and advertising expenditure is impossible and the National Centre for Tourism Policy Research at Limerick University has openly questioned the correlation between this expenditure and increased tourism.

Perceived Weaknesses/Critical Success Factors.

For the first time in 16 years Irish tourism numbers declined in 2001. Foot and Mouth, September 11th and problems with the world economy all contributed. There was also evidence that the UK and US markets were declining in growth particularly over the period 1999–2001. This may be attributed in part to the perception that Ireland is now a relatively expensive destination in respect of costs of food, beverage and accommodation and that the fascination with/fashionability of Ireland as a destination is beginning to wane.

The Irish model has its problems. Factors such as the escalation of property values in the city centre, the high cost of living and Dublin as arguably the most expensive EU capital could create problems. Euro membership has meant Euro-zone tourists can make easy price comparisons and can appreciate the relatively poor value for money obtained. Thus, both nation and capital may have lost some appeal in terms of price competitiveness.

Furthermore the failure of some of the larger scale tourist attractions in the city (developed utilising EU structural assistance) and their problematic relationship to tourist demand is a concern. In initial analysis it would appear that such developments are simply not a factor for deciding to visit the city. Furthermore a number have experienced problems of low-visitor numbers and low-satisfaction rates making their operation marginal. In Dublin, the Dublin Viking Village closed in 2001, the IMAX screen closed within 12 months of launch in 2002 and more recently Ceol (the Irish folk music centre) ceased trading.

Although the findings of the Policy review were considered largely positive, it is too early to tell how successful the new tourism support system and administrative structure in Ireland is. Although there are indications that early problems are being rectified and some cohesion is evident, it does appear that the tourism situation in Ireland seems to have become more complex. The relative simplicity of the former structure — which was seen as very successful — has been complicated by the politicisation of issues, not least the pan-Ireland tourism marketing.

The ongoing review of the NITB may encourage the Northern Ireland Government to rethink its joint marketing and promotion with the Republic of Ireland. Certainly, the fact that there is clearly duplication of effort is not beneficial to the industry. Tourism Ireland is supposed to act as the agent of Fáilte Ireland and the NITB, but the latter two agencies continue to undertake internal marketing.

The value for money, quality perception and the dilution of the authentic experience all have to be tackled immediately and to this end, in February 2004, the Tourism Action Plan Implementation Group (comprising seven full members from the public and private sectors) held their inaugural meeting.

Chapter 9

The Netherlands

The Netherlands' Recent Tourism Performance

The stable political and economic climate of the Netherlands has been a major contributor to its appeal as a tourism destination. Yet it has a number of other attractions — from its rich cultural heritage to its windmills and tulips and, until recently at least, its liberal drugs policy. In addition, its easy accessibility — particularly through the development of Amsterdam's Schiphol airport — has also boosted tourism demand from abroad. While the majority of Dutch people on holiday in the Netherlands stay at campsites or in bungalows, some 56% of foreign bed-nights were spent in hotels in 2002. This compared with 16% in camping sites, 25% in individual holiday villas/cottages (in holiday parks) and 3% in group accommodation (Table 9.1).

Inbound tourism performance is assessed mainly on the basis of the registration of guest arrivals and room-nights recorded by hotels and other forms of registered commercial accommodation (TCE). A substantial number of bed-nights are clearly from business visitors, but it is difficult to provide a breakdown of arrivals or overnight volume by purpose of trip as surveys of inbound visitors are conducted very infrequently — the last was five years ago.

The situation may change following the merger of the Netherlands Convention Bureau (NCB) and the Netherlands Board of Tourism (NBT) into the Netherlands Board of Tourism & Conventions (NBTC) at the end of 2003. But detailed statistics on Dutch domestic trips and overnights have until now been restricted to leisure tourism as domestic business tourism was not part of the NBT's research remit.

The NBTC also says that data on expenditure/receipts is unreliable as it does not include the spending of same-day travellers, whether Dutch or foreign. Some research has been conducted on this sector (see below) but there are still reportedly problems of definition.

International tourist arrivals in all forms of commercial accommodation (TCE) totalled 9.6 million in 2002, but the NBTC estimates frontier arrivals at 11.6 million. TCE arrivals were expected to fall by 5% in 2003 and overnights by more than 3%. Meanwhile, domestic travel stagnated, in terms of both trips and overnight volume (Table 9.2).

The top two foreign markets for the Netherlands, Germany and the UK, account for some 48% of total arrivals and the top five markets (including the USA, Belgium and France) generate close to 70% between them (Table 9.3).

More than 85% of overnights were generated by Europeans (2002 data), with the Americas accounting for an 8.2% share, Asia Pacific 5.3% and Africa 1.4%.

Table 9.1: The Netherlands: Key facts — 2002.

Population	16.1 mn
GDP	£281.2 bn
International arrivals (TF est)	11.6 mn
International arrivals (TCE)	9.6 mn
International overnights (TCE)	26.4 mn
Average length of stay (TCE nights)	2.8
International arrivals per inhabitant	0.7
Domestic arrivals (holidays)	18.7 mn
Domestic overnights (holidays)	108.9 mn
Average length of holiday trip	5.8 nights
Domestic receipts (holidays only)	£1.83 bn
Domestic receipts (total est)	£3.41 bn
International receipts (holidays only)	£5.15 bn
International receipts	£5.81 bn
(total estimated excl same-day travel)	
as a % of GDP	2.0%
per tourist arrival (TF)	£501
per tourist arrival (TCE)	£605
per overnight	£220
per inhabitant	£361
Total tourism receipts	
as a % of GDP	3.3%
per arrival	£305
per overnight	£68
per inhabitant	£573
Tourism's total contribution to GDP	NA
Estimate 1999 according to preliminary TSA	2.5%
WTTC estimate (T&T industry GDP)	3.3%
NTO's total tourism budget (% annual change)	£22.5 mn
	(−4.2%)
State contribution (% share)	£14.2 mn
	(62.9%)
Marketing budget (% share of total budget)	£10.9 mn
	(48.5%)
Rate of exchange	£1 = €1.58

NA, not available.

Table 9.2: Growth trends in tourism to and in the Netherlands, 2002–2003.

	2002 Actual ('000s)	2003 Estimated ('000s)	% Change 2002–2003
International			
Arrivals (TCE)	9,596	9,115	−5.0
Overnights (TCE)	26,368	25,538	−3.1
Tourism receipts (£ mn)	5,814	5,803	−0.2
Domestic			
Trips (holidays only)	18,700	18,600	−0.5
Overnights (holidays)	108,870	108,500	−0.3

Source: Netherlands Board of Tourism & Conventions (NBTC).

Table 9.3: The Netherlands' leading international markets, 2000–2002 ('000).

Market	2000	2001	2002	% Share 2002
Germany	2,884	2,657	2,755	28.7
UK	1,838	1,939	1,851	19.3
USA	999	993	886	9.2
Belgium	677	629	705	7.3
France	512	455	511	5.3
Italy	374	343	346	3.6
Spain	250	259	276	2.9
Japan	194	183	187	1.9
Switzerland	144	122	128	1.3
Sweden	134	118	112	1.2
Australia	127	114	107	1.1
Denmark	119	104	103	1.1
Ireland	77	81	98	1.0
Canada	97	93	96	1.0
Norway	89	78	71	0.7
Austria	56	56	60	0.6
Finland	43	40	45	0.5
Poland	50	49	44	0.5
Luxembourg	25	23	37	0.4
Czech Republic	26	23	25	0.3
Other Europe	659	504	425	4.4
Other Americas	120	116	118	1.2
Other Asia Pacific	401	380	437	4.6
Africa	108	141	173	1.8
Total[a]	10,003	9,500	9,596	99.9

[a]Tourists in all forms of commercial accommodation (TCE).
Source: NBTC.

MICE Business

The Netherlands is an important international conference destination. In 1997 — the last year for which accurate figures are available — some 686 conferences were recorded in the country generating 912,025 delegate days. Over the 1990s the number of international conferences reportedly grew by an annual average of nearly 10% and the number of delegate days by about 7% — well above the average for tourism generally.

A survey conducted by the consulting firm LA Group, meanwhile, suggests that the value of the meetings, incentives, conferences and exhibitions (MICE) business overall for the Netherlands in 2002 was more than £0.65 billion, or 11.4% of total international receipts (excluding receipts from same-day travel) (Table 9.4).

Events

The results of research conducted over the past 12 years by the NBTC/NBT/TRN highlight the value of special events and exhibitions to the country, both in terms of visitor numbers and their contribution to economic growth. The Netherlands hosts more than 5000 local events annually, plus 1000 or more small regional events, 500 regional events with wider impact (e.g. floral processions), 10–20 big national events (e.g. Sail Amsterdam and pop festivals) and one major international event (e.g. Euro2000 or Floriade 2002).

The tourism demand generated by all these different events (excluding demand for overnight tourism from abroad) is estimated by the NBT at 1 billion day-trips.

A detailed report on the events business for the Netherlands and its preliminary strategy for the future is included in the Marketing Strategy section of this chapter.

Tourism's Economic Contribution

The Netherlands does not yet have a fully fledged Tourism Satellite Account but estimates by the NBTC — based on data collected from all the different research institutes and industry organisations measuring tourism trends — suggest that tourism accounted for 450,000 jobs in 2002, of which 280,000 were full-time jobs. Tourism's total contribution

Table 9.4: The value of international MICE business for the Netherlands, 2002.

Sector	£ mn
Meetings & conventions	283
Exhibitions	83
Incentives	22
Individual business travel	272
Total	660

Source: LA Group; NBTC.

was estimated at £22.6 billion, including spending in the Netherlands by Dutch tourists related to foreign travel.

Organisation of Tourism in the Netherlands

The Netherlands' tourism support system has undergone many changes over the past 15 years — not least since 2002. In the late 1990s/early 2000s, the NBT was the body responsible for promoting tourism. Funding was provided by the Ministry of Economic Affairs and by the Dutch tourism industry. The NBT's budget allocation for 1999 from the state/central government was G40 million (£12.8 million).

The NBT's promotional efforts were focused on domestic as well as international tourism but its main goal was to increase international tourism receipts and, particularly, foreign exchange. Also involved in domestic tourism promotion was the Stichting Toerisme & Recreatie (AVN) and the provincial and local tourist information offices (VVVs), which worked closely with the NBT and the AVN — in the case of the VVVs, through the Dutch Association of Tourist Offices (ANVV).

In addition to these different bodies, the National Convention Bureau (NCB), based in Amsterdam, assumed a large part of the responsibility for selling the Netherlands as a conference destination.

In 2002, the NBT had its name changed to Toerisme Recreatie Nederland (TRN) (but only in Dutch as offices abroad reportedly had problems working with the new name since it appeared to involve only leisure tourism), at the same time merging with the AVN. The plan was for TRN also to absorb the ANVV but, although the latter's staff moved into TRN's offices, the merger could not be effected immediately because of the legal structure of the ANVV — it was a membership organisation.

The decision was therefore taken to restructure it and merge it with TRN in mid-2002. However, because of delays due to financial problems at the ANVV and reported tensions between the different organisations, the planned merger was abandoned and the ANVV staff moved out of TRN's offices.

Meanwhile, the ANVV has become the VVV Nederland and, since the beginning of 2004, the national tourism organisation (NTO) has been merged with the NCB and become the NBTC. The new structure, which was only announced in late-2003, will also mean a cut in staff numbers of an estimated 47 — or about one-third of total staff employed in the Netherlands (see below) — and a reduction in responsibilities for the NTO.

Many of the comments in this report refer to the TRN/NBT and the tourism structure in the Netherlands pre-2004. Although the new structure is discussed, details are not finalised, which makes it difficult to comment on its likely effectiveness (Figure 9.1).

National Tourism Administration (NTA)

The Ministry of Economic Affairs is ultimately responsible for tourism in the Netherlands, although there is no specific sectoral policy on tourism — in fact, there has

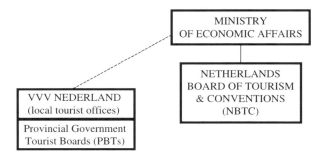

Figure 9.1: Structure of Dutch tourism support system. *Source*: Authors.

no longer been one since 1999 and the so-called Division of Tourism Policy comprises only two people.

Tourism policy is now included within the area of spatial and regional economic policy — thus in combination with regions and cities. The state's main role is to ensure an efficient economy with a strong and dynamic private sector. An internationally competitive economy is considered absolutely vital if the Netherlands is to realise its goals in areas such as employment, social security, education and the environment.

The Ministry of Economic Affairs employs just a handful of people in tourism, and this is only one of their responsibilities. In addition to funding allocated to the NBTC, some £142,200 is allocated annually to the Ministry for tourism matters. This covers the annual fee for the Netherlands' membership of the World Tourism Organisation. The Ministry is responsible for co-ordinating with other ministries on all issues affecting, or affected by, tourism. However, there are no formal inter-ministerial committees or councils.

As in some of the other northern European countries, a number of management tasks formerly carried out by the Ministry responsible for tourism, or NTA, were handled by the NBT/TRN — at least until end-2003. Examples include specific dissemination of knowledge, strategic research and non-physical product development. (NB Product development is one of the key tasks that will no longer be the responsibility of the new NBTC.)

New Industry Vision

Following consultations with the industry, different government and parastatal bodies and other private sector organisations, including the assistance of an external consultancy, the Ministry of Economic Affairs admitted in 2003 that its disengagement from tourism had been excessive and that it should do more to support and promote the industry for the benefit of all stakeholders. As a result, a White Paper was produced at the end of 2003 — a *FutureVision Plan* — which is intended to be the global framework for policy-making in the coming years.

Provincial Government Tourist Boards (PBTs) and the VVV Nederland

No formal, institutionalised relationships exist between the state and the PBTs or local/city tourism organisations (now operating under the name VVV Nederland), although their views are taken into account when formulating policy, say, re transport infrastructure — roads that connect regions — and other similarly important issues.

Due to reorganisation — in most cases, to cut costs and stimulate efficiency — both the number and structure of PBTs fluctuates sharply — even from month to month. At the time of writing, six PBTs currently serve seven provinces, and there are no PBTs in the remaining five provinces. The PBT for the Northern province was liquidated in 2003. Meanwhile, a merger of three regions to create a new PBT, the Southern province, was due to take place at the end of 2003.

Within the framework of provincial policy-making each province has its own autonomy on tourism. The provincial governmental level deals mainly with policy-making, spatial planning/infrastructure, sometimes facilitating commercial investments and supporting the PBTs.

The level of involvement in tourism of the provincial/local government depends on the importance of tourism for the provincial economy, existing problems and the level of provincial political interest. Within the political area the economic aspects of tourism are more closely connected to policies on well-being that relate to facilitating outdoor recreation for the region's population. Facilitating outdoor recreation is a specific regional task.

Provincial policies on tourism may fall in line with the national policy, but there is no obligation for national policy to be followed. In principle, of course, national views influence those of the regions. However, as national views and policy-making have tended to become less explicit, regions — which cannot count on specific financial support anymore — have tended to go out on a limb and develop policies on their own.

Funding of the PBTs has traditionally come from both the respective regional/provincial governments and the private sector of the industry — or through the PBTs' own commercial activities. While the PBTs have been responsible for their own marketing and promotion, they have tended to link with the NBT/TRN for major international campaigns, trade fair activities, etc.

As has been the case with the NBT over the past few years, the PBTs have been allocated additional tasks that were formerly carried out at national state level, and these responsibilities have resulted in extra funding from the regional governments.

The marketing of provinces has in some cases been delegated to the sub-regions, or even local/municipal tourist authorities within each province. This makes sense since, with the exception of the better-known western part of Holland, most tourism demand for the Netherlands is domestic, or from Germany and Belgium. So this is clearly reflected in regional/local marketing and promotion.

The local tourist offices — comprising the VVV Nederland — are financed partially by their respective cities and partly by the local private sector.

The relationship between some PBTs/VVVs and the NBT/TRN has traditionally been based on 'low-key contracts', or on agreements for joint marketing activities — drawn up in the same way as between the NBT/TRN and the private sector of the tourism industry. Foreign offices of the NBT/TRN have also been closely involved in these activities.

Netherlands Board of Tourism and Conventions (NBTC)

Role and Responsibilities

The remit of the NBT/TRN from the late-1990s to the end of 2003 was to promote travel to and within the Netherlands. The meetings, incentives, conferences and exhibitions (MICE) market was the responsibility of the NCB during this period. Now that the two organisations have merged, business travel of all types is included in the NBTC's remit.

The NBTC aims to achieve its goal of promoting travel to and within the Netherlands through close co-operation with the travel trade and the PBTs, government departments and intermediary organisations, as well as by stimulating co-operation between these parties.

The NBTC (and the NBT and TRN before it) is an autonomous foundation under Dutch law. The Ministry of Economic Affairs and the NBT/TRN signed an annual contract, specifying the tasks to be carried out by the Board and the amount of funding the government was prepared to pay for the different tasks. The Board had to report to the Ministry twice yearly, highlighting progress and re-assessing budgets.

Relations between the Ministry and the Board have reportedly always been very strong. The division of tasks and competencies has been very clear — and all contained within the contract — and additional decisions, or changes to the contract, have been made as needed. The NBTC says this worked well in practice.

Given the recent merger between the NBT/TRN and the NCB, the Ministry is to sign a new contract with the NBTC which, according to the NBTC, is currently being negotiated and will be a lot simpler than the previous one.

Offices and Staff

The following details were supplied in October/November 2003 and updated in January 2004. But they still relate to the office/staff status prior to the completion of the merger between the NBT/TRN and NCB.

In addition to one office in the Netherlands (HQ), the NBT/TRN (and also the NBTC) has representation in 15 locations abroad — either through fully owned/operated NBTC offices, or through GSAs and other arrangements. Paris is the only walk-in office serving the public.

10 full offices:

- Europe — Brussels, Cologne, London, Madrid, Milan, Paris, Stockholm (the Stockholm office is located in the Dutch Embassy);
- Outside Europe — New York, Taipei, Tokyo.

Representation/GSAs (4):

- Gliwice (Poland), Prague, Los Angeles, Toronto

Consultancy (1):

- Beijing

A new office is currently planned for Shanghai in 2005, and there are tentative plans to close Taipei at the same time. The Israel office was closed in 2002 and the Jakarta office in 2004. The trend over the past few years has been to reduce the number of offices abroad in an effort to cut costs and free up funds for new offices/representation in key emerging markets.

The offices closures were also in line with enforced cuts in the NBT/TRN's marketing and promotions budget two years ago, at a time when the Ministry decided it was better for the TRN/NBT to step up its activities in product development and knowledge transfer.

Staff numbers: There are currently a total of 214 staff at the NBTC — 141 in the Netherlands at HQ (141.4 full-time employees/posts) and 73 (71.7 full-time posts) — 34% — in its offices abroad.

Over the next few months HQ staff will be reduced by one-third (47 posts). The department that will suffer the largest number of cuts is product development, but other sectors such as research, domestic tourism and media sales are also expected to suffer. Because of current sensitivities (court cases are reportedly pending and the legal situation is unclear), it has not been possible to obtain an organigram — either for the pre-merger NBT, or for the post-merger NBTC. However, the following is a breakdown of staff by activity/responsibility before 2004 (Table 9.5).

Staff in offices abroad: All the staff in the NBTC's offices abroad work in the area of marketing and promotions, or are support staff. An increasing share of staff abroad, including management, are locally recruited, i.e. the trend is away from employing expatriate staff with all the associated costs. There are no expatriates at all in the Swedish office, for example. The representatives/GSAs are all locally recruited.

Resources and Funding

In 2003, the NBT's budget was £23.5 million, a 4.5% decline on 2002 in euro. Of this, 65% (£15.2 million) was 'grant in aid' funded by the state — up from 62.9% the previous

Table 9.5: Netherlands tourist board staff responsibilities.

CEO	1.0
Facilities	6.2
Strategy & corporate communications	8.2
Finance & control	10.9
Human resources	4.9
Non-profit relations	3.7
Domestic tourism (incl. sales)	14.8
MICE	4.4
Internet & media sales (includes organisation of trade fairs, etc.)	46.0
International operations	24.2
Research	4.9
Product development	12.2

year — with the balance coming from industry and provincial/local tourist authority contributions to marketing and promotional campaigns (35.3%, or £8.3 million) and contributions in kind (3.8%, or £897,000). Contributions in kind have been falling over the past few years and now only relate to air fares (Table 9.6).

The total budget was expected to fall by a further 7% or so in 2004.

The share allocated to marketing and promotions (42.4% in 2003) seems low by comparison with the situation in other countries. However, it is important to note that the balance is not all fixed/operating costs. In 2002 and 2003 a significant share went towards product development and other activities totally unrelated to marketing and promotions. Examples are quality assurance — which from 2004 is the responsibility of VVV Nederland and the private sector — and, to a lesser extent, skills training.

Note: The grant in aid from the government is expected to decrease by 25% over the next five years — from its present £13.9 million (provisional 2004 funding) to around £10.5 million.

Domestic Tourism

An estimated 6% of the NBT's total budget in 2003, or £2.1 million — down from just under 8% in 2002 — was allocated to domestic tourism promotion, almost exclusively for national campaigns. Most thematic/product promotions in the domestic market are carried out at regional/local level. National campaigns are conducted at trade and consumer fairs and exhibitions, and on TV.

The NBTC's efforts in domestic tourism promotion will decline further over the next few years, and will be limited to general promotions. Marketing of products and regions will be the responsibility of the industry and PBTs.

Table 9.6: NBT/TRN's budget, 2002–2004.

Year	Total budget (£ mn[a])	% Annual change (in euro[a])	State's contribution	% Share to marketing & promotion[b]	Actual M & P budget (£ mn)
2002	22.5	NA	62.9	48.5	10.9
2003	23.5	−4.5	65.0	42.4	9.9
2004[c]	21.8	−7.1	63.9	NA	NA

Note: The NBT/TRN/NBTC's budget is net of VAT. NA, not applicable.
[a]€1 = £0.632 in 2002, £0.690 in 2003 and 2004 (estimated).
[b]The balance between the share allocated to marketing and promotions and the total budget — i.e. 51.5% in 2002 and 57.6% in 2003 — covered a range of activities/responsibilities included in the NBT/TRN's remit as well as fixed costs (estimated at 25% of the total budget every year).
[c]Provisional.
Source: NBTC.

Activities

As already indicated, the NBTC's prime role is to promote inbound tourism to the Netherlands with the aim of increasing international tourism receipts and, particularly, foreign exchange.

Until its merger with the NCB in 2004, which also resulted in a name change to the NBTC, the NBT/TRN's responsibilities were fairly broad. In addition to marketing and promotion, it was also closely involved in product and knowledge development. As a result, much of its research was also linked to product development. And it was also responsible for a number of tasks that would normally be assumed by the national tourism administration in a country, i.e. in this case the Ministry of Economic Affairs.

Over the past two years, the organisation's marketing activities have involved (to quote its publicly disseminated strategy):

Marketing and promotion
The focus of marketing and promotion was on three areas:

- coastal tourism — mainly from the German market;
- major cities in the western part of the country — primarily for cultural short breaks and events tourism;
- the MICE business.

Research
The NBT/TRN said it:

- monitored developments on the demand side through in-house research and via its international network of offices abroad;
- monitored trends and processes of interest to the tourism and leisure product, in co-operation with branch organisations;
- provided links with other knowledge centres;
- was a broker and intermediary;
- propagated knowledge;
- used international benchmarking and effect measurement.

Innovation
The NBT/TRN stated that it:

- improved and innovated the marketing process by working with other stakeholders;
- stimulated flexible product development, aimed at the market *(this will no longer be part of the NBTC's remit)*;
- monitored the development of opportunities;
- developed and propagated one vision, one policy *(task will be re-assumed by the Ministry)*;
- tried to find (new) sources of finance *(this will no longer be part of the NBTC's remit)*;
- offered support to the tourism and leisure sector *(ditto — the Ministry will be responsible for SMEs)*;
- enhanced co-operation with provincial and regional tourist information offices.

Distribution and Information Dissemination
The NBT/TRN:

- ensured that local businesses were given good publicity in the media *(no longer part of the NBTC's remit)*;
- enhanced specific multi-channel distribution through joint efforts;
- made efficient use of its offices abroad and their relations with third parties;
- made efficient use of the local tourist information offices and the ANWB (National Automobile Association) distribution channel;
- developed on an ongoing basis the role of the internet and other new media.

NBTC's Marketing Strategy, 2004-?

The following is an estimate of the likely strategy and action plan to be adopted by the NBTC from 2004 onwards. Details are based on comments made in an interview in January 2004 by the NBTC's Directors of Marketing and Research.

With the exception of a few national institutional campaigns, marketing and promotions will primarily focus on activities abroad in future. Current thinking is that investment will continue to be prioritised as follows:

- **Key markets** (for which most of the spending will be allocated): Germany, Belgium, the UK, France and the USA.
- **Secondary markets** ("defensive marketing"): Italy, Spain and Scandinavia.
- **Low level of marketing**: Japan and (even lower level) Czech Republic, Poland and other former East European markets. (NB: some of these could be termed emerging markets.)
- **Emerging markets**: Given the fact that funds are limited, emerging markets are not really part of the NBTC's core strategy at the moment. The main focus is on China — the NBTC now has one person in the country and will probably step this up to an office, or representative office, once the ADS starts producing results. It is unlikely to consider sharing an office with other Eurcopean NTOs (as the Nordic countries are thinking of doing) as it says there is a lack of trust among NTOs generally.

Marketing strategy will continue to be drawn up by HQ, but the offices abroad will be given increasingly more responsibility to interpret strategy and translate it into actions that meet the needs of their specific local markets. But they will also be given targets based on the results of the NBTC's research, and if they fail to meet those targets, there will be some kind of penalties.

Competitor Analysis and Benchmarking

Targets — and, to some extent, the level of marketing investment — are based on competitor analysis and benchmarking, which is expected to be stepped up in the future. The NBTC uses a competitor set comprising the UK, Denmark, Germany and Belgium, benchmarking the Netherlands' share of key markets across the whole of the competitor set. Targets are assessed on what research suggests the Netherlands' share ought to be.

Research key and emerging markets involves the offices abroad. Their input can be particularly valuable in determining opportunities for growth. The NBTC also works closely with other NTO members of the European Travel Commission (ETC), sharing expertise and knowledge and commissioning joint studies on emerging markets.

Studies on all key emerging markets have been conducted over the past few years. And in 2003, a study on urban tourism and culture was commissioned jointly by the ETC and European Cities Tourism.

New Media and e-Marketing

Over £2 million has been invested by the NBTC (under its former names) to develop the Holland platform www.Holland.com, which is hailed as one of the best examples of public–private sector co-operation in e-marketing/e-distribution in Europe, if not the world. It is regularly cited in the media.

What the Dutch have succeeded in doing — that so many other NTOs failed to do — has been to bring together a dedicated group of partners under the public sector banner of the NBT/NBTC to provide the required investment to develop the site and provide a one-stop shopping platform, or virtual marketplace. Traditional marketing is used to attract people to the site.

Its success is also attributed to the fact that it was carefully planned at each stage of development and it was able to rely on a core base of public and private sector founders to fund its initial launch. Its approach has been much broader than that of most other NTOs, or destination marketing companies, in that it counts — among its many partners — non-tourism companies, such as a newspaper group, banks, a beer manufacturer and television company.

www.Holland.com was launched on 1 September 1998, although the first strategic partners were signed up as early as June/July 1995. These were in addition to the founding partners who provided the necessary investment to launch the brand, and they included major city tourism organisations (the Hague, Amsterdam and Rotterdam), as well as key players in the Netherlands tourism industry — P&O North Sea Ferries, Stenaline, Golden Tulip Hotels, the Floriade, etc. The first reservation partners were Amsterdam Reservation Centre (ARC), the National Reservation Centre (NRC), Hotelnet, Hotelcontact, Travel Service International, Ticket Service Netherlands, Advantage Travel Partners and Roompot.

The site took 18 months to develop and, since it was launched, it has regularly been enhanced, upgraded and extended, with new regional and city sites added. Each additional site within the umbrella of holland.com has been the result of co-operation with existing or new partners — e.g. the flight booking capability was developed with KLM and the Amsterdam site in co-operation with the Amsterdam Tourist Board and Heineken.

An increasing share of interest in the Netherlands, as well as business, is due to the internet, especially since sites are tailored for local markets. The Japanese and South Koreans have their own, local-language, sites.

Brand Development and CRM

The Netherlands' tourism brand — the distinctive green and orange website name www.Holland.com plus tulip — is used widely in advertising by small and large companies, especially those involved in e-distribution and marketing and through the Holland platform. This includes a growing share of non-tourism companies. So, as already indicated, all promotions steer respondents to the website.

Brand promotion is very much tailored to suit different markets since Holland has a very different image in different parts of the world. For Americans, for example, it is seen as a cosy, but relatively expensive, place to visit for a couple of days. But for European markets on short breaks, it is perceived as a relatively inexpensive destination.

The NBT/NBTC has carried out customer relationship management (CRM) and e-marketing for about five or six years now, growing its customer base significantly as a result. It moved into CRM because the cost of direct marketing by mail was prohibitive. Also, it is more effective — people respond faster than they do to traditional marketing.

B2B marketing was developed first, as well as marketing to the corporate world for conferences and other meetings. It is only now really moving strongly into B2C marketing and consumer CRM. Neighbouring markets have been targeted first since these are the people most likely to visit Holland independently.

Event Tourism

The results of research conducted over the past 12 years by the NBT/TRN/NBTC confirm the value of special events and exhibitions, both in terms of visitor numbers and their contribution to economic growth. The Netherlands hosts more than 5000 local events annually, plus 1000 or more small regional events, 500 regional events with wider impact (e.g. floral processions), 10–20 big national events (e.g. Sail Amsterdam and pop festivals) and one major international event (e.g. Euro2000 or Floriade 2002).

The tourism demand generated by all these different events — in addition to demand for overnight tourism from abroad — is estimated by the NBT at 1 billion day-trips of two hours and longer. Small regional events alone contribute more than 75 million visitors (7% of day trips), around £380 million (between 2.5% and 3.0% of total tourism spending) and nearly 7000 full-time jobs (2% of total tourism employment). This makes them attractive as an addition to the existing product supply, especially since they provide variety and authentic local colour, meeting visitors' needs for added value (Table 9.7).

Visitors to Events have Grown Faster than to Attractions Generally

Between 1995 and 1998 visits to events actually declined by 0.4% per annum, while visits to other attractions rose by a modest 0.8%. From 1998 to 2001, however, events attracted 2.4% growth in annual attendance as against stagnation for attractions in general. This would tend to suggest, the NBTC says, that events are competitors for permanent tourist attractions, in terms of numbers of visitors. But they do not seem to cannibalise demand when it relates to variety in local or regional supply (Table 9.8).

Events are important additions to the overall tourism product of a destination, according to the NBTC, since they provide new experiences and can easily be adapted to changes in demand.

Table 9.7: Economic significance of small regional events in the Netherlands, 1990–2002.

	Visitors (mn)	Spending (£ mn)	Full-time jobs
Small regional events	75	380	7,000
% Share of total tourism counts	7.0[a]	2.5–3.0	2.0

[a]7% of day trips.
Source: NBTC.

Table 9.8: Increase in visitors to events and other attractions in the Netherlands, 1995–2001.

	% Annual increase	
Years	**Events**	**Other attractions**
1995–1998	−0.4	0.8
1998–2001	2.4	0.1

Source: NBTC.

Mega Events Reinforce a Country's Identity...

Major international events and exhibitions held in the Netherlands over the past 13–14 years have all been successful, in differing degrees, at boosting international tourism demand. The majority of these events, whether major art exhibitions, or the Floriade, last from at least four to six months.

NBTC research confirms that such events tend to strengthen the destination's image as a cultural destination, as well as generating extra demand and tourism expenditure. This is not only the result of the widespread media publicity surrounding such events — but is also due to the fact that they support the country's identity. The master-pieces of Rembrandt and Van Gogh and Holland's colourful tulip fields are known the world over.

... as well as Boosting Visitor Numbers and Expenditure

The year 2002s Floriade/flower exhibition in Amsterdam attracted more than 1 million fewer visitors than it did last time it was held, 10 years ago, in Zoetermeer, a city of 100,000 inhabitants around 10 k from the Hague in South Holland. However, the drop in numbers was mainly due to a decline in domestic demand. International visitor interest was reportedly sustained.

The Floriade is nonetheless the Netherlands' major international event followed, in terms of visitor numbers and spending, by the Van Gogh exhibition held in 1990 (close to 1 million visitors and £120 million in receipts) and Euro2000 (620,000 visitors and £88 million). Van Gogh was repeated in 2003, celebrating at the same time 150 years of the world-famous artist (Table 9.9).

The following table compares the share of foreign visitors to major exhibitions and events in the Netherlands. While the Van Gogh exhibition attracted huge numbers of foreigners, who made up 68% of the total visitor count, the foreign share was a much lower 45% for the 1991 Rembrandt exhibition and an almost modest 37% at the 1992 Floriade (Table 9.10).

Many Foreign Visitors Choose the Netherlands for Specific Events

A significant share of visitors come specifically for the events in question, according to data collected by the NBTC regarding the three important exhibitions/events held in the country between 1990 and 1992.

Foreign visitors to these three events were 9.2 million nights in the Netherlands and spent £379 million. Some 2.3 million nights (around 25%) and £115 million (30% of the total) were generated by visitors who came specifically for the events in question, and they would not have been spent if the events had not taken place. The NBT/NBTC research also showed that those who travelled to the Netherlands especially for the events stayed in more expensive accommodation. By comparison, the Dutch spent only £43 million visiting the three events — mainly on day-trips (Table 9.11).

Table 9.9: Selected major international exhibitions/events in the Netherlands, 1990–2002.

Event/Exhibition	Year	Visitors ('000)	Spending (£ mn[a])
Van Gogh	1990	950	120
Rembrandt	1991	440	41
Floriade	1992	3,500	259
Vermeer	1996	420	38
Rembrandt	1999	200	15
Euro2000	2000	620	88
Floriade	2002	2,300	NA

NA, not applicable.
[a]2002 exchange rate used throughout the table.
Source: NBTC.

Table 9.10: Visitors at international exhibitions/events in the Netherlands, 1990–1992.

	Van Gogh		Rembrandt		Floriade	
	('000)	% Share	('000)	% Share	('000)	% Share
Domestic	300	32	240	55	1,980	63
Foreigners	650	68	200	45	1,170	37
Total	950	100	440	100	3,150	100

Source: NBTC.

Table 9.11: Importance of international exhibitions/events in foreign visitor motivation, 1990–1992.

Motive	Van Gogh ('000)	% Share	Rembrandt ('000)	% Share	Floriade ('000)	% Share
Of total foreign visitors attending the specific events, those who						
Came specifically or the event	300	46	110	55	327	28
Would have come anyway	350	54	90	45	790	72

Source: NBTC.

The foreign share of total visitors at events since 1992 has varied sharply — from as low as 27% for the Rembrandt exhibition in 1997 to 57% for the Vermeer exhibition in 1996 and 60% for Euro2000. Vermeer attracted the highest percentage of visitors from abroad specifically for the event (69%).

A High Share of First-Timers

On average, therefore, between 35% and 40% of all foreign visitors at mega events and exhibitions in the Netherlands have come specifically for the event, and around 50% have not visited the country before. The first-timers who come especially for the event tend to stay for a shorter length of time and spend less than average. Nevertheless, their importance should not be underestimated since, in terms of nights and expenditure, they account for shares of around 25% and 30% respectively of total tourism business.

The NBTC and the Dutch travel industry are so convinced as to the importance of mega events and exhibitions in the country's overall tourism product that a national policy has been drawn up for the organisation of events and festivals, and a special fund is being considered to support their development and marketing/promotion. Financial support for such events is also received from other ministries, e.g. Culture, Agriculture and Sports.

Case Study — the UK Office of the Netherlands Board of Tourism and Conventions

Staff and Responsibilities

Despite the high share of redundancies planned at HQ, offices abroad will not lose staff. In fact, some, like London, are seeing an increase in staff counts — in line with the change in emphasis in marketing approach. Each overseas office has a different structure, geared towards its particular target market.

London currently has 12 staff and there have been recent important changes. The last UK director (for five years) has been appointed head of core markets (UK & Ireland, France, Germany, Belgium) at HQ. His main focus will be the development and execution of the marketing strategy for this area, as well as the Holland Brand strategy and branding programmes, which will include an extensive image campaign (under planning).

The new Director in London was at VisitScotland and then worked in the London office as marketing manager. The new structure has two new marketing managers who have been appointed to focus on consumer marketing (the respective manager was formerly at Royal Mail) and business marketing (he was in New York for the NTB/TRN and before that, he worked in various Dutch hotels). The team overall is very young (average age mid-30s or younger).

Responsibilities/Activities

The UK office's remit is to:

* Raise funds from the private sector (tourism and non-tourism companies) for marketing activities — its role is basically to 'bundle' partners' funds to maximise the contributions of all stakeholders in a campaign. The ultimate goal is to increase trips and spending in the Netherlands by the UK market;
* Initiate and manage campaigns with any number of partners;
* Produce, with partners, brochures and other forms of media, including radio (unfortunately, TV is too expensive);
* Liaise with the UK trade, organise road shows and workshops, produce a trade newsletter, etc. (A new member of staff is being recruited for this.);
* Organise the Dutch participation (provinces, cities and the industry) in consumer and trade shows;
* Raise brand awareness and visibility through different image campaigns. (The office plans to expand this activity — see below);
* Handle press promotions.
* Answer public enquiries by phone, email, etc.

The office would like to carry out travel agent training, but it does not have sufficient resources to do so at present.

Niche segments in the UK are: cycling, gardens, family travel — of interest to AB&C1 target markets.

Partnership Marketing

Partnerships are the crux of NTBC's marketing approach — in London as in all other offices abroad. Each campaign has a different balance of partners, although some — like KLM, VLM, Ryanair, easyJet, Basiq Air, Golden Tulip, the three ferry companies (P&O, DFDS Seaways, Stena) — are established partners.

The Netherlands has been successful in bringing in non-travel partners, like Amstel beer and Frico cheese — both of which are trying to develop their UK markets. Frico is integrated in most UK activities at the moment, including e-marketing. It has managed to get

Café Nero — not a Dutch company, but one that wants its brand in the UK to be associated with the arts — into a 2004 campaign for Holland/Vermeer (see below).

HQ will provide some funding if the campaign is related to the current core segments — coastal, city tourism (including culture) and MICE business. However, it does not in principle contribute funds to marketing and promotional campaigns initiated by its offices abroad. But it of course pays for the office rentals, staff salaries and all fixed costs.

Among the different campaigns carried out using these themes, one particularly innovative co-promotion with the German National Tourist Office (DZT) for 2004 should be mentioned — the promotion of self-drive holidays in Holland and Germany in the UK market… 'Drive Dutch — Drive Deutsch!' The bulk of funding for this campaign is from Dutch interests. The campaign has a special website, and will run for three years, focusing on creating product awareness and interest in the lesser-known parts of Holland and Germany with internet, direct mail, door-drop and tactical press and PR.

How does the NTA Decide when to Develop a Marketing Partnership?

The NBTC's London office says it has to look for partners all the time. This is a fundamental role of NBTC's overseas marketing managers. Basically, all activities should be self-liquidating. If no partners can be found, then there is no promotion.

Brand Promotion/Development

Because of the need for private sector, or city/provincial, partners in all marketing efforts, the UK office says it is very difficult to carry out any marketing, which is purely about selling the Holland brand. There must be something in the promotion to attract the partners — e.g. the ferry lines need to see direct results etc. — so the advertising/promotion is inevitably biased.

The *Holland Magazine* — free to travellers to the Netherlands from the UK and Ireland and produced in the UK — carries advertisements, but the 'Dutch Perspectives' articles in this are more brand-oriented.

In 2002, London carried out a Holland image campaign — including celebrity endorsement with Van Nistelrooy, Bobby Robson and Bill Bryson — but it is more difficult to get the private sector to support brand image campaigns since there are less tangible results for partners. However, the new managers in London would like to do more of this.

All offices abroad have to use the same logo — in fact, London has had to change its modified logo back to the HQ version. The London office initiated the distinctive 'orange' for its brochures, but developed its own logo (slightly different from the current one) at the same time.

Managing Positive/Negative Publicity

The London office monitors the media closely through a clippings agency. It can react very quickly to new opportunities — e.g. a campaign centred around the launch of the film in January 2004, *The Girl with the Pearl Earring*, was set up in two weeks. Partners are the film distributors, The Hague (which wants to promote its Vermeer context), café Nero (it wants an 'arts' image for its coffee shops) and travel partners (KLM, etc.).

The London office got the whole campaign together through funding — it just offers the resource. The campaign comprises a small brochure, with detachable postcards to enter a competition to go to the Hague to see the Vermeer picture for real. For the first time, the London office is also experimenting with accepting text message responses. The website is also given prominence in the campaign.

Negative publicity includes the seedy side of Amsterdam (red-light district and drugs). It attempts to deflect attention to more positive aspects of the city — it believes it is best not to draw attention to the downside.

Overcoming Barriers to Effective Marketing

Examples include problems with the dominance of Amsterdam and the lack of knowledge of other city destinations. The London office initiated and encouraged other cities to participate in the 'City-break' campaign and produced a Holland City Break Guide for the UK & Ireland market.

Cities that are less well known paid more towards the campaign than Amsterdam — e.g. Eindhoven, Maastricht, The Hague, Groningen. There was a 3 million brochure print-run, distributed through newspaper inserts and at World Travel Market. Partners also include KLM, NH Hotels, P&O, DFDS, easyJet, Basiq, VLM, Ryanair, Frico and Accor.

Business Tourism

The NCB — now incorporated into the NBTC:

- offers support for potential organisers of international meetings and exhibitions in Holland;
- gives neutral and independent advice — on regional convention bureaux, venues, PCOs, DMCs;
- provides some financial support to international meetings which meet certain criteria; and
- provides online services, such as an international congress calendar, a step-by-step guide to organising a meeting in Holland, venue searches, etc.

Current Trends

A changing environment   Since there are still a number of uncertainties regarding the changes due to be implemented in the whole support structure of tourism in the Netherlands, and especially at the NBTC, it is difficult to make meaningful comments as to the effectiveness of the Dutch NTO.

A frequent criticism by the Dutch travel industry and provincial/local tourism authorities — in common with comments in other countries surveyed — is that there is a lack of appreciation of tourism's economic importance. However, tourism does seem to have received more press in the Netherlands today, and the Ministry of Economic Affairs has attracted more attention than usual, since it has admitted that the state's lower level of involvement in tourism over the past few years was almost certainly too low.

Current discussions and debates seem to be on the subject of which tourism sectors can really be influenced, in terms of demand, by which forms of marketing and promotion, and whether or not the state should be involved at all in domestic tourism. This is seen as especially pertinent when it involves the use of taxpayer's money just to stimulate day trips in some cases. The debate may lead to a policy in which domestic marketing activities executed by the NBTC have to be fully financed by participating private sector companies. Certainly, there is likely to be a decline in domestic tourism promotion at state level, except in the case of national campaigns

Role of the NBTC

There seems to be general agreement that the NBTC should stick to marketing, promotion and research, rather than get involved in areas such as product development, which is best left to the industry.

However, most recognise that there needs to be some kind of support and guidance from government since the industry is made up of so many small players who neither have the money nor the knowledge/experience to handle product development themselves. For this reason as well, some stakeholders suggest that — similarly to what is now happening in Denmark — country-wide marketing and promotion should focus more on activities and experiences possible in Holland rather than on small destination regions in the country. That way, more stakeholders are likely to benefit.

Continuous Need for Cost Cutting

Despite the government's renewed recognition of the importance of state support of tourism, the NBTC's grant in aid is being reduced by 25% over the next five years. True, the rationalisation of tasks allocated to the NBTC — it will focus almost exclusively on marketing and promotion — will free up funds to increase and strengthen its efforts in foreign markets. But the budget will remain tight and the trend towards office closures, restructuring, sharing with third parties, etc. is likely to continue.

An Unequal Playing Field

It is true that the different PBTs and municipal tourist offices all operate under very different conditions. This does not favour co-operation and partnership between the different stakeholders because it creates resentment and jealousies. As an example, Rotterdam receives 90% of its funding from the city government and 10% from the private sector. The latter's contribution is split between membership fees — to belong to Rotterdam Marketing (the city's destination management organisation) — and funding to participate in advertising and promotional campaigns, etc.

By comparison, The Hague's Visitors & Convention Bureau (Den Haag Marketing) gets a maximum of one-third of its total budget only from the city. This means it is much less beholden to the city and can operate more independently — i.e. in the commercial interests of its members. It is also therefore much more into generating its own revenues — e.g. through the sale of vouchers, which brings in £9.5 million a year — and participating in country-wide marketing and promotion led by the NBT.

Lessons from the Netherlands

Among the critical success factors of the NBTC (and its predecessors, the NBT and TRN), the most important would seem to be:

- It is rated highly by competitor NTOs;
- It has a very strong brand, recognised around the world;
- Its brand steers customers to its highly acclaimed website, the Holland platform, which groups tourism and non-tourism partners and enables customers to book online, bringing business to its partners;
- As a result, its partners believe they get good value for money from their partnership with the NBTC, which provides a platform for the industry and regions of the country to sell, but which does not compete with them;
- The NBTC's overseas offices are respected by HQ and the industry — both in the local country and in the Netherlands. Staff are considered experts in their respective markets and in specific sectors as well, and they are very successful at bundling partners' funds into marketing and promotional campaigns without incurring any costs for the NBTC;
- For a small country with a relatively modest budget, the NBTC and its predecessors have been particularly successful at promoting the country as an events and MICE destination.

Chapter 10

New Zealand

New Zealand's Recent Tourism Performance

Tourism plays a key role in the growth of the economy through employment, foreign exchange investment and regional development. Indeed the tourism industry of New Zealand saw 85% growth in international visitors over the period 1991–2002 and a 40% growth in domestic tourism over the same period. It is one of the country's largest export earners generating 16% of all exports. Similarly, New Zealand's global share of tourism is growing at between 0.25% and 0.45% and it would appear to have developed a balanced portfolio of generating markets. The New Zealand Tourism industry is dominated by 10 major public listed companies and between 13,500 and 18,000 small to medium enterprises. Tourism supports approximately 1 in 10 jobs (Table 10.1).

International and Domestic Tourism

Performance is highly comparable in terms of trips numbers with a similar balance of overseas and domestic tourism trips and expenditure. What is important about New Zealand however is its relatively recent appearance as a major destination given its relative remoteness from tourism-generating markets (Table 10.2). The growth and declining cost of air travel has been a major contributor to New Zealand tourism growth, as have some of the other factors discussed below.

Clearly, given New Zealand's location it is defined as a long-haul destination. It is some 8 hours away from most tourism-generating markets. However, at a government and popular level tourism is seen as a primary industry, which provides:

- Regional economic benefits;
- Environmental protection of landscape assets;
- Community Services and facilities (developed for visitors and used by the host population).

For the year 2003, international arrivals are recorded as 2,106,229 (3% increase on 2002) with December 2003 being 12% higher than December 2002. Overnights are also forecast to increase to around 46 million. The medium- to long-term outlook for tourism remains positive with international arrivals forecast to increase by an average 6.3% by 2007. In addition, international expenditure is forecast to increase at an annual rate of 7.8% by 2007 by which time international tourism is expected to contribute £2.5 billion to the economy per annum.

The graph in Figure 10.1 illustrates the forecast growth for tourism to New Zealand. According to most analysts the country will continue to benefit from the increased accessibility of air travel and growth in the long-haul market.

Table 10.1: New Zealand: Key facts (2002).

Population	3.9 m
GDP	£39 bn
International arrivals (TF)	2 mn
International overnights (TCE)	43.6 mn
Average length of stay (approx)	21.8 nights
International arrivals per inhabitant	0.51
Domestic arrivals	18.3 mn
Domestic overnights	52.4 mn
Domestic receipts	£2.22 bn
International receipts	£1.88 bn
as a % of GDP	4.8
per tourist arrival	£940
per overnight	£43
per inhabitant	£482
Total tourism receipts	£4.1 bn
as a % of GDP	10
per tourist arrival	£202
per overnight	£43
per inhabitant	£1051
Tourism's total contribution to GDP	9.0%
WTTC estimate for T&T industry GDP	6.1%
NTO's total tourism budget	£17.0 mn
State contribution	£17.0 mn (100%)
Marketing budget (% share of total budget)	£13.6 mn (80%)
Exchange rate	£1 = NZ$3.24

Table 10.2: Comparative tourism indicators, New Zealand (2000–2002).

	2000	2001	2002
Total overseas tourists (mn) (trips)	1.8	1.9	2.0
International overnights (mn)	35.9	38.8	43.6
Total domestic tourist (mn) (trips)	17.0	16.6	18.3
Domestic overnights (mn)	53.6	50.3	52.4
Domestic expenditure (£ bn)	1.9	2.1	2.2
International expenditure (£ bn)	1.5	1.6	1.9
Tourism share of GDP (%)	9.7	9.4	9

Source: Tourism New Zealand (TNZ)/Tourism Research Council New Zealand (TRCNZ).

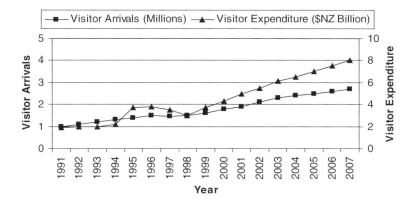

Figure 10.1: New Zealand Tourism projections. Source: Adapted from Tourism New Zealand.

Table 10.3: Type of visitor.

Type of visitor	New Zealand (%)
Holiday	53
VFR	26
Business	11
Other	10

Source: TNZ/TRCNZ.

The main purpose of overseas visitation (by volume of overseas trips) to New Zealand is detailed in Table 10.3.

The importance of holiday and VFR visits is clearly evident with New Zealand evidencing a more limited development in the business market. This is primarily as a result of its location in respect of major international centres of commerce.

The main generating markets for visitation to New Zealand are detailed in Table 10.4.

Some 56% of arrivals are first time visitors. In addition 88% of arrivals indicated that they would re-visit. In 2002, arrivals reached a new high of 2 million with the Auckland region attracting 35% of international visitors, followed by Canterbury (15%) and Otago (10%).

Australia dominates arrivals, although it is evident that the Lord of the Rings film trilogy has increased awareness and influenced visitation from other tourism-generating countries. It is notable that the US market recovered well in the first half of 2002 with arrivals up by 6% confirming New Zealand's status as a safe haven. Similarly encouraging levels of recovery were noted in the Canadian market.

The Asian market grew strongly with significant growth evident in South Korea following good recovery since the Asian financial crisis. New Zealand is also starting to profit from in-bound Chinese tourists following designation of Approved Destination Status.

Table 10.4: Main visitor markets for New Zealand (1999–2002).

Nation	1999	2000	2001	2002
Australia	523,428	573,862	630,549	632,470
UK	168,271	200,250	211,646	236,986
USA	180,881	195,781	187,381	205,289
Japan	147,345	151,373	149,085	173,567
South Korea	43,234	66,581	87,167	109,936
Germany	46,243	51,451	52,482	48,951
Canada	33,296	32,971	36,694	39,669
Singapore	33,903	35,725	32,808	34,019
Taiwan	40,228	40,848	36,188	38,358

Source: TNZ/TRCNZ.

Table 10.5: Average length of stay (nights) for international visitors (2000–2002).

Country	2000	2001	2002
Australia	13	11	12
Americas	16	18	19
Japan	16	16	15
Other Asia	23	23	25
UK/Nordic/Ireland	30	30	31
Other Europe	33	34	35
Rest of World	30	30	30

Source: TNZ/TRCNZ.

Numbers have grown by 59% in 2001 and are expected to exceed 70,000 in 2002. Other notable emergent markets for New Zealand include the Middle East Arab States (particularly United Arab Emirates and Saudi Arabia) as the Far East has now replaced America and Europe as the favoured choice of Arab families for holidays.

The holiday market is by far the most important market for New Zealand and it has seen significant growth as a specialist/niche destination given its distance from major tourism-generating markets. The VFR market remains important and it generates the longest stays (24.3 days) but relative expenditure particularly in the area of accommodation remains low. The average length of stay in New Zealand is significant but this is primarily related to the distance travelled. It is a remote destination that is aspirational for many tourists. As a consequence, dwell times and internal travel undertaken is significant (see Table 10.5 for comparative length of stay).

Clearly, those tourists travelling relatively longer distances to New Zealand have a tendency to stay for longer periods with Australian and certain South East Asian markets evidencing a shorter relative dwell time.

Table 10.6: Expenditure of major international visitors, 2001–2002 (£ m).

Nation	2001	2002
Australia	292	288
Americas	311	307
Japan	199	217
Other Asia	291	432
UK/Nordic/Ireland	252	324
Other Europe	138	178
Rest of World	133	148

Source: TNZ/TRCNZ.

Major sources of visitor expenditure are detailed along with recent trend data in Table 10.6.

Performance over this period was strong with rises evident in most major Pacific, Asian, USA and European markets. Japanese expenditure reflects the ongoing problems of that economy although it is notable that New Zealand has targeted Japan very aggressively in its 2003–2004 marketing campaigns.

It is forecast that the growth in tourism to New Zealand will continue to gain momentum given the value for money perception encouraged by poor performance of the New Zealand Dollar and relatively low cost of living. The low crime and terrorist activity record on the islands will reinforce the destination's perception as a safe haven.

MICE Market

New Zealand is not a major business and conference destination given its distance from major financial and business centres. Business tourism accounts for 11.8% of total overseas trips in 2001 with Australia the main business tourism-generating source. The gateway cities of Auckland and Christchurch are the destination for most international business trade and it is here that the greatest growth in infrastructure (conference, exhibition centres and associated hotels) is likely.

Domestic Tourism

The domestic market is growing slowly. By 2008 it is expected to increase by 2.3% per annum. The market has shown some evidence of downturn in recent years, however there was some growth during 2002 with 18.3 million overnight trips and visitor overnights also increasing to 52.4 million. Main causes for the previous reductions in domestic tourism included increasing fuel costs within New Zealand which effected the day-trip market and increasing numbers of New Zealand residents taking holidays overseas. For overnight trips the most popular region was Waikato with 17% of the total domestic visitors, followed by Auckland with 15%.

The late 1990s saw significant concern with oversupply of accommodation (reflected in relatively low-occupancy levels) and quality of accommodation. The New Zealand response at a policy level was to focus on strong brand-led marketing and quality improvement. This seems to be working as does appear to have moved matters forward. Relatively good results have been recorded in government's efforts to communicate the benefits of tourism development to host communities and getting the message across that tourism is the business of all the New Zealand residents. The oversupply issue has also been somewhat eased by the success of the county in increasing international visitors and successfully hosting major international events.

Organisation of Tourism in New Zealand

In 1901, New Zealand created the first National Tourism Organisation (NTO), the 'Department of Tourist and Health Resorts'. New Zealand now benefits from a Ministry of Tourism, which aims to maximise the benefits to New Zealand from the sustainable development of the tourism industry. The Ministry forms part of the Ministry for Economic Development as represented in Figure 10.2.

The Ministry analyses issues impacting on tourism and provides advice to the Minister of Tourism, government departments and agencies in order to develop appropriate policies.

The Ministry provides:

- Core policy advice;
- Research and statistics (via the Tourism Research Council New Zealand);
- Advice on crown entities, land and grants;
- Advice and assistance on major events;

Figure 10.2: New Zealand Ministry for Economic Development. Source: Adapted from New Zealand Ministry for Economic Development.

- Ministerial correspondence and questions;
- Land and property management.

The Ministry does not have a direct role in marketing New Zealand.

The **Tourism Research Council of NZ** (TRCNZ) is the division of the Ministry that provides research and data for industry and the government on performance of tourism. The government recognises that a solid body of data and analysis is essential for decision-making. TRCNZ's functions include:

- Research and development strategy development;
- Enhancing the provision of tourism research;
- Advising on the management of core data;
- Advising on data management and dissemination through the internet;
- Contributing interpretation and analysis of data, research and forecasting.

They have a very useful website that provides a comprehensive range of tourism data including data on special interest, policy and national markets (see www.trcnz. govt.nz and www.tourisminfo.govt.nz). TRCNZ works very closely with the National Tourism Agency; Tourism New Zealand (TNZ). The Core Tourism data set is shown in Figure 10.3.

TRCNZ's purpose is to "define, champion and pursue an integrated research strategy to ensure the co-ordinated provision of consistent, authoritative and reliable research, information and forecasting". The Council is an advisory body comprising senior representative from the public and private sector. The Ministry of Tourism provides the secretariat to TRCNZ.

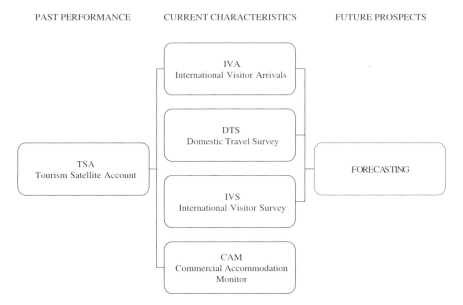

Figure 10.3: New Zealand Core Tourism data set. Source: Tourism New Zealand.

New Zealand first produced tourism satellite information in 1997 highlighting tourism's contribution to the economy and over the past six years has recorded an increase in expenditure of 27% with international expenditure increasing by 43%. It confirms tourism's position as New Zealand's second largest export industry behind the dairy industry. Over 7000 users of research and data during the year to June 2003 (against a target of 6000) with, in addition, almost 6000 recipients of the bimonthly Tourism News.

The lead industry body is the Tourism Industry Association of New Zealand, which represents the interests of over 3500 tourism businesses. The purpose of the organisation is to provide leadership, guidance services and benefits to members. There are a number of sector-specific organisations including the Inbound Tour Operators and the Hotels and Accommodation Parks Association.

Tourism New Zealand

Structure

New Zealand Tourism Board trading as TNZ is the national tourism organisation. The Executive Structure is shown in Figure 10.4.

The TNZ board is appointed from the private sector by the Minister for Tourism. TNZ handles all marketing in co-operation with the 28 Regional and Local Tourist Boards and there would therefore appear to be some major overlap/duplication in key areas such as business, area and urban-destination marketing.

The Executive Structure is divided amongst five departments: Corporate Services, Marketing, Operations, Tourism Development and Corporate Communications.

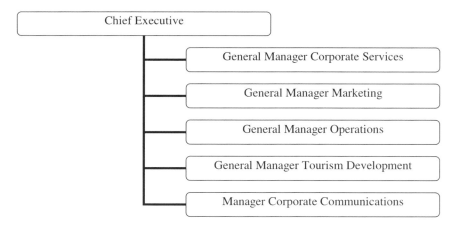

Figure 10.4: TNZ Executive Structure. Source: Adapted from Tourism New Zealand.

Staff and Offices

There are three offices based in New Zealand at Wellington (Head Office), Auckland and Christchurch. In addition there are 12 international offices as follows:

* China — Shanghai and Hong Kong;
* Japan — Tōkyo and Osaka;
* Singapore;
* Taiwan — Taipei;
* Thailand — Bangkok;
* India — Mumbai;
* Australia — Sydney;
* UK — London (also responsible for Europe);
* USA — New York and Santa Monica (also responsible for Canada).

There are also two general sales offices in South Korea (Seoul) and South Africa (Randburg). While there are no offices shared with embassies etc., Trade New Zealand and Foreign Affairs and Trade are contracted to provide services in some markets where TNZ does not have a presence such as Argentina, Brazil and UAE. There were no plans to open or close any offices during 2004.

Some of the offices have responsibility for wider areas. For example, the North American offices have responsibility for seven different areas comprising the areas of

* East Coast Canada, East Coast and Mid-west, USA;
* West Coast Canada and US;
* Kiwi Bag and Kiwi Specialist;
* Explore New Zealand;
* Media relations;
* North American newsletter;
* New Zealand companies visiting North America.

The London office responsibilities have been divided into the following areas:

* Explore New Zealand;
* France and Netherlands;
* German-speaking countries;
* Information distribution;
* Ireland;
* Italy and Spain;
* Nordic countries;
* Overseas marketing initiatives;
* PR in German-speaking countries;
* PR in all other Western European countries;
* UK market.

Included within the services these offices offer to the public the provision of a self service brochure area. Brochure orders are mainly handled through www.newzealand.com by contracted mail houses.

Table 10.7: TNZ staff responsibilities.

Activity	Number of staff
Corporate communications	7
Corporate services	8
Executive	6
Operations	8
Tourism development	9
Marketing	27

People calling TNZ's Offices for holiday information from Austria, Australia, Canada, Germany, Switzerland, the US and the UK are referred to the website www.newzealand.com and their call centre in New Zealand.

Travel agents with New Zealand expertise in each country are the main source of face-to-face information for people planning New Zealand travel. TNZ's role is to focus on marketing activities which include organising New Zealand's presence at selected travel trade events, international media and travel agent visits to New Zealand and travel agent training in market.

There are a total of 59 permanent staff and 6 temporary staff within TNZ based in New Zealand itself. The distribution between activities is shown in Table 10.7.

The marketing staff can be divided by responsibility as follows:

- Marketing communications;
- International Media Programme;
- Events management;
- Online website management;
- Product research;
- Trade development/training;
- International promotion.

The balance of staff are involved in administrative or corporate service functions within New Zealand Head Office.

There are 34 permanent staff based abroad, of which 15 are currently employed on visas and/or work permits. All of the expatriate staff are involved in tourism marketing and promotions in the broader sense.

Resources and Funding

TNZ is a crown entity with 100% public funding. The Regional Tourism Organisations are funded separately from rates (local taxes). Funding for the years 2002–2003 was £17 million with a similar amount projected for 2004. The year end is June each year. Some 80% of the total budget is allocated for marketing and promotions with the remaining 20% for administration and operations. Salaries are included within the administration portion of the budget. There is no budget allocation for the marketing and promotion of domestic tourism.

Within the New Tourism Strategy 2010, discussed later in this chapter, it is anticipated that future funding will come from a range of sources to support the requirement for set-up or one-off costs; for the ongoing costs of activities and; for investment in capital and infrastructure. The one-off funding alone to implement the major development initiatives from the strategy are estimated at between £1.5 million and £3.4 million.

For marketing it is considered essential that spend will grow in line with tourism growth and on this basis it is estimated that marketing spend will be around £30.2 million in 2010. It is however stressed that while Government will contribute to tourism funding in the short term, the overall funding required to achieve targets in the medium to long term will be spread across the private and public sectors. As stated in the strategy document, "It will not simply be the responsibility of Central Government. Without all sector participants pulling their weight, these results will not be achieved".

Role and Activities

TNZ handles all marketing with significant central government funding going into this area. TNZ has an annual budget of £17 million; approximately £6–8 million is allocated to overseas marketing. Future marketing strategy remains focused on:

- International marketing;
- Brand building;
- International event location;
- Building and developing market research.

TNZ's statutory functions are to:

- develop, implement and promote strategies for tourism; and
- advise the government and the New Zealand tourism industry on matters relating to the development, implementation and promotion of those strategies.

Activities undertaken in the year to June 2003 include the following:

- Consumer advertising;
- Internet;
- Events;
- Public relations;
- Marketing research;
- Trade facilitation and education;
- Stakeholder communication;
- Product development;
- Tourism strategy and development;
- Market support offshore;
- New Zealand market support.

Performance is measured as Quality, Quantity and Timeliness of the action undertaken, set against objective targets where possible. For example, one target during the year was to host 250 media individuals. This was exceeded as 487 attended from overseas during the year to June 2003.

Partnerships

Forms of co-operation and partnership include the following:

The private sector supports the International Media Programme and travel agent familiarisations by offering a discounted product to encourage visitation. The private sector also has access to the 100% Pure New Zealand branding in their offshore advertising. In addition, the Qualmark (www.qualmark.co.nz) quality grading system for accommodation, retailers visitor attractions and transport providers is a joint project with the New Zealand Automobile Association (www.aa.co.nz). TNZ has a 51% shareholding in Qualmark New Zealand Limited which is the official quality agency.

Activities carried out jointly with regional/municipal tourism organisations include an international Media Programme and travel agent familiarisation visits to New Zealand. Participation in selected international travel trade shows and roadshows. In addition, local government and the Department of Conservation fund and manage New Zealand's network of 90 visitors's centres. However, TNZ helps set quality standards for these 'I Sites' operations.

Communication is maintained with key stakeholders via consultation groups and local government. For example, industry updates were used as a forum to present TNZ's three-year focus and explain marketing campaigns and strategy. Other communication channels used include:

- The website www.tourisminfo.govt.nz;
- Tourism News bimonthly publication;
- 'Regional Rap' electronic newsletter issued 10 times during the year to June 2003;
- Annual Report (2000 copies issued plus available on the internet);
- TNZ updates (meetings which are to be organised in future in co-operation with the Regional Tourist Offices);
- Eighty regional seminars in the year to June 2003.

In addition to training, in excess of 12,700 overseas trade officials in 2002, TNZ is involved in familiarisation visits plus producing CD-Roms, Powerpoint presentations, Video clips and Online training modules (in Australia).

Partnerships are also formed overseas with particular success in North America, Japan, North Asia and the UK/Nordic Countries in the year to June 2003. In addition to the 100% Pure campaign, a 'Dual Destination' project progressed in North America with the Australia Tourist Commission, Air New Zealand and North American wholesales. Furthermore an advertising project with Quantas progressed in North America. In 2002/2003, £3.74 million was received from partners involved in tactical projects, whereas the target set was £1.16 million.

Marketing

TNZ handles all marketing with significant central government funding going into this area. There are industry contributions to the marketing campaigns but it is primarily state-funded. The great success has been the 100% Pure New Zealand Campaign (www.purenz. com) launched in 1999. It is directed to develop a unique brand identity, which should convert:

- Quality;
- Warmth/friendly people;
- Authenticity;
- Diversity;
- Natural attractions (scenery and landscape);
- Relaxation, respite, escape;
- Adventure;
- Safety;
- Abundant wildlife (land and marine).

It is the foundation of medium- to long-term brand building in the key generating markets: Australia, Japan, Singapore, Taiwan, USA, UK and Germany.

The campaign combines advertising, Internet, international media coverage, events and trade training to market destination New Zealand to key target markets. The use of events to promote the nation and gain media coverage along with the sales training is perhaps the most innovative element. Close liaison with events sponsors for the purposes of maximising publicity and trade-training tools are worthy of further investigation (particularly in respect of the emergent work of the industry Tourism Innovations Group). In order to build on the success of the campaign, key marketing opportunities have been developed such as 'Explore New Zealand' programme, developed as an incentive to encourage international agents, wholesalers and media to experience the Country.

The campaign continues to receive recognition as demonstrated in January 2004 as it received an American award for International Public Relations for Destination Marketing, as a result of a £4.6 million investment over three years in a US campaign.

The use of the internet is a key component of the campaign. The website, www. purenz.com, is an essential part of the potential visitor's travel decision. The site has over 6000 accommodation, transport, activities and visitor attractions with up-to-date information on events. The site attracts an average of 1.8 million page impressions each month.

Generally the website, www.newzealand.com, is validated by increasing usage. Users more than doubled to 176,392 in January 2003, the highest ever for the site. The average monthly usage is 122,300, which is increasing due to factors such as partnership agreements such as with Discovery Channel Asia and publicity from Lord of the Rings and the America's Cup. Average monthly page impressions have reached 1.93 million. The site is also used to support events and campaigns and to build upon promotions.

The internet was also used by TNZ to counteract potential negative publicity following the Bali bombing and SARS. For example, special editions of the 'Regional Rap' electronic newsletter were issued to provide additional information. A survey conducted in February 2003 found that 98% of users rated the site information as 'good' or 'very good'. The additional site, www.tourisminfo.govt.nz, has an average monthly user rate of 13,530 (against a target rate of 6000), with an average session lasting for 5.12 minutes.

Recent evolutions in this area include short-break marketing directed at Australia. The campaign, which will operate for 18 months, is the largest ever undertaken by

New Zealand in a single country. Its headline advertisement 'In 5 days you'll feel 100%' has shown good results in early 2002.

Cultural and urban attractions are secondary marketing icons used less frequently and this reflects the relative merits of the New Zealand product. The country's strengths lie in the quality and diversity of the natural landscape as opposed to any developed or constructed attraction base.

Domestic marketing   It is the preserve of the 25 regional and local tourism organisations. Campaigns are funded directly by taxpayers and supplemented by local member's contributions and membership fees. In urban regional tourism organisations, some effort is also directed at targeting international visitors, conferences and conventions business.

Film tourism   It has been significant for New Zealand. The government has injected some £1.4 million into a campaign with the Lord of the Rings film trilogy distributor New Line Cinema. Such positive exposure is being reinforced by the joint locations of The Last Samurai and the Steven Spielberg mini series on King Arthur. In addition, the film 'Whalerider' has been used as a destination promotion in Whangara in the East Coast Region with a focus on Maori culture. TNZ has also developed a valuable relationship with Discovery Channel Asia.

Specialist Market Niche Performance

New Zealand enjoys a strong reputation as a good niche performer with a number of developed segments described below.

The New Zealand offer has significant appeal to back packers who contributed some £216 million to the economy in 2001. They are long-stay visitors (39–40 nights) and a traditionally youthful market. However more than 10% were aged over 40 years in 2001.

In the field of adventure tourism, the ski market accounted for some 100,000 visitors in 2001 spending £101 million and averaging 24 nights in the country. The growth in snow boarding and the quality of the snow and slopes has contributed to the 25% increase in 2002 bookings.

Wine tourism has emerged as a substantial new tourism product both internationally and domestically. It is estimated that there are over 3 million visitors to New Zealand's wineries each year and of these between 20% and 25% are international visitors. This is a high-yield market with an average stay of 20 days or more. It is a niche taken very seriously by government and the producers. Cellar door sales to visitors are worth £46 million and wineries are part of a differentiated and more sophisticated range of offers to the tourism. The concept of combining New Zealand quality wines with a visitor experience that incorporates food, art, retail, etc. is building on strong foundations in Australia and the USA (particularly California). This type of tourism activity helps to move the perception away from the view of the country as a youthful, adventure tourism destination only.

Honeymoon tourism has attracted some 20,000 newly weds to the 'exotic and the familiar' with significant appeal to lucrative Eastern and Western markets. The opportunities for skiing, sailing and white water rafting mean that the adventure capital of Queenstown remains a popular destination. Expenditure is about 13% more than the average arrival and reflects the desire among such tourists to experience as much as possible during a relatively short time.

New Zealand also benefits significantly from dual destination travel. In 2001, about 62.5% of New Zealand's tourists had incorporated another country as part of their tour. Australia and Singapore were the most common destinations followed by the USA, Fiji and Thailand reflecting air routes and relative popularity of such destinations.

Visitor Attractions and Activities

Activities often located in areas designated as attractions have been a hallmark of advertising and visitor perception of the country's product. This has led to some confusion in their documentation a situation further hampered by the relatively unsophisticated approach to attraction visitation monitoring.

A large number of international visitors are interested in adventures and activities when visiting New Zealand and the promotion of key niche products around activities have been very successful. International strengths in activities are recognised in:

- white-water rafting;
- jet boating;
- skiing;
- snow boarding;
- bungee jumping;
- mountain biking;
- para-gliding;
- scuba diving;
- golf;
- wilderness experiences.

Large proportions of such activities are found in South Island although winter sports/activities are available in both islands. Safety issues are a concern with such activities and efforts to improve safety and security of tourists are likely to continue at a sectoral and national level. Interestingly, recent research has indicated that adventure alone was found not to be a driver of satisfaction among holidaymakers to New Zealand. It should be combined with scenic experiences and relaxation. Cost and safety re-emerge as vital elements of ensuring high levels of satisfaction. Other opportunities to enhance the visitor's experience include introducing flexibility, greater choice and a range of options (in addition to 'hard' adventure) as part of holiday packages. For the future, scenery, relaxation and better visitor management in more remote destinations are seen as vital improvements necessary for this element of the tourism product.

Attraction data do however remain relatively undeveloped with little data on major paid and unpaid attractions. Other difficulties occur as activities are merged with attractions in certain locations (see Table 10.8).

Some very strong niche focus has occurred with an emphasis on arts. For example, Nelson is promoted around New Zealand creative arts, which are sold in unusual gallery and public space areas throughout the town. Other success areas include Casino introduction in

Table 10.8: Major attraction visitation (1999–2001).

Attraction	**1999**	**2000**	**2001**	**2000–2001** **(%)**
Geothermal	372,068	402,588	410,799	+2.0
Beaches	295,098	305,281	371,931	+21.8
Sightseeing tours	333,656	320,569	365,481	+14.0
Museum/gallery	332,203	367,930	336,876	−8.4
Maori cultural	310,376	357,632	332,492	−7.0
Scenic cruises	289,059	349,318	298,205	−14.6
Sky Tower	198,009	230,532	292,660	+26.9
Botanical Gardens	229,949	257,629	247,394	−3.9
Gondola Ride	190,976	244,282	229,703	−5.9
Trekking	165,121	234,489	200,158	−14.6

Source: TNZ/TRCNZ.

the late 1990s with significant clusters in Auckland and Christchurch, which has assisted in developing the relative attractiveness of these urban destinations.

Events and Building Destination Profile

The government has been very keen to use events to promote the nation and give it increasing international prominence. Particular success stories were:

- The America's Cup 2002/2003;
- The America's Cup 1999/2000;
- The Millennium 2000;
- The APEC Summit in 1999.

TNZ as part of their Events and International Media Programme undertakes marketing via events and increasing destination awareness. Getting increased broadcast media coverage is the primary aim of the programme. In the year to June 2002, the programme hosted 472 media organisations, including 52 TV crews from all target markets and hosted more than 300 visiting media across 27 NZ events. For the year to June 2003, the programme reached an estimated audience of over 1 billion. Success in hosting TV crews from National Geographic contributed a projected 80 million audience, together with Channel 5 and GMTV (both UK) each contributing an 11 million audience. Circulations also took place in for example:

- France — Le Figaro with a circulation of 600,000;
- Japan — Bungei Shunju (450,000);
- Germany — Vogue/Elle/Marie Claire (502,000);
- UK — The Telegraph (995,000).

TNZ had a presence for the first time in the Louis Vuitton Media Centre in Auckland, during the America's Cup 2002–2003. This allowed TNZ staff access to the 1500 media and allowed them to directly assist with filming locations, travel, itineraries and general information on New Zealand. In addition, during the build up to this event, £19 million was generated of which some £18.5 million supported 1100 jobs.

Appreciation of direct and indirect expenditure as a consequence of these events is well understood at government level. New Zealand benefits from Tourism Satellite Accounts, which have adequately demonstrated at a national level the importance of tourism to the economy. At a political level, this has helped build support for tourism forthcoming and helped focus attention on the winning and hosting of major events.

Following the events of 11 September 2001, the New Zealand government effectively 'bailed out' Air New Zealand and launched a £0.62-million campaign to restore confidence in the important Japanese market. Currently, TNZ is pressing for government commitments towards investment in education, training and infrastructure and an investment of about £6.17 million to overhaul the New Zealand website.

There is great reluctance among the industry to develop any form of government taxation-funded promotional budget given the relatively small population. According to the Chief Executive of TNZ, if the marketing budget were doubled, the earnings from tourism would quadruple — a claim that thus far has fallen on deaf ears in government circles.

Product mixing is also considered important for development. Advertising is now including tourism scenarios where for example, adventure and culture holiday experiences or wine and urban tourism are combined as one package.

Developing a Brand with Real Industry Buy-in

New Zealand has achieved significant coverage for the success of its '100% Pure NZ' brand yet its formation and development was predicated upon achieving macro participation with host communities. At the basic level the consumer can be reached from a variety of mediums including:

- Advertising;
- Internet;
- Events;
- Trade;
- Media;
- Directly (through contact);
- Word of mouth.

New Zealand's use of filmic incentives including a 12.5% taxable repayment for films on location generating more then £15.4 million are clearly inspired and capitalise on the value of film coverage of the landscape and people. However, it is the buy-in to the brand of non-tourism sectors (such as agriculture, food, carriers, retail, etc.) that merits further exploration for an agency such as VB that is seeking to build brand awareness.

Imagery is central to effective marketing and this is very important in an increasingly sophisticated market. TNZ had effectively targeted a consumer profile that can be summarised as follows:

- Lived in world's largest cities;
- Well educated;
- Well travelled;

- Well read;
- Stressed;
- Seeking time out;
- Seeking natural experiences;
- Seeking rejuvenation.

The initial key was to use images to communicate to this profile but also communicate a national identity. Evidence that TNZ had collected suggested an image predicated upon:

- Maori culture;
- Expanses of open country;
- A charming but dated and possibly boring destination.

Such an image if used to market the nation was seen as inappropriate and potentially offensive to New Zealanders. Thus, TNZ sought to conduct a brand campaign which met internal and potential customer needs. This was achieved by playing to the New Zealand strengths as detailed below in ascending order:

1. Country/landscape
2. Adventure
3. People
4. Culture.

These four areas provide the conduit and guide for image development. Research was conducted to ascertain the most popular images of New Zealand and these included:

- a Maori meeting a child visitor (traditional greeting); and
- a range of landscape and water images emphasising vastness and purity/nature.

From this positioning of advertising occurs around the thematic areas of the brand and its unique positioning as detailed in Table 10.9.

Table 10.9: New Zealand thematic brands.

Brand position	New Pacific freedom
Emotional value	New found freedom Exhilarating involvement Warmly welcomed
Attributes	Young/adventurous Pacific culture Dramatic diversity of environment A breathtaking and beautiful land
Mission	Come now, do more, come back
Vision	The ultimate destination and the world knows it
What	New Zealand as a tourism destination

Source: TNZ.

Table 10.10: New Zealand image positioning.

Positioning	Focus	Characteristics for imagery
The people	New Pacific voyagers	Ingenious Passionate Inspiring Straightforward
The landscape	New Pacific land	Young Mystical Tempestuous Refreshing
The adventure	New Pacific invigoration	Intense Innovative Touched by Nature Inner-vigorating
The culture	New Pacific identity	Natural Vibrant Sensual Contemporary

Source: TNZ.

Accordingly images to populate the set would be developed around focused advertising that would achieve high international recognition and strong buy-in from domestic resident population and industrial sectors. In the case of images of the people of New Zealand this was achieved under the categories detailed in Table 10.10.

Consequently, the images used provide a contemporary illustration of brand positioning that now enjoys a level of buy-in from the people and industry of New Zealand that is hard to find replicated elsewhere.

Future Development and the New Tourism Strategy 2010

The 2010 strategy was produced in 2001 and was developed by the Tourism Strategy Group under a joint industry and Government initiative. It has incorporated significant input from the employers groups (most notably the Tourism Industry Association) and the Maori Tourism Advisory Group (MTAG). It is built around the key challenge:

> "…to ensure that the industry's growth potential is maximised whilst ensuring cultural, social, environmental and economic sustainability".

The document is interesting because of its relatively simple set of objectives, which underpin a serious and very systematic approach to tourism. The mission and vision (detailed below) are underpinned by four key objectives (which have their origins in a sustainable approach to tourism development).

TNZ new vision

Visitors and their host communities understand and embrace the spirit of
manaakitanga (hospitality) while
New Zealander's environment and culture is conserved and sustained in the
spirit of kaitiakitanga (guardianship) and
Tourism is a vibrant and significant contributor to the economic development
of New Zealand.

TNZ new mission

Welcome visitors
Protect our environment
Celebrate our culture

TNZ New Objectives

 (i) Securing and conserving a long-term future (this involves environmental protection, Maori participation, heritage promotion and increasing levels of community goodwill and support for tourism).
 (ii) Marketing and managing a World Class Visitor Experience (this involves further development of the brand positioning around culture, lifestyle and environment, increasing destination awareness, optimising yield, combating seasonality and regional spread of benefits).
(iii) Working smarter (this involves improving business capacity and quality, increasing efficiency and ensure public sector intervention is co-ordinated, responsive and effective).(iv) Being financially and economically prosperous (this involves maximising the financial returns from tourism by investing in yield management, developing value pricing, utilising assets more effectively, and ensuring airline yield and capacity issues are adequately taken into account in targeting visitors and developing products).

It is envisaged that a new sector structure will be created to:

• Streamline processes and programmes;
• Strengthen functions and partnerships.

The new TNZ will lead international branding and marketing plus having responsibility for destination management. It will be a public/private sector entity with public and private sector ownership and funding. The board members will be appointed by central/local government and industry. The Regional Tourist Offices will also have an enhanced role integrating destination marketing and management. There will also be consolidation of the various functions of the Regional Tourist Offices to create a more effective spend. In addition specific Maori tourism representation bodies will be created.

The strategy also proposes significant development of the small- and medium-sized enterprise (SME) sector to improve standards and quality and proposes a number of sources of development funding for the tourism industry. It represents a unified vision for progress and provides joint development agenda for industry and state bodies through to 2010.

Other vital areas for development include e-commerce (linked to a national government development strategy) and the funding and advancement of research. Online research and statistical sources are strong and rapidly updated although key gaps exist in product areas such as attraction visitation where data is woefully inadequate. However, in other areas there is a real will to drive standardisation of methodologies in the development of economic impact assessment, etc. Notably, benchmarking is seen as a vital element of building quality and value as part of the portfolio.

The document ends with a forecast of the characteristics of tourism in 2010:

- The New Zealand experience will stand out as a unique global offering;
- Tourism products will have been developed in a way that protects the environment, culture and built heritage;
- The strong New Zealand brand will be marketed through both physical and virtual distribution channels and joint public/private sector initiatives;
- Improved research and development will underpin decision-making and drive innovation;
- Communities will understand the benefits of tourism and will be welcoming hosts;
- In excess of 220,000 people will work in tourism. It will be an exciting and dynamic sector to work in and it will be a highly desirable career choice.

Lessons from New Zealand

What is interesting in reviewing the New Zealand approach to tourism is the significant buy-in that TNZ enjoys from industry, airlines and the general population. Campaigns such as '100% Pure NZ' enjoy support from retail, wholesale, agriculture, transport, etc. as well as from directly involved areas such as accommodation, food and beverage. Similarly, the new New Zealand tourism strategy to 2010 has been collectively authored and enjoys strong support from both community and industry. A mutually supportive relationship appears to help underpin a very positive experience for most tourists.

The positive elements of the New Zealand approach and tourism product are detailed below:

- An innovative approach towards business development with minimum public sector involvement;
- Strong brand-led marketing — increasing buy-in from all sectors in the country to pure NZ position;

- Strong buy-in from the industry to the role of the NTO and the marketing — there is a healthy scepticism about the effectiveness of government but it is not carried through to TNZ by most commentators;
- The marketing spend is high as a proportion of the overall budget;.
- Aggressive marketing in key generating nations: Australia, Japan, etc;
- Development of balanced visitor portfolio reduces reliability on one source, such as activity holidays;
- Guerrilla marketing tactics employed using film locations, events, niche identification;
- Good emphasis on sustainability, purity, natural beauty for an increasingly sophisticated traveller — seriousness of approach reflected in legislation and good practice;
- Good diversified target markets (Asia, SE Asia, Australia, Europe, USA and Canada) reducing risk of over dependence on one visitor source;
- Strong public sector support for tourism recognised as vital to New Zealand economy as demonstrated by Tourism Satellite Account;
- Recognition of value of forecasting, measurement and research in decision–making;
- Appreciation of vital importance of airlines in tourism;
- Good partnership and collaboration in evidence between industry and state to develop new strategy;
- Simple but systematic new tourism strategy in place built around sustainable framework;
- Appreciation of need to win community buy-in to tourism in order to engineer and develop genuine hospitality.

The less effective elements of the New Zealand approach and tourism product are detailed below:

- Twenty five Regional and Local Tourism organisations that currently duplicate and over-lap with many of the marketing and promotional activities of the national agency TNZ;
- The lack of built heritage, quality differentiated urban products and world renowned cultural attractions limit the marketing message;
- The distance from major tourism-generating markets necessitate reliance on air-borne visitation which is vulnerable to fuel costs, terrorism and international conflict;
- The perception of the country as a youthful destination associated with activity/high-adrenaline sports has had to be redressed in recent marketing strategy;
- The poor performance in the business and conference markets strongly effected by the geographical isolation of the location;
- Possible future concerns raised on sustainability as key sites grow.

Clearly, New Zealand is an example of strong proportional growth over a relatively short period and given the distance from generating markets this growth is all the more remarkable. Dwell times are extensive (in excess of three weeks) and the destination is seen as aspirational.

The targeted growth will create problems for the destination in terms of balancing its legislative environmental concerns and growing private sector leverage for marketing and operation. Currently, private sector leverage is minuscule although government has intimated a will to decrease state funding for tourism replacing it with industry partner funding. Such an ambition may prove difficult when advanced environmental legislation is fundamentally concerned with minimising impacts.

The lack of developed business and conference tourism is likely to continue largely as a function of location and facilities for the MICE sector are relatively undeveloped. This leaves the nation dependent upon leisure tourism and VFR predominantly, which of course increases the risk of maintaining and increasing visitation across a non-balanced portfolio.

This aside New Zealand offers many lessons and is clearly a strong competitor with large growth potential. It offers pristine natural heritage, good value for money and a range of activity and experiential type products. Urban offers are perhaps the weakest but given current distance from tourist-generating markets short/urban breaks are simply not in demand for New Zealand at this stage.

Marketing, branding and cross-sectoral buy-in all offer a model of co-operation and brand recognition that many countries only aspire to. Certainly, a nation and NTO to continue to observe over the next 5–10 years.

Chapter 11

South Africa

South Africa's Recent Tourism Performance

Inbound Tourism Trends

While tourism expansion in many of the world's leading destinations has been disrupted by global terrorism and the economic downturn over the past three years, South Africa's tourism performance has impressively bucked the trend. In 2002, it recorded 11% growth in international tourist arrivals, bringing its total count to 6.6 million. And preliminary figures for 2003 suggest that the growth trend has continued, albeit at a slower pace (Table 11.1).

The turnabout in 2002 — described as 'gravity-defying' by the Minister of Environmental Affairs & Tourism — followed four years of little change, with 5.7 million arrivals in 1998, 5.9 in 1999, 6.0 in 2000 and 5.9 in 2001.

In terms of international tourism receipts, South Africa recorded some £3.2 billion in 2002 — a massive increase of 38% on the previous year. However, preliminary estimates based on actual performance during the first nine months suggest that 2003 will have suffered a decline — at least in rand.

Performance has clearly been affected by the huge fluctuation in exchange rates in recent years, not least against sterling. The value of the rand to £1 fell from R10.51 in 2000 to R12.41 in 2001 and to a low of R15.80 in 2002. In 2003, it picked up to R12.70 again. This means that the data on tourism receipts, budgets, etc., used in this report is somewhat confusing. But year-on-year changes are provided in rand (Table 11.2).

Undoubtedly, a range of factors contributed to South Africa's strong performance in 2002, not least the weak rand, which made South Africa a very competitively priced destination for many international visitors. But equally important, in terms of the destination's appeal, was the perception of South Africa as a country relatively safe from terrorist attack. This 'safe' image was in complete contrast to its image immediately after the end of Apartheid, and also perhaps explains why there was suddenly evidence of strong pent-up demand for the destination.

The global perception of the peaceful transition has certainly been important, but the country also has a number of major attractions, notably its diversity of tourism products — and especially its potential for ecotourism and adventure travel.

Arrivals in 2002 were also boosted by two major events held that year — the World Summit on Sustainable Development in Johannesburg, or Rio+10, which attracted an additional estimated 37,000 visitors, and the African Union Summit in Durban. Encouragingly for the tourism authorities, this was also the year that South Africa's new Tourism Growth Strategy was implemented.

Table 11.1: South Africa key facts — 2002.

Population	45.0 mn
GDP	£69.6 bn
International arrivals (VF)	6.6 mn
International overnights (TCE)	79.2 mn
Average length of stay (nights)	12
International arrivals per inhabitant	0.15
Domestic arrivals (est)	37 mn
Domestic overnights	NA
Average length of stay (nights)	NA
Domestic receipts	NA
International receipts	£2.7 bn
as a % of GDP	3.9%
per tourist arrival	£412
per overnight	£35
per inhabitant	£61
Tourism's total contribution to GDP	7.1%
WTTC estimate (for T&T industry GDP)	2.9%
NTO's total tourism budget (FY 2001/02)	£26.1 mn
State contribution (% share)	£16.1 mn (65)
Marketing budget (% share of total budget)	£20.5 mn (83)
Rate of exchange	£1 = R15.80 (2002)
	£1 = R13.54 (FY2001/02)

Table 11.2: South Africa's international arrivals and receipts, 2000–2003.

Year	Arrivals ('000)	% Annual change	Receipts (£ mn)	% Annual change[a]
2000	6,001	1.9	2,513	NA
2001	5,908	−1.5	2,501	17.5
2002	6,550	10.9	2,719	38.4
2003[b]	6,720	2.6	3,115	−7.9

[a]Year-on-year changes in rand.
[b]Estimates based on actual performance in first 9 months.
Source: SAT and WTO.

One of the keys to the new marketing strategy was its focus on a smaller number of source markets. But this also involved taking a more pro-active approach to them, targeting carefully identified segments, and also being more active in encouraging promising new markets like India and China.

In 2002 more than 69% of South Africa's total international arrivals were intra-regional. Europe generated 20%, Asia Pacific and the Americas 4.0% each, and other sources 3%.

The general trend since the end of Apartheid has been an increase in long-haul arrivals. (Note: the respective shares quoted here are different from the 2001 breakdown used in the comparative analysis in Part I of this report.)

Main International Markets

There was particularly strong growth from European markets in 2002, with arrivals up 24%. Arrivals from the Asia Pacific region increased by 16% and the Americas were up 5%. Africa and the Middle East, meanwhile, rose by just under 8% (Table 11.3).

In terms of arrivals volume, South Africa's largest five markets are neighbouring countries — Lesotho, Swaziland, Botswana, Zimbabwe and Mozambique — accounting for 60% of total international arrivals between them. But excluding South Africa's immediate neighbours, Zambia is South Africa's main source from the African continent, with Malawi and Angola the only other African countries to feature in South Africa's top 20.

Table 11.3: South Africa's leading international tourism markets, 2000–2002 ('000).

Market	2000	2001	2002	% Change 2001/2002	% Share 2002
Lesotho	1,559	1,288	1,163	−9.7	17.8
Swaziland	743	752	789	5.0	12.0
Botswana	563	644	782	21.4	11.9
Zimbabwe	477	502	613	22.1	9.4
Mozambique	492	506	580	14.6	8.9
UK	358	364	449	23.5	6.9
Germany	215	208	253	22.1	3.9
Namibia	206	204	217	6.6	3.3
USA	182	176	188	6.4	2.9
Zambia	76	97	123	27.3	1.9
France	93	86	115	34.0	1.8
Netherlands	93	98	112	14.4	1.7
Malawi	71	78	96	23.0	1.5
Australia	57	62	71	14.7	1.1
Italy	39	38	48	28.7	0.7
Belgium	42	35	40	13.5	0.6
Switzerland	34	33	38	13.3	0.6
India	28	30	35	19.9	0.5
Canada	29	28	35	22.2	0.5
Angola	28	27	31	14.8	0.5
Total (incl. others)	6,001	5,908	6,550	10.9	100.0

Sources: Statistics South Africa and WTO.

Among the non-African, long-haul, markets, the UK is by far the most important source for South Africa — accounting for a 7% share of the arrivals count. The UK was followed by Germany, France and the Netherlands, all of which are relatively small at present, but which showed healthy growth in 2002 and are considered important potential sources. The USA, which performed poorly in many destinations in 2002, increased by more than 6% in volume in 2002, although its share of South Africa's total arrivals remained the same as in 2001.

Preliminary Data for 2003

Preliminary estimates point to some 6.7 million international arrivals for 2003 — an increase of 2–3%. Despite the Iraq war, growth in the first quarter of the year — when the World Cricket Cup was staged in South Africa — averaged 5%, according to WTO figures. Arrivals continued to increase in the second quarter — by 4% — but they fell by nearly 2% in the third quarter and were expected to continue to fall in the last three months of 2003.

Key Competitors

Research commissioned from The Monitor Group in 2001/2002 identified four countries as South Africa's main competitors in its key future growth markets. These are Australia, Thailand, Kenya and Brazil.

Domestic Tourism

The domestic tourism sector has been given little attention to date, but this is set to change, with South African Tourism (SAT) pledged to play a more proactive role in boosting domestic tourism demand. Little data on domestic tourism exists, although SAT and the Department of Environmental Affairs & Tourism (DEAT) conducted a domestic tourism survey over the 12-month period July 2000–June 2001. The survey results suggest that 67% of all tourism in South Africa is derived from domestic travel.

During the period under survey, South Africans took 34 million trips, 59% of which were visits to friends and/or relations (VFR) and 21% holidays/leisure trips. Of the remaining 20% share, 14% were for pilgrimages, 4% for health treatment and 2% business trips. The province of KwaZulu-Natal attracts 44% of domestic tourists.

The DEAT's Strategic Plan for 2003–2008 called for an increase in domestic tourism of 15–20% by 2006.

Purpose of Trip

Not surprisingly, purpose of trip is very different for international and domestic tourists. Visits to friends and/or relations (VFR) dominate domestic travel, with business attracting a mere 2% of all trips. But holidays and business travel are both important for international visitors. For Europeans, the share of holidays of total arrivals volume averages over 70%, and is as high as 85% for some markets (Table 11.4).

Average length of stay for international tourists is longest, at 18.2 nights, for VFR, followed by holidaymakers (15.2 nights). MICE visitors — those attending conferences,

Table 11.4: Purpose of trip.

Purpose	% Share of trips	
	Domestic	**International**
Holidays	21	40
Business	2	35
VFR	59	15
Other	18	10
Total	100	100

Source: SAT.

exhibitions, etc. — stay the shortest length of time in South Africa, averaging eight nights per trip.

Tourism's Economic Contribution

South Africa is working towards establishing a TSA, but first results are not expected until 2004. Figures from a simulated TSA developed by the World Travel & Tourism Council (WTTC), however, suggest that tourism contributed £4.6 billion, or 7.1%, of GDP, and accounted for 3% of total employment (a little under 500,000 jobs) in 2002.

Organisation of Tourism in South Africa

SAT, the country's national tourism organisation, comes under the aegis of the DEAT. The country's nine provinces — Western Cape, Northern Cape, Free State, Eastern Cape, Limpopo, North West, Mpumalanga, Gauteng and KwaZulu-Natal — all have their own tourism authorities, which work fairly closely with DEAT and with SAT in promoting the destination in foreign markets.

Department of Environmental Affairs & Tourism (DEAT)

The Tourism Branch of the DEAT comprises 52 full-time management staff (i.e. excluding support staff and staff working in corporate and financial services or HR). They are spread across the Office of the Director General, two programmes — Tourism Support and Tourism Development — and four operational units: Quality Assurance, International Tourism Liaison & Inter-governmental Co-ordination, Research & Development and Business Development.

DEAT leads and directs tourism policy formulation and implementation towards national tourism growth. It works in partnership with SAT, the marketing arm of the department, the provincial tourism authorities, the tourism industry and other stakeholders. As detailed in DEAT's Business Plan 2003–2004, it aims to ensure and accelerate the practical delivery of tourism benefits to all South Africans, while maintaining sustainability and quality of life (Figure 11.1).

The *Tourism White Paper*, drawn up at the beginning of the decade, provides the policy framework and contains a number of programmes that contribute to the key tourism objectives:

Tourism growth:

- Facilitating increased tourist volumes, tourism spend and the geographical spread of tourism;
- Facilitating investment in infrastructure and product development in tourism priority areas;
- Creating awareness of the economic potential and impacts of tourism;
- Promoting domestic tourism;
- Monitoring tourism trends and providing timely information to the public and private sectors.

Human resource development:

- Enhancing training interventions focused on tourist guiding;
- Promoting tourism training and awareness creation among teachers and learners.

Employment:

- Engaging the tourism industry to employ trained and registered tourist guides;
- Providing support to entrepreneurs to establish and/or grow their tourism enterprises;
- Promoting infrastructure and product development in priority tourism areas.

SME development:

- Providing a package of support services to small- and medium-sized tourism entrepreneurs (SMEs), including funding information, marketing, business linkages;
- training and mentorship.

Figure 11.1: Structure of the South African tourism support system. *Source*: The Travel Business Partnership.

Black economic empowerment:

- Setting targets and monitoring public sector procurement from black-owned tourism enterprises;
- Marketing potential tourism investment opportunities to black investors;
- Monitoring investment by black entrepreneurs in tourism products and services.

Increasing competitiveness:

- Identifying and developing products that are aligned to market need;
- Promoting tourism awareness domestically;
- Ensuring quality of service through training and grading interventions.

Integrated sustainable rural development and urban development:

- Identifying tourism priority areas, both urban and rural;
- Promoting infrastructure and product development in these areas;
- Facilitating training and quality assurance interventions in these areas.

New partnership for Africa's Development (NEPAD):
Developing and implementing a Tourism in NEPAD programme.
DEAT's core services include the:

- Provision of tourism enterprise marketing assistance, both internationally and domestically;
- Facilitation of access to financing and business support for tourism enterprises;
- Provision of market intelligence to inform planning and decision-making;
- Facilitation of access to tourism training instruments;
- Convening and conducting tourism awareness creation activities; and the
- Facilitation of quality assurance within the tourism industry.

DEAT oversees the management and financial aspects of the operations of SAT, the Tourism Hospitality, Education & Training Authority (THETA) and the South African Tourism Institute (SATI). It is also responsible for monitoring and evaluation of delivery against their respective business plans.

It was announced that DEAT has been allocated a total of £128 million (@ a projected R12.70 to £1) for fiscal 2004/2005 (ended 31 March 2005), up from £114 million in 2003/2004. According to the budget report on environmental affairs and tourism, the allocation for the tourism role of the department has increased by 17% to £29.6 million and is now forecast to rise to £33.2 million by 2006/2007. SAT will receive 91% of the DEAT's tourism allocation — down from 92% — and, of this, 76% (74% in 2003/2004) will be for marketing.

The budget also calls for £0.9 million to be allocated to the Tourism Enterprise Programme (TEP) in 2004/2005 — up from £0.8 million in 2003/2004 — and £1.2 million in 2005/06. The TEP, a programme to develop skills capacity in South Africa, has created more than 10,000 jobs, assisting 646 black-owned tourism enterprises. The increase in turnover of enterprises assisted by TEP since its inception in July 2000 has exceeded £46 million.

The International Tourism Marketing Assistance Scheme (ITMAS), a tool to finance SMEs to attend exhibitions, such as London's World Travel Market and ITB Berlin, has now been absorbed into the TEP programme.

Expenditure on bio-diversity and conservation is expected to increase from £17.0 million in 2003/2004 to £21.8 million in 2004/2005 — and to £24.9 million by 2006/2007. Among the key reasons for this growth are the funds spent on the Trans-frontier Conservation Areas Sub-programme, which is expected to grow at an average of 33.5% per year over the next three years in order to increase the area of land under conservation and to implement the Protected Areas Bill in the medium term (Table 11.5).

Consultative and other related bodies:

Although not apparently formalised, inter-ministerial committee meetings addressing tourism issues are reportedly frequent and effective. There is also a Parliamentary Committee on Tourism.

The Tourism Forum

Established in December 1998, the Tourism Forum acts as an advisory body to DEAT. Its membership comprises leaders from government, business, public institutions and labour, with the common purpose of ensuring the growth and development of the tourism sector. The Forum agreed to support the following areas:

- Sustainable funding mechanisms;
- Information systems;
- HR development programmes;
- International marketing; and
- Welcome Campaign.

The Welcome Campaign was launched in December 1999, aimed at increasing South African awareness about the importance of tourism to the growth of the national economy. It encourages South Africans to make visitors feel safe and welcome.

The Tourism Grading Council of South Africa, like SATI, trains teachers and provides learners from disadvantaged backgrounds with tourism internships. The Council sits within SAT, but appears to operate separately from the international marketing body.

Table 11.5: DEAT's annual budget, 2003/2004 to 2004/2005[a] (£ mn[a]).

	2003/2004	**2004/2005**	**% Annual change[b]**
Total budget	114.2	127.6	11.7
of which, for:			
Tourism	25.3	29.6	17.1
Allocation to SAT	23.3	26.9	15.3
Tourism marketing	17.3	20.5	18.2
Fixed costs	6.0	6.4	7.1
Tourism Enterprise Programme	0.8	0.9	20.0

[a]FYs ended 31 March — rand converted at constant R12.70 to £1 over the period.
[b]% annual change in rand.
Source: South African Government Budget Speech, February 2004.

The Tourism Business Council of South Africa is the private sector partner of DEAT and SAT. It administers the Tourism Marketing South Africa (TOMSA) levy — a levy paid voluntarily by its members — which significantly boosts the funds available for the international marketing of South Africa as a preferred tourism destination.

In the context of the government's Transformation Strategy — the transformation and empowerment of black South Africans — a Transformation and Empowerment Index is being developed jointly by DEAT and the Tourism Business Council to determine, measure and monitor transformation in the tourism industry.

The Business Trust — representing big business in South Africa — is also an important partner of DEAT and SAT, having provided significant financial support over the past few years.

Trade and Investment South Africa (TISA)

In line with Cabinet's identification of tourism as one of the top five priority areas for the promotion of economic development and job creation in South Africa, a tourism investment promotion/facilitation strategy is being developed in collaboration with Trade and Investment South Africa (TISA).

South African Tourism (SAT)

Role and Activities

SAT is the official international marketing arm of South Africa as a tourism destination. It markets South Africa's scenic beauty, diverse wildlife, kaleidoscope of cultures and heritages, the great outdoors, sport and adventure opportunities, ecotourism and conference facilities. Marketing is undertaken via SAT's international offices located in nine strategic markets on three continents.

SAT's vision for tourism mirrors that of the DEAT:

> 'As an integral part of the African continent, to competitively market South Africa internationally as a preferred destination, for the sustainable economic and social empowerment of all South Africans and to make tourism the leading economic sector in South Africa.'

SAT's stated mission is:

- to increase the number of international visitors;
- to increase export earnings;
- to increase the dispersal of all visitors across South Africa to spread the economic benefits and encourage development;
- to co-operate with all stakeholders to promote a suitable national tourism culture and environmental awareness and consolidate partnerships to maximise resources;
- to promote a unique African experience;
- to demonstrate leadership, integrity, responsibility, creativity and excellence in all we do;

- to promote southern Africa as a tourism hub through regional co-operation, for the benefit of the whole region;
- to co-ordinate, where appropriate, data, research, statistics and product information for the industry nationally; and
- to offer visitors a quality experience.

During FY 2002/2003, SAT adopted and rolled out a Tourism Growth Strategy that allows it to focus its marketing activities on specific segments of tourists outside South Africa:

- who are most likely to travel to South Africa; and
- whose value for South Africa will be highest, taking into consideration the size of the segment. (Value is calculated as the days spent in South Africa multiplied by the spend per day, multiplied by the number of provinces visited, multiplied by the time of year the tourist will be visiting.)

These specific segments have been identified through extensive research since the second half of 2001. Research is continuing.

Staff and Offices

SAT has 12 business units at its HQ, each with its own business plan and budget, reporting to a Business Unit Manager. The units are: Americas, Europe, Asia, Africa, Central Marketing, Research & E-business, Communications & PR, Finance & Administration, Human Resources, office of the CEO, Strategic Relations and the tourism Grading Council of South Africa (Figure 11.2).

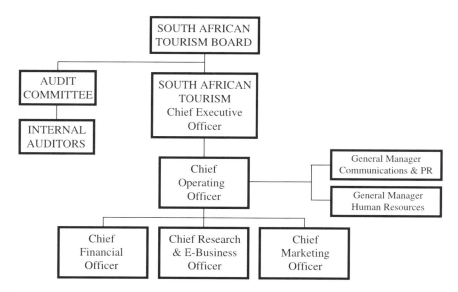

Figure 11.2: Structure of South African Tourism's HQ. *Source*: The Travel Business Partnership.

SAT has a total of nine offices — all overseas, i.e. in long-haul markets.

- Europe — Amsterdam, Frankfurt, London, Milan and Paris;
- North America — New York; and
- Asia Pacific — Beijing, Sydney and Tokyo.

During 2002/2003 it closed down non-value adding operations, such as its offices in Vienna, Harare and at Johannesburg International Airport (this last one has been taken over by the Gauteng Tourism Authority). In addition to its fully manned offices overseas, SAT has set up local information and brochure phone lines for the trade and consumers in 10 countries: Austria, Belgium, France, Germany, Ireland, Italy, the Netherlands, Sweden, Switzerland and the UK.

Resources and Funding

Government grants contributed 71% of SAT's total budget in FY 2003/2004 — down from 73% the previous year, but up from 62% in 2001/2002. The total budget this FY is 38% higher than in 2002/2003. Of the remaining funds, £4.3 million has come from formal business contributions — i.e. from the Tourism Business Council of South Africa through the voluntary TOMSA levy (see above) and the Business Trust — and £3.8 million from other sources. These include deal-driven campaigns with airline and trade partners and the sale of exhibition space at international trade fairs, exhibitions and similar events (at which South African exhibitors are grouped under the umbrella of SAT) (Table 11.6).

Marketing — SAT's prime activity — accounts for around two-thirds of the total budget and salaries and administration for the balance. The financial contribution committed by the Business Trust reflects the success of the public-private sector partnership set up for tourism marketing and promotion.

Marketing Strategy

The marketing mandate of SAT is 'to position South Africa as the world's preferred tourist destination of choice'.

Table 11.6: South African Tourism's budget, 2001/2002 to 2003/2004.[a]

Year[a]	Total Budget (£ mn[b])	% Annual change (Rand[b])	Government grants (%)[b]	% Share to marketing & promotion	Actual M&P (£ mn)
2001/2002	26.1	NA	62	78	20.5
2002/2003	20.5	−14.3	73	67	13.8
2003/2004	32.8	37.5	71	NA	NA

[a]FY ended 31 March of respective years.
[b]Converted at estimated average exchange rate for respective FYs — i.e. £1 to R13.54 in 2001/2002, R14.77 in FY2002/2003 and a projected R12.70 in FY2003/2004. But % annual change calculated in Rand.
Source: SAT.

SAT is currently in the throes of changing the way it goes about its marketing and developing the country as a destination. It has been through a lengthy and in-depth strategy development process, which culminated in the publication of its Tourism Growth Strategy in May 2002. This laid out a completely new strategy for marketing the country, together with an action plan and a new scheme to redefine and reposition its tourism brand. These plans are now gradually being implemented.

SAT is at pains to show that its new marketing and branding decisions are research led, and it takes every opportunity to emphasise the need to describe and understand its source markets and the consumers through up-to-the-minute methodologies.

As already noted, SAT's core business is as the international marketing arm of South Africa. To date there has been little emphasis on domestic tourism marketing, although several recent research papers from different bodies highlight its importance. SAT is currently inviting tenders for research on the domestic market in 2004, with a view to understanding and doing more for domestic tourism.

Marketing Activities

Marketing is initiated and undertaken from both HQ and in SAT's nine international offices. Campaigns/events involve:

- Initiating and co-ordinating marketing campaigns 'to create a positive climate for effective marketing';
- Producing promotional material — printed media brochures, newsletters; promotional videos, CDs, DVDs;
- Participating in exhibitions — both trade and consumer — and presenting workshops to the travel trade. Organising INDABA, which is an annual tourism market held in South Africa for international buyers. (A new exhibition organiser has recently been given a three-year contract to handle this and other SAT trade events.);
- Organising PR events and hosting press and familiarisation trips;
- Co-ordinating the website (a webmaster is employed at SAT HQ) and distributing e-newsletters; and
- Improving relations with the trade by offering an e-training programme for agents. The specialist destination Fundi training, which is divided into eight modules, is delivered via the website, with the final module delivered by email. SA Fundi graduates get additional support from SAT and become eligible for a range of incentives. They can also benefit from SAT's lead referral system.

SAT is currently drawing up new contracts with the private sector to contract out a range of marketing activities. In December 2003, four private sector agencies were appointed to work with SAT over the next three years on:

- PR communications;
- Media intercept;
- Integrated campaigns; and
- Design and visual identity.

SAT will maintain overall control of brand aesthetics and identity, but the agents will provide expertise on a sustained basis and supplement and compliment SAT's existing resources and skills base. Other recent developments include the appointment of a new company to handle SAT's exhibition presence around the world — the first roll-out being WTM 2003.

Market Prioritisation

SAT has commissioned a substantial volume of research over the past few years to help it identify and decide which core international markets it should target. SAT realised it could not afford to sustain aggressive marketing efforts in all the markets, which currently yield most volume and expenditure for South Africa, nor could it mount campaigns in all the world's top outbound leisure markets. (These are defined by SAT as markets that produce over one million leisure visitors a year.) But through analysis — particularly by viewing potential markets in terms of effort versus gain — SAT has identified a limited number of markets and segments for focus.

Tough choices had to be made about the countries on which it should focus, and which segments within those countries to target. Having selected key countries for its marketing effort, SAT also identified those which offered the greater opportunity for growth and those which should just be defended. SAT also identified a range of visitor segments, and again divided these into 'growth' and 'defend' categories. SAT's strategic focus by country currently comprises:

- **UK and Germany** — defend established position, and aggressively focus on growth;
- **The Netherlands** — relative gains are less significant than from other markets, so SAT is defending existing position in key segments, but will look to build growth in other markets;
- **USA and Japan** — the potential gains are seen as greatest from these two markets, but the effort required will be significant. Both are major investment targets for SAT. The USA is the first market where SAT will be going into building the long-term effort for growth. Japan will follow in the medium to longer term;
- **China, Sweden, Italy, Canada, France, Australia** and **India** are the focus of more targeted efforts — 'picking off' key valuable segments in the short term. China represents a particular opportunity. South Africa obtained approved destination status (ADS) in 2002, and tried to act immediately to ensure early gains from this market. Its early efforts seem to be paying off.

Africa is viewed as a separate market with a different strategy — over 70% of arrivals are from Africa with the majority from neighbouring countries. SAT's approach for Africa is not so much to grow volume, but rather to extract further value (e.g. encourage Africans to stay longer, spend more and convert the business visitor to become a returning holiday-maker, etc.). Source countries offering the best growth opportunities are Egypt, Nigeria, Kenya, Tanzania and Mauritius.

In addition to the target countries, SAT also has a list of 20 or more countries which are not included in their marketing strategy, but which are being watched and re-assessed annually.

Market Segmentation

As noted above, SAT has already conducted considerable research to help identify segments clearly. It has decided to break away from what it views as the more traditional segmentation groupings, which can be too broad to be of any real use in targeted market-ing, and has developed a more detailed list of segments, which are based on a closer under-standing of the consumer. SAT currently has 16 'growth' segments (including four MICE segments) and 17 'defend' segments.

Growth segments:

- **USA**: Next Stop South Africa; Upscale Wanderlusters; Convertible Positive Apathetics; Family Explorers'. The USA is seen as a prime long-term market and will receive most investment, according to SAT;
- **UK, Germany, France, The Netherlands**: Luxury Tour;
- **UK**: Confident Golden Relaxers; Short-stay Organised Break; Next Stop South Africa;
- **Germany**: German Medium Tour;
- **Italy, France**: High-end Package Combined;
- **France**: Active Independent Explorers;
- **India**: Wealthy Indian Segment; and
- **Kenya, Nigeria, Tanzania, Mauritius, Zambia, Egypt**: Businessmen (35–44, profes-sional with or without family, high income).

   The **MICE** sector is treated independently from the other segments, and is viewed as a very important segment to pursue. SAT is targeting:

- **MICE worldwide, but mainly Western Europe and North America**: Medium-sized conferences with 100–1000 delegates, lasting an average of four days, and with a 1–3 year lead-in time;
- **North America**: Incentives groups, mostly with fewer than 100 delegates and a lead-in time of less than 12 months;
- **Western Europe**: Incentives;
- **Rest of World, especially Eastern Europe, Asia and Australasia** : Incentive groups with fewer than 100 delegates and with a relatively short lead-in time of 2–6 months.

Defend segments:

- **UK**: Working Explorer, Midlife Working Break, Backpackers;
- **The Netherlands**: Budget Package, Comfort Tour;
- **Germany**: Bargainer, High Independents, Medium Package, Low-end Budget Tour;
- **Italy**: High-end Tour, Package Adventure;
- **Neighbouring states and the rest of Africa**: The Focused Trader, Low Budget Business Person, Professional Businessman, Freeloading VFR, Holiday VFR;
- Medium Budget Holidaymaker.

The MICE Sector

SAT sees its role as co-ordinating the marketing efforts of the six key MICE bureaux in the country. The bureaux do their own marketing, but SAT provides a platform in the form of web-site links, co-ordinating South Africa stands at trade exhibitions, brochure dissemination, etc.

In global terms, the MICE sector is still relatively small — South Africa has been in the lower levels of ICCA's rankings of the top 20 countries that hold international conventions. But MICE is being viewed as a priority sector with considerable potential, and four recently appointed MICE special representatives are just coming on board in overseas offices in the UK, USA, France and Germany. (The London office's MICE specialist, for example, started work in October 2003.)

Niche Segments

SATs strategy is to provide market intelligence and ongoing support for niche products, but not to actively market them — this is being left to the industry.

The main niche segments that the industry is either developing or has already established are: Golf, Spa, Gourmet (wine), Adventure, Adventure Sports, Wildlife, Gardens, Festivals, Events, Backpacking and Water.

Shopping (especially from African visitors) and medical tourism (elective surgery/procedures from the developed world and trips from other African countries with poor medical facilities) were initially identified in the International Tourism Marketing Strategy Development Project Phase 1 as priority segments for SAT. However, SAT has now decided that both should be treated like other niche segments, and are better left for the industry to develop.

Marketing Partnerships

SAT has recently changed the way it handles its marketing partnerships. The earlier system of forming Joint Marketing Agreements with the private sector, which could lock the partners into three-year partnerships and were built around rigid investment: outcome ratios, has proved too inflexible and bureaucratic and has not always been successful. Now, SAT is entering into one-off agreements with a range of partners for specific campaigns, and this seems to be working much better.

This more flexible approach has led to, for example, the Sunsation Campaign 2004 — a major marketing campaign to target two core segments of UK travellers — Next Stop South Africa (the product criteria is a 13-day package from around £1400) and Wanderluster (7-day package from £850). UK tour operators were invited to join the SAT/South African Airways multi-faceted campaign, which involves printed, online and direct mail advertising.

SAT is putting £700,000 into the campaign, and South African Airways £350,000, while each operator will contribute £8000. For the PR and promotional component, SAT is linking with a non-travel partner (not yet identified) — as in 2003 when Land Rover dealerships carried SAT brochures and a DVD about South Africa.

Because of its limited funds, SAT is restricting itself to leading the marketing in its core markets only. For other markets, SAT aims to facilitate packages.

Steps to Overcome Barriers to Effective Marketing

SAT's strategy is to facilitate unlocking barriers — lobbying to expand air capacity, for instance, or trying to find a way to resolve visa difficulties for nationals of some target countries.

Brand Development

The development of a stronger brand image for South Africa is an important element of SATs new growth strategy, although work on this is really only just beginning. Recent research showed that, in most target countries, the South Africa brand did not own any key attributes in the mind of the consumer.

SAT is now in the process of re-defining its brand. It has categorised the growth/defend segment portfolio (see above) into four 'brand audience' categories: Luxury in Africa, Africa as Hip, South Africa for Entertainment and Business and Value for Money in Africa.

Market Intelligence and Research

SAT only established a strategy and research capacity within the organisation in 2001, so 2002/2003 was the first full year for the Strategic Research Unit (SRU). Its main efforts to date have been to set up the basics for reliable measurement systems. As an example, it will soon be able to monitor and track industry indicators, thus generating the kind of data essential to the development of a Tourism Satellite Account.

In the past SAT only carried out summer and winter surveys at airports, so only understood four months of the tourism year. In 2002/2003, over 12,000 foreign tourists were surveyed in its first full-year inbound visitor survey. SAT also provided custom data cuts and analysis to the industry. Land border post surveys were carried out for the first time in all four quarters of the year.

The SRU has also now developed 'smart' tools and systems that are beginning to create a virtual portal, where staff from anywhere in the world can download and access data reports and strategic information at the touch of a button.

Competitiveness Survey

SAT, in partnership with DEAT, the Department of Trade and Industry (DTI) and Trade and Investment South Africa (TISA), have engaged The Monitor Group again to assist government in assessing the competitiveness of the tourism industry in South Africa. This follows SAT's intensive and sustained efforts over the past three years to analyse potential markets outside South Africa and connect the SAT industry to the most profitable market segments.

SAT believes that the strategic agenda now needs to shift to an analysis of the ability of the different players in the industry — both individually and holistically as a system — to satisfy the needs and desires of the target segments. This, it maintains, will engender yet higher growth rates for the SAT industry, whether through increased arrivals or value.

New Media, e-Marketing and CRM

Different overseas offices used to have their own websites but, in 2002, these were pulled together into a single website, operated out of South Africa. The webmaster is employed by SAT from HQ. The website, www.southafrica.net, which reaches consumers and the trade from a single site, is regarded as crucial by SAT, particularly as the budget for its overseas presence and marketing efforts is relatively small.

However, SAT is still working on more basic aspects — broadband speed is currently very slow, for example — but this is being changed. These are early days, and much needs to be done to expand the website to match the size and capabilities of, say, Australia's. Other language versions are also being developed.

In 2002/2003 (ended 31 March 2003), visitor hits on the website averaged 1.5 million hits monthly, having risen from 3000 a month in May 2002 at its launch.

The website does not house an electronic booking engine, but offers a virtual 'travel bag', which facilitates bookings through the user's preferred travel agent or a specialised South African agent known as a 'Fundi'. Travel bags can be e-mailed to friends and relatives so that they can make their travel plans.

An intranet was also developed in 2002/2003 specifically to serve the internal information needs of SAT staff worldwide.

SAT is now marking the country's 10 years of freedom with the launch of a new website, www.southafrica.net/heritage. The website is designed to offer a dynamic window into the trademark culture and heritage that makes South Africa one of the world's unique and authentically inspirational destinations. Visitors to the site can travel through time to learn about the earliest beginnings of the country and chart the progress on the road to freedom. They can 'visit' South Africa's United Nations-designated World Heritage Sites, including Robben Island, the long-time prison home of Nelson Mandela. Thirty-nine cultural routes are showcased, with detailed descriptions and historical data given about each location and its environs.

It is interesting to note that the Western Cape Tourism Board — representing the second most visited province in South Africa in terms of international tourism, after Gauteng — has opted to buy a readymade software package from the Austrian destination management software provider, Tiscover, instead of investing in developing its own portal.

Case study — UK Office of South African Tourism

The London office has seven staff — a managing director, deputy managing director, marketing manager, manager joint trade marketing, marketing communications executive, marketing services executive, financial officer and despatch administration officer. It is located outside central London, in Wimbledon, where office rental is more economic.

Handling Enquiries

Enquiries are received by e-mail, via the website and by telephone call and, as with other overseas offices, there is no overt walk-in enquiry desk for the public. The UK telephone brochure/information line is manned by South Africans — with four or five staff are on duty at any time — but, as in other countries with trade/consumer phone lines, the team is not part of the marketing operation and is located in a separate office away from the main marketing office.

Marketing Activities

One fundamental focus for the London office is raising awareness of the destination. SAT's research in the UK has shown that many UK residents do not know where South Africa is, let alone knowing anything about its history, geography and range of possible holiday opportunities. SAT is therefore trying to raise awareness in the UK of the range of products, destinations and activities South Africa can offer, as well as the price and time-zone advantage compared with competing destinations such as Canada, Australia and Thailand.

SAT's visibility campaign in the UK in 2002 has generally been regarded as a notable success. With a £499 Sunsational holiday offer a focal feature, the visibility campaign used billboards, the internet, associate marketing, plus the '£499 Sunsational offer' available from 1 May to 31 July 2002 as the focus. An imaginative range of marketing associates/events in 2002 included the following:

- London cabbies were used in a South Africa Taxi Campaign highlighting the destination. This involved 80 London cabbies who were offered holidays in South Africa, and they, in return, displayed South African flags on their cabs, and talked about the destination with their passengers. Their enthusiasm and experience — describing the destination, commenting on how exaggerated crime in South Africa is, etc. — was passed on to a wide range of customers. In addition, the cabbies' feedback to SAT was very valuable;
- South Africa had a big presence at the Chelsea Flower Show. Its stand was co-funded by Kirstenbosch Botanical Gardens, Cox & Kings and the National Botanical Institute of South Africa;
- The Big Braai was organised. This was the biggest braai (BBQ) to be held by South Africa in the UK, with 17,000 attending. It took the form of a celebration of South Africa as a destination — its culture, music, food and its people;
- Promotion of the Scandinavian Masters Golf Tournament (held in South Africa);
- SAT co-ordinated stands at the Holiday World Consumer Show, the Great Yorkshire Show and the Destinations Holiday Show.

Targeting the trade in 2002:

- SA Tourism had a strong presence, with 100 exhibitors, at WTM;
- Selected UK retailers, tour operators and the media were invited to Indaba in South Africa;
- Joint marketing initiatives with tour operators were used to help expand the promotion of South African products through brochures, via the internet and through the retail travel chain;
- Educating the trade — seminars and workshops were held in co-operation with tour operators and partners such as SATOA (South African Tour Operators Association);
- The number of educational tours to South Africa for travel agents was increased;
- A monthly product newsletter was developed, and delivered electronically to the travel trade to improve communication and to create awareness for co-operative opportunities between SAT and the UK trade.

New campaigns in 2004 are targeting three core segments identified by specific research in the UK market.

Wanderlusters — 18–29 year olds, earning over £23,000 a year, who are already experienced long-haul travellers, but not to South Africa. They want to experience wildlife and culture in an active way as well as relax on the beach. Childless, some 30% are based in London. Value for money is important, and there is some concern for personal safety. SAT is focusing on building up knowledge of South Africa in this group, on highlighting value for money, and showing that South Africa is a country of warmth, contrast, surprise and vibrancy.

Upper Wanderlusters — 18–49 year olds (average age 36), with an income over £50,000. Childless, and 67% are based in London. They have visited South America and/or Africa but not South Africa. Regarded as the most easily convertible segment, but they must be convinced there is something out of the ordinary about the destination. They are interested in an active, luxury holiday, but other destinations have priority over South Africa. SAT is focusing on the need to see South Africa soon, and on the range of experiences possible — whale-watching, cycle tours, etc., as well as more established wine and safari tours. The safety issue is being addressed through highlighting the positive aspects of Africa.

Next Stop South Africa — 50–64 year olds, with middle to high incomes. They have travelled long haul recently, but have never been to South Africa. Over half are London based and they want relaxation, time to visit friends, quality time with their partners and to explore, luxury accommodation and a safe environment. The main barriers would be AIDS and crime, and the fact that other destinations have a higher priority (especially Australia). SAT is focusing on excellent value for money and the image of South Africa as a preferred destination for comfort and convenience vs. safety and health issues.

Managing Positive and Negative Publicity

SAT is increasingly aware of the need to leverage events in which South Africa has a high profile. When Nelson Mandela was in London in 2001 for the Trafalgar Square concert and to receive the Freedom of the City of Leeds, for instance, SAT mounted 30 events over a 6-week period to leverage the impact of Mandela's visit.

Interestingly, South Africa's image as a destination with excessive crime and problems with safety and security for tourists was wiped out almost overnight by the events of 11 September. Suddenly South Africa was seen as a destination outside Islamic terrorist risk areas.

Nonetheless, there are still issues of personal safety in the three target segments for 2004 outlined above, and SAT is adopting particular strategies to address this. In general SAT has decided it is best to avoid all mention of the crime/security issue in promotions — there is little point in reminding markets of the more negative sides of South Africa's image.

MICE Marketing in the UK

The UK is regarded as South Africa's strongest market for incentives and conferences — particularly as many non-UK clients use the international expertise of organisers in the UK. The UK is one of only four countries where a specific MICE marketing manager has been recruited.

For non-discretionary business travel, SAT is focusing on attracting business visitors back on another occasion for a leisure trip, or encouraging them to extend a business trip to take a short leisure break (e.g. wine country tour, week-end safari, etc.).

Lessons from South Africa

Weaknesses

According to the former Minister of the Environment & Tourism of South Africa one of the problems with the current set-up (i.e. regarding DEAT and SAT) is that there has been too much restructuring and too many reviews. This has destabilised staff out in the field that have little contact with management at HQ, with the latter being much more involved in political issues than in having a hands-on approach to marketing operations. A number of former high-level DEAT and SAT (formerly SATOUR) staff resigned from their positions as a result.

The good news for tourism is that significant funds have been invested in research over the last few years. But questions remain as to whether it was money well spent. Research into market segments carried out by The Monitor Group reportedly cost well in excess of £1 million, and a new £1 million-plus research project has just been commissioned to look at SAT's image in different markets.

Another concern, recently voiced by South Africa's then Minister of Tourism, is that there is not sufficient collaboration between SAT and the provincial tourist offices, with the result that there is no common brand and message being marketed. A new brand is due to be launched by SAT in May at the South African travel trade fair Indaba.

Key strengths include the following:

- Tourism has a high priority in South Africa. Within government, it has been identified as one of the five pillars of growth for the country. The industry is very supportive of SAT, providing funding for the NTO and for joint marketing/promotional campaigns. And considerable efforts have been/are being made to ensure buy-in by South Africans generally;
- SAT focuses heavily on scientific research to develop its marketing and market segmentation strategies — and it receives a large budget for this from DEAT. Both SAT and DEAT recognise the value of forecasting, not least for the development of a Tourism Satellite Account and to provide valuable ongoing trends data for their partners — all stakeholders in South Africa's tourism industry;
- Market segmentation — redefining the more traditional market segments to pinpoint target customers more clearly — makes sense given the NTO's limited funds;
- Innovative campaigns — e.g. the visibility campaign (trade and consumer) pulled in a number of non-tourism partners (e.g. London cabbies) and was promoted in some interesting venues (e.g. The Chelsea Flower Show);
- SAT has wisely decided to keep out of niche product development — this is being left to the industry — but it provides strong support in terms of market research and promotion;

- The country has a wide variety of attractive tourism products, and SAT is making efforts to ensure that there is improved awareness of the diversity of its offer in key target markets;
- SAT only has nine overseas offices, but its decision to close offices not showing a good return on investment seems to have been a wise one. As a result, each office has greater responsibilities — not just regarding different markets, but also specific sectors, such as MICE.

Chapter 12

Spain

Spain's Recent Tourism Performance

Spain is the world's second most popular destination behind France, in terms of international tourist arrivals, and second after the USA in international tourism receipts (Table 12.1). In 2002, tourist arrivals from abroad increased by 3.3% to 51.7 million, which followed a 1.6% rise the previous year. Receipts fell by a similar percentage to £22.4 billion, but were still comfortably above 2000's level.

Preliminary results for 2003 show a 1.4% increase in arrivals and, based on actual performance for the first 10 months of the year, a 4% growth in receipts (Table 12.2).

Table 12.1: Spain key facts — 2002.

Population	39.9 mn
GDP	£439 bn
International arrivals (TF)	51.7 mn
International overnights (total)	550.3 mn
International overnights (TCE)	221.6 mn
Average length of stay (TCE/TF)	10.6 nights
International arrivals per inhabitant	1.3
Domestic arrivals	124.3 mn
Domestic overnights (THS)	86.7 mn
Average length of trip (nights)	NA
Domestic receipts	NA
International receipts	£22.4 bn
• as a % of GDP	5.1
• per tourist arrival	£433
• per overnight	£41 (£101 TCE)
• per inhabitant	£561
Tourism's total contribution to GDP	11.8%
• WTTC estimate for T&T industry GDP	7.1%
NTO's total tourism budget (% annual change)	£55.5 mn (NA)
State contribution (% share)	£48.5 mn (87.5)
Marketing budget (% share of total budget)	£33.3 mn (60.0)
Rate of exchange	£1 = €1.58

Table 12.2: Spain's international tourist arrivals and tourism receipts, 2000–2003.

Year	Arrivals ('000)	% Annual change	Receipts (£ mn)[a]	% Annual change[b]
2000	47,898	NA	20,705	NA
2001	50,094	4.6	22,793	7.8
2002	51,748	3.3	22,463	−3.2
2003[c]	52,478	1.4	25,502	4.0

[a] Converted at EUR1 = £0.608 in 2000, £0.621 in 2001, £0.632 in 2002 and £0.690 in 2003.
[b] % change in EUR.
[c] Preliminary estimates — total for receipts based on actual data for Jan–Oct.
Source: Spain's secretary of State for Trade and Tourism.

Tourism's Economic Contribution

Spain developed its first Tourism Satellite Account (TSA) in 2002 (covering 2000–2001). Estimates from the latest TSA put the total contribution of tourism — inbound, domestic and spending in Spain by Spaniards travelling abroad for tourism — at 11.8% of GDP.

Transport

Tourist arrivals by air, which account for a 70% share of the total arrivals count, increased by close to 6% in 2002 — no doubt stimulated by the increased availability of flights from low-fare carriers. But road travel to Spain fell by 13% and arrivals by rail were down 11%.

Purpose of Trip

Business travel, including meetings, incentives, conferences and events (MICE), generated a modest 9% of all arrivals, with holidays and other leisure travel (excluding visiting friends and/or relations (VFR)) accounting for the bulk of demand, with an 82% share. VFR and health combined totalled 3.2 million trips, or 6%.

The MICE business has expanded considerably since 1995. According to the Spanish Convention Bureau, some 12,563 meetings were held in 2002 attracting 2.5 million delegates — increases of 23% and 27% respectively. The number of congresses rose by 27% to 1750, and these attracted 730,388 participants — the highest figure ever recorded and 53% higher than in 2001.

Accommodation

Hotels attracted 65% of all tourists and just under 20% stayed in non-paying accommodation — either their own holiday homes, or those of family and friends.Rented apartments and villas accounted for 9% of demand.

Key Markets

The UK is by far the most important source of tourism for Spain, generating a 28% share of arrivals in 2002. Preliminary estimates suggest that its share for 2003 was even greater thanks to a 10% increase — the third consecutive year of growth.

Apart from the UK, all key markets either declined or stagnated in 2003. Germany, in second position in the ranking, suffered its fourth consecutive year of decline, recording a drop of more than 3%.

The UK, Germany and France (in third position) account for nearly two-thirds of Spain's total international arrivals (Table 12.3). It is interesting to note that, since 1990, UK arrivals have increased by over 130% and Germany's by around 45%. Over the same period, arrivals from France have fallen by one-third.

Table 12.3: Spain's leading international markets, 2000–2002 ('000).

	2000	**2001**	**2002**	**% Share, 2002**
UK	13,239	14,012	14,564	28.1
Germany	11,171	10,783	10,111	19.5
France	5,681	6,712	8,030	15.5
Italy	2,098	2,412	2,503	4.8
Netherlands	1,968	2,148	2,390	4.6
Belgium	1,680	1,717	1,757	3.4
Portugal	1,490	1,632	1,710	3.3
Switzerland	1,198	1,233	1,209	2.3
Sweden	1,210	1,184	1,127	2.2
USA	1,146	1,136	931	1.8
Norway	636	747	764	1.5
Denmark	614	670	632	1.2
Austria	462	421	456	0.9
Finland	431	437	427	0.8
Russia	237	299	268	0.5
Japan	301	265	238	0.5
Mexico	228	173	211	0.4
Argentina	242	179	165	0.3
Canada	118	144	154	0.3
Brazil	203	165	144	0.3
Venezuela	92	137	132	0.3
Chile	92	66	61	0.1
Other Europe	2,384	2,419	2,807	5.4
Other Americas	397	174	261	0.5
Other/not specified	579	827	697	1.3
Total[a]	47,897	50,092	51,749	100.0

[a] International tourist arrivals at frontiers (TF).
Source: Secretary of State for Trade and Tourism.

Table 12.4: Inbound tourist arrivals in Spain by main destination region, 2003.

Autonomous Region	Arrivals ('000)	% Change on 2002
Catalonia	11,817	1.1
Canary Islands	10,669	−0.8
Balearic Islands	9,608	−0.5
Andalucia	7,579	1.1
Valenciana	4,963	−0.6
Madrid	3,093	1.5
Other	4,748	1.3
Total	52,477	1.4

Source: Secretary of State for Trade and Tourism.

Main Destination Regions

Catalonia (in which Barcelona is located) was the most popular region of Spain for foreign tourists in 2003, with the French generating the highest share — 3.4 million, or nearly 30% of total arrivals. However, the UK showed the best growth — largely as a result of low-fare flights — boosting demand for urban tourism.

Product and Market Diversification

Although city tourism *per se* (mainly short city breaks) attracts a modest 10% share of total arrivals in Spain from abroad, it is one of the fastest-growing sectors of demand. This is partly due to the rapid rise of low-fare/low-cost airlines operating to Spain in recent years, but it is also the result of aggressive marketing and promotion by Turespaña and regions such as Madrid and Barcelona to diversify the destination's tourism products and markets.

Nevertheless, sun & beach tourism continues to dominate, as reflected by the high demand for the Balearic and Canary Islands. But there are concerns that Spain is losing ground in this sector to cheaper destinations in the eastern Mediterranean, as well as former Central and Eastern European nations such as Bulgaria (Table 12.4).

Organisation of Tourism in Spain

Tourism in Spain appears to be highly structured, but most people working within the system say that, despite the perception, this is not the case. The national tourism administration has undergone little change since 1996 — a very unusual situation for European countries. And those changes that have been made have reportedly not been logical ones, which means that the system does not work well in practice. In particular, communication and co-operation between the different institutes and sub-directorates involved in tourism at national level are poor and, in some instances, non-existent — a weakness attributed to personalities as well as politics.

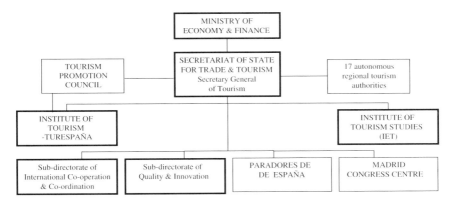

Figure 12.1: Structure of the Spanish tourism support system.
Source: The Travel Business Partnership.

Following the recent elections, a major restructuring of the whole tourism support system in Spain is likely (Figure 12.1).

Tourism in Spain currently comes under the aegis of the Secretariat of State for Trade & Tourism within the Ministry of Economy & Finance. The Secretary General of Tourism, who reports directly to the Secretary of State for Trade & Tourism, is the Director General, or President, of the Institute of Tourism — Turespaña, the national tourism organisation (NTO).

The post of Secretary General of Tourism in fact replaced that of Director General of Tourism in 1999 — a position abolished in an effort to streamline operations. Since then, the Director General of Turespaña has effectively only had the powers of a Deputy Director — at the same level as the head of the Institute of Tourism Studies and the Deputy Directors in charge of the sub-directorates responsible for International Co-operation & Co-ordination and Quality Control & Innovation.

The Secretary of State for Trade and Tourism (the post used to have small- & medium-sized enterprises within its portfolio until the beginning of the decade) is also ultimately responsible for the Spanish Paradors — managed as a separate organisation — and the Madrid Congress Centre.

The Paradores de España are the state-owned and managed hotels — mainly restored castles, palaces and convents — which are representative of Spain's historical and cultural heritage. There are currently 87 paradors, the first having opened in 1929. The government is in the process of upgrading the properties and improving facilities, infrastructure and the chain's distribution system. The total cost of this investment, which is due to be completed in 2004 is estimated at £120 million (Table 12.5).

Tourism Policy

The overall framework for tourism policy is provided by the Spanish Tourism Quality Plan (Plan Integral del Turismo Español — PICTE 2000–2006), launched in 2000, and which

Table 12.5: Budget of the Secretary General of Tourism, 2002–2003 (£ mn).

	2002	**2003**	**% Change (in EUR)**
Total budget	73.8	91.7	13.9
Budget allocated to Turespaña	48.5	60.9	15.0
Allocation for other institutes and sub-directorates	25.2	30.8	11.8

Note: The Paradors and Madrid Congress Centre have separate budgets and it seems likely — although we have not been able to conform this — that fixed costs are shared (see Turespaña's budget).
Source: Turespaña.

called for an investment of over £45.4 billion (€71.9 billion) in tourism-related infrastructure and promotion in the seven years from 2000 to 2006 (inclusive).

The objectives of the plan are the:

- medium- and long-term consolidation of the position of leadership held by Spain's tourism;
- increased profitability;
- socio-cultural and environmental sustainability of tourism activity;
- diversification of supply and demand;
- more equitable spread of tourism across the different regions of Spain;
- enhanced quality of employment in the tourism sector;
- increased international presence of Spanish tourism companies; and
- recognition of tourism as a key sector of the national economy.

The Secretary General for Tourism is responsible for drawing up the basic guidelines for, and general planning of, tourism policy in consultation with the autonomous regions, municipal tourism authorities and the tourism industry in general. Consultation is effected through a number of different institutionalised consultative bodies. These include the Inter-ministerial Tourism Committee (ITC), Tourism Sector Conference (TSC) and Consejo promotor del turismo (CPT)/Tourism promotion council.

Inter-ministerial Tourism Committee (ITC)

Set up in January 1994, the ITC was primarily conceived as a channel for co-ordinating the actions of the various organs of the national tourism administration (NTA). Chaired by the Minister of Economic Affairs, the ITC includes representatives of a variety of ministries (including Education, Employment, Foreign Affairs and the Environment) whose actions can either impact on, or be impacted by, tourism. Different Working Groups are set up by the ITC to address issues of concern.

Tourism Sector Conference (TSC)

The TSC acts as a discussion forum for all those involved in tourism, particularly addressing interests of common concern to the national and regional tourism authorities. Apart from sitting in plenary session, the TSC has a technical arm, the *Tourism Roundtable of the Directors General.* This body, chaired by the Secretary General for Tourism, and comprising the DGs of Tourism of the different autonomous regions and cities, is used as the basis for forming the different Working Groups.

Consejo Promotor del Turismo (CPT)/Tourism Promotion Council

Chaired by the Secretary of State for Trade & Tourism, the CPT is actually more closely linked to Turespaña than to the Secretariat of State. Turespaña's Director General acts as one of the two vice-presidents. The CPT comprises nine members representing the Spanish regions — four permanent members and five drawn from an annual rotation among the other regions.

The Council's prime role is to ensure that public and private-sector interests have a voice in decision-making regarding the shaping of Spanish tourism products and policies for marketing and promoting these abroad. The CPT operates largely through working groups. In July/August every year each member of the Council prepares a regional marketing plan, structured by generating market. After discussions and debate, the plans are incorporated into the annual Turespaña Marketing Plan (Plan Marketing del Turismo Español).

Relations with the Regions

Spain's 17 autonomous regions enjoy total autonomy/competence for the management and marketing/promotion of tourism within the confines of their respective territories. Many of Spain's regions, for example, receive substantial EU funding through the Structural Funds Programme, especially the one for Objective 1 regions (e.g. Extremadura, where tourism is being used as a means of economic diversification for a region formerly dependent on agriculture.)

In addition to the autonomous regions, the country has two city enclaves — Ceuta and Melilla on the coast of North Africa — and each of these is also governed by a statute of autonomy.

The regions and city enclaves are free to carry out their own marketing and promotion abroad — and frequently do, as can be seen by their independent stands at international fairs like WTM. But they also carry out joint campaigns with Turespaña and are increasingly using the same brand — e.g. as in the Spain Marks campaign.

Institutes/Sub-Directorates Reporting to the Secretary General of Tourism

Apart from the Paradors and the Madrid Congress Centre, the institutes/sub-directorates reporting directly to the Secretary General of Tourism and which are all — in theory, at least — units of support to Turespaña — include Institute of tourism studies (IET), Sub-directorate for tourism quality & innovation and Sub-directorate for tourism co-operation and co-ordination.

Institute of Tourism Studies (IET)

The IET, which is responsible for most of the key market research conducted in the field of tourism at national level. This includes the inbound tourism survey, *Frontur* (a frontier survey costing upwards of £1.1 million a year to conduct), and the national travel survey, *Familitur* (£0.9 million in 2002), which measures travel by residents of Spain — whether for Spanish destinations or abroad.

The IET has also been responsible for data collection and analysis, etc., for the country's TSA development since March 2002, as well as for the database of ongoing trends in Spanish tourism. It conducts other *ad hoc* surveys on tourist behaviour, accommodation usage and occupancy, travel organisation, etc. In 2002, its total budget for surveys was over £2.5 million.

According to Turespaña, there has historically been very poor co-operation between the NTO and the IET, largely attributed to a clash of personalities. However, the new DG of Turespaña is reportedly trying to improve relations so that Turespaña can benefit from the IET's work and can at the same time influence the ad hoc surveys it conducts.

Sub-directorate for Tourism Quality & Innovation

The department, which appears to work totally separately from Turespaña, is responsible for improving the quality of tourist products and enhancing technological innovation among Spanish firms. It has drawn up a number of different plans/programmes, including the Tourism Excellence Plan — aimed at helping mature sun & beach resorts in Spain to regain their competitiveness — and the Tourism Dynamic Development Plan, which is geared to ensure the coherent development of emerging destinations, notably in Spain's hinterland/interior.

The sub-directorate has also been the driving force behind what has become known as the 'Q' seal of quality through the Spanish Tourist Quality Institute (ICTE by its Spanish initials), affiliated to the Spanish Standards Association (AENOR) as a corporate member since March 2002.

Sub-directorate for Tourism Co-operation and Co-ordination

This sub-directorate handles all liaisons with the autonomous regions, local authorities, the ministry and the tourism industry in general, to define tourism policy on behalf of the Secretary General for Tourism. It serves as the secretariat for the Tourism Roundtable of the Directors General. Its responsibilities also extend to dealing with information opportunity analysis and support for the expansion outside Spain of Spanish companies. As an example, some 32% of all Spanish-owned hotel chain bed capacity is located in countries outside Spain.

Turespaña

Role and Activities

Turespaña is an autonomous body within the State Secretariat for Trade and Tourism, reporting to the Secretary General for Tourism. Its remit is to promote Spain as a tourism destination abroad and to co-ordinate all international promotional activities initiated/sponsored by the national tourism administration, the autonomous regions and the local/municipal authorities.

The post of Chairman of Turespaña is held ex-officio by the head of the State Secretariat, with the Secretary General for Tourism and the Director General of Turespaña acting as first and second deputy chairmen respectively.

Turespaña's activities include:

* Planning, developing and implementing actions for the promotion of Spanish tourism in international markets (Marketing Plan, Media Plan, advertising campaigns, etc.);
* Providing marketing support for Spanish tourist products abroad;
* Liaising with the autonomous regions, local authorities and the private sector in respect of programmes designed to promote and market their products abroad;
* Managing and promoting the potential of individual tourist venues, in particular the Madrid Convention Centre; and
* Drawing up the action strategy and marketing plan for Spain's Paradors.

It should be noted that hotel classification is the responsibility of the autonomous regions and education and training — in which Turespaña used to be involved — is now looked after by the universities and educational institutes, with input from the relevant ministries.

Staff and Offices

Headquarters   Turespaña comprises three units/sub-directorates at its HQ in Madrid, with a total of some 400 staff, handling respectively:

* International marketing and Spanish tourist offices abroad (approx 25% of staff);
* Public relations and media, including all brochure production — even brochures for the offices abroad (30%); and
* finance and administration (45%).

A diagram of the organisational structure (Figure 12.2) of the NTO follows:

The 31 offices abroad, all of which are fully fledged Turespaña offices (whose directors have diplomatic status) and are open to the public, are located in:

* *Europe* — 20 offices (65%) — Austria (Vienna), Belgium (Brussels), Denmark (Copenhagen), Finland (Helsinki), France (Paris), Germany (Berlin, Düsseldorf, Frankfurt and Munich), Italy (Milan and Rome), Netherlands (The Hague), Norway (Oslo), Poland (Warsaw), Portugal (Lisbon), Russia (Moscow), Sweden (Stockholm), Switzerland (Geneva and Zurich) and UK (London);
* *Americas* — 8 offices (26%) — Argentina (Buenos Aires); Brazil (São Paulo), Canada (Toronto), Mexico (Mexico City), USA (Chicago, Los Angeles, Miami and New York); and
* *Asia Pacific* — 3 offices (10%) — China (Beijing), Japan (Tokyo), Singapore.

Only two new offices have been opened since 2000 — in Warsaw and Beijing. However, Spain is one of the few countries that has not closed any offices, and there does not appear to be any thought of reducing staff and office numbers to cut costs. In fact, there are plans to open two new offices in 2004 — in Dublin and another east European city. Ireland, until now has been covered by the London office.

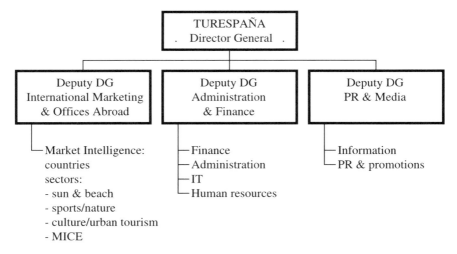

Figure 12.2: Organisational structure of Turespaña's HQ.
Source: The Travel Business Partnership.

Of the 250 staff employed abroad, 210 are local (largely support) staff, with most of the 40 directors/deputy directors enjoying diplomatic status (and referred to as 'Their Excellencies').

As is indicated in the case study of the UK office later in this chapter, the whole marketing operation is very centralised. HQ decides on strategies — although the offices abroad can adapt these to their particular markets — and even prints market-specific brochures for all the different offices.

Resources and Funding

Turespaña's funding comes 100% from the public sector — 87–88% from the state/central government through the Secretary of State for Trade & Tourism and the balance from EU Structural Funds through the EU's Regional Development Programmes (Table 12.6).

Around 40% of the total budget is spent on fixed costs (salaries, administration, etc. — it is not clear whether the admin staff are shared with the IET and two sub-directorates, or not) and 60% goes directly to marketing and promotion. Note that the development of the Spanish web portal (see below) has a separate budget — i.e. it does not come under Turespaña.

Allocation of Total Budget to Marketing

Although Turespaña says that 60% of its total budget is allocated to marketing every year, this information should be interpreted with caution. An earlier study on European NTO budgets conducted by the Netherlands Board of Tourism & Conventions in its last incarnation (i.e. as Toerisme Recreatie Nederland) from July to October 2003 suggests that, in 2003, only 49% of Turespaña's total budget went towards marketing and promotion — down from some 53% in 2002.

Table 12.6: Turespaña's budget, 2002–2004.

Year	Total Budget (£ mn)[a]	% Annual change (in Euro)[a]	State's Contribution (%)[b]	% Share to Marketing & Promotion[c]	Actual M&P (£ mn)[c]
2002	55.5	NA	87	60	33.3
2003	72.8	20.2	88	60	43.7
2004[d]	78.4	7.7	88	60	47.0

[a] EUR1 = £0.632 in 2002, £0.690 in 2003 and 2004 (estimated).
[b] The state is the central government — the balance of funding comes from the EU Structural Funds — the EU Fund for Regional Development.
[c] Estimated share.
[d] Provisional.
Source: Turespaña.

Domestic Tourism Promotion

Domestic tourism promotion is not the responsibility of Turespaña. It is handled by the tourism authorities of the autonomous regions and the local/municipal authorities.

Marketing Strategy

Although it is drawn up through a consultative process — with input from its own offices abroad, the autonomous regions, local tourism authorities and the private sector of the industry — Turespaña's annual Marketing Plan is the responsibility of its HQ. And everything carried out by the offices abroad has to be approved by HQ.

Turespaña's Deputy Director of International Marketing and Offices Abroad and the former Director General of Tourism both say that the major weakness of the Marketing Plan is the centralisation of key decisions and the lack of concrete actions contained within the plan. In addition, although lip service is paid to the opinions of the private sector, there is no real industry involvement in marketing strategy. And, until such time as a decision is taken to generate private sector funding for tourism marketing and promotion at national level, the industry is not likely to be given a real voice by Turespaña and the other public sector bodies.

2004 Marketing Plan

The 2004 Marketing Plan will be allocated a budget of £36.6 million, up 20% on 2003's level (in euro). Spending on advertising campaigns — the basis of which is again the Spain Marks campaign — will receive an additional 12%.

The main objectives of this year's Plan are to:

- stimulate the recovery of European markets that have performed badly in the last year or two, notably Germany;
- consolidate the position of strong markets such as the UK and France; and
- woo back the USA.

Online marketing and promotion through www.Spain.info will receive about the same budget as in 2003 — i.e. £2.8 million.

Of the total advertising planned for 2004 — some £18.6 million for online and offline — online advertising will get 15% and the following countries will benefit from the biggest shares of the budget (in percentage terms): UK and Ireland (18.1%), Germany (16.8%), France (11.8%), USA (5.9%), Italy (4.9%) and Portugal (4.7%).

Turespaña will ensure a Spanish presence at some 160 international trade and consumer fairs — not just fairs specifically for tourism, but also specialist events for golfers, retail business, etc.

Travel agent training will be undertaken in the USA, UK, Canada and Germany, and this will be supplemented by 250 agency familiarisation trips from all over the world.

Identifying Priority Markets

Decisions regarding the definition of priority markets are not really based on scientific research, according to Turespaña. And there are currently no formal mechanisms for determining potential or actual return on investment. Countries with the largest number of offices (Germany and the USA) cost the most to run. But there is some consideration of returns (arrivals, overnights, spending, etc.) over previous years, current market trends and expressions of interest in specific markets by the travel trade.

Market Segmentation

The UK, Germany, France and the USA are currently seen as the top priorities in terms of marketing efforts. Key emerging markets are China, Singapore and East Asia in general, Poland, Russia and South Africa.

Segmentation is both by country of residence and purpose of visit — i.e. leisure or business. VFR is not treated as a marketable segment. Leisure is further segmented by activity/interest, e.g., city tourism, sun & beach and rural tourism. Turespaña is trying to focus on higher-yield social groups — in the UK, for example, most marketing and promotion is geared towards AB socio-economic groups.

Sun & beach is not being ignored in its attempt to diversify, but it is trying to attract higher spenders to sun & beach holidays in Spain.

MICE is increasingly seen as a segment to market, but its importance was only formally recognised a couple of years ago. Before that, all marketing and promotion abroad of MICE business was left to the Association of Convention Centres and individual venues and cities.

Assessing Performance

The main method used to assess the impact of advertising campaigns is to pre-test them in key markets. But the situation varies from one market to another, e.g., some markets do not buy ad space in media. As far as promotional campaigns are concerned, Turespaña evaluates their success by asking the opinion of people taking part in the campaigns.

Competitor Analysis

Competitor analysis has been facilitated by the development of Spain's Tourism Satellite Account. It is likely to become more important in the future.

Brand Development

In November 2002, Turespaña launched a huge global campaign — which is still ongoing — to change/extend the brand image of Spain from a mass-market sun & beach destination to a destination offering a diversified range of products/regions to appeal to a much wider group of visitors. These include inland urban and rural destinations, as well as different niches such as culture, sports (golf and sailing particularly), learning Spanish, wellness, etc.

Central to this branding is the high-profile 'Spain Marks' campaign, which is characterised by 12 core images that are being used globally, and can be adapted to suit various markets/products, in print material, on billboards and online — either via the website/portal (they can be sent as postcards from the website), or as online advertisements.

The Spain Marks campaign, which has costed to date some £25.3 million — 50% of which has been funded by the autonomous provinces and local authorities such as the city of Madrid — follows a number of other successful branding campaigns. From 1998 to 2002 there was Bravo España and, before that, Passion for Life. Perhaps the most famous of all was the first real branding campaign, Everything under the Sun, which ran for nine years in the 1980s, turning Spain into the world's favourite sun & beach destination.

In fact, Everything under the Sun was intended to show the world that Spain had a variety of attractions on offer, including culture, sporting possibilities, etc. But the perception was very different — it came over as a campaign promoting Spain's sun and beaches.

Bravo Spain was the first attempt at moving away from Spain's dependence on sun and beach and developing new brand images for the country — e.g. as a cultural and gastronomic paradise.

Spain Marks — which highlights the different attractions and activities available to tourists in different parts of Spain — goes a few steps further, positioning the destination in terms of lifestyle as well as attractions. Turespaña says that there is plenty of statistical evidence that buying patterns in major markets are changing, and that leisure visitors are becoming more independent, preferring self-tailored holidays to package tours. The changes are fuelled by low-fare/low-cost airlines and changing preferences of activity. Even the seven major Spanish islands now have low-fare services and independent beach/island breaks are growing. Spain Marks is intended to show the country's flexibility/ability to adapt to this changing market.

Both its branding and marketing strategy are intended to respond to these trends. The change in image is justified to some extent by statistics, but it is also driven by the NTO's strategy of changing Spain's visitor profile to the higher spender, who is interested in a much wider range of travel products/Spanish destinations.

Interestingly, the Spain Marks campaign — and specifically the new focus on the higher-yield, independent tourist — has caused, and is continuing to cause, some problems with the volume operators (e.g. TUI), who say that the Spanish government needs to invest where the bulk of the benefit is going to accrue — i.e. in beach products. But the London office, for example, is adamant that trends in arrivals in Spain from the UK, as well as buying patterns, etc., confirm that the approach is right.

Use of the Spain Marks brand in advertising is increasingly being adopted by the autonomous provinces (e.g. Andalucia) and local authorities (e.g. Comunidad de Madrid). But there has always been lots of competition between the NTO and the regions, resulting in overlapping and duplication of efforts — particularly in terms of exhibiting at trade and consumer fairs. A number of the regions/cities have substantial marketing funds of their own and continue to see no reason for buying into the national brand.

Partnership Marketing

There is no private sector involvement in marketing activities, but the autonomous regions sometimes join in specific campaigns. As an example, the Tourism and Sports Council of Andalucia, through its promotional arm Turismo Andaluz, conducted a 50:50 joint marketing campaign with Turespaña from September through December 2003. The campaign was intended to help Andalucia recoup visitor losses in its three main segments — sun & beach, golf and gastronomy — especially from North America and Scandinavia.

The total budget for this is was £1.3 million. Some £0.6 million was put into ads, using Andalucia Marks, in prestigious publications in the USA, Canada, Denmark, Finland, Norway and Sweden — general upmarket news press and consumer travel magazines and some trade publications, and around £380,000 was allocated to the USA. This covered ads in publications such as *Conde Nast Traveller*, *Food&Wine*, *Saveur*, *Art News*, *Gourmet and Elite*).

Research

As already indicated, the relationship between Turespaña and the Institute of Tourism Studies (IET) is not as good as one might expect — especially given that they are located in the same building in Madrid. Turespaña's involvement in research is primarily to develop market intelligence about demand trends in foreign markets. It does have a huge budget, however, for the purchase of surveys from third parties.

As an example, Turespaña is one of the few NTOs in Europe that still spends up to £320,000 a year buying European Travel Monitor data (the German National Tourist Office (DZT) is the other one), although there are signs that there may be a change of strategy with the new Director General, Piñanes.

New Media and e-Marketing

New Portal being Launched   A new Spain portal www.spain.info had a soft launch in 2002 and was due to be fully functional, after a total investment of more than £5.7 million, by the end of 2003. The full launch has been slightly delayed but, once up and running in its final version, the site is expected to handle over 20,000 users a day — it has already attracted over 90 million site visitors.

The Spanish view the portal as a crucial part of their marketing and promotion of Spain, and have set out to establish 'the most complete and advanced guide in existence on the web'.

Its database of information contains 56,000 photos, 230 video clips, 754 maps and 21 virtual tours. It is available in four languages — Spanish, English, French and German — but a certain amount of information will also be available in Japanese, Russian, Portuguese and Chinese.

For the consumer, the portal aims to provide information on a complete trip to Spain — car hire, excursions, hotels, routes, maps, etc. — and allows the user to establish a personalised guide. Tourists can send photos and comments to friends and family, and contact other travellers with similar preferences. The website/portal is becoming increasingly interactive.

Extranet Development   Although it will remain predominantly consumer-oriented, the site will also have an extranet, which will be used by the trade as a kind of meeting point, 'to obtain and exchange information'. Lisbon has already come online and Milan is scheduled to be next.

Country-Specific Sites   Spain/Turespaña also has websites operated for specific large markets by the respective overseas offices — e.g. www.tourspain.co.uk for the UK market. This doubles up on some material available through the new portal.

The website, www.tourspain.co.uk, which has been running much longer than the portal, offers online brochure orders for UK addresses only, and has some agent/operator information as well. A monthly (usually) newsletter, different from that available from www.spain.info, is compiled by staff at the London office. It covers basic tourist information, useful practical info, events, places to visit, UK tour operators and agents, sports, advice on getting around, info on 'green' Spain, learning Spanish, accommodation, disabled access, a bibliography and weather. None of the pages carry advertising and the site does not allow transactions — this is being left to the private sector.

Website Reflects NTO's Strategy of Diversification

The Spain website attempts to be comprehensive and objective in terms of destinations/products. As an example, the beaches in all regions are given equal weight. The website does not give particular prominence to the destinations or products which attract most visitors — i.e. sun and beach, and city breaks in Madrid and Barcelona.

The site reflects the key NTA-led strategy of encouraging tourists inland, away from straightforward sun & beach holidays, and it attempts to present the whole variety of niche markets. Links to the autonomous regions, etc., are comprehensive and easy to use.

WAP-enabled technology is currently a priority area for development, as is customer relationship management (CRM). However, there is little evidence that CRM is already used as a tool for e-marketing by the NTO.

Case study — the UK office of Turespaña

Structure and Activities

The London office is one of Turespaña's largest offices abroad, with 30 staff, three of whom deal exclusively with the media. It is housed in the Spanish Embassy building (offered to tourist office when the Embassy's commercial section moved out) but the lease is now running out, and the tourist office is thinking about new premises. The decision has not yet been made.

The London office follows the strategy drawn up at HQ. However, offices abroad are free to select the most appropriate elements of the marketing strategy for their own particular national market — for the London office, as already indicated, this means both the UK and Ireland. HQ is involved in many aspects of the foreign offices' activities — e.g. all brochures are produced at HQ, even those specifically for the UK market — and all additional activities and related funding, etc., have to be approved on a case-by-case basis by HQ.

The London office stressed nonetheless that HQ relies on individual staff creativity and energy in its offices abroad, and does not want to cramp their style too much. One example is STEPS, the two-day trade show held in London, which is a unique event among the different activities of Spanish offices abroad. It only came about because of the initiative of UK director Manuel Butler. Depth of experience of staff is also viewed as crucial — the man handling MICE marketing in the UK has been promoting Spain in London for 20 years.

Marketing Activity

Marketing activities comprise:

- advertising campaigns — mainly in the printed media;
- press trips and agency fam trips (20 fam trips alone in 2003);
- the production of trade and consumer brochures and newsletters — printed and online;
- organising Spain's participation in regular fairs for the trade and consumers;
- organising and participating in other promotional events; and
- agent training programmes.

As far as agency training programmes are concerned, a Spain Specialist Programme online training scheme is organised annually in the UK (as well as in the USA, where the programme originated) — it is administered by TTC Training in London. In 2003, some 345 agents bought the programme — although only 28 graduated! The explanation for this is that travel agents tend to be busy, move on, or lose interest. Nonetheless, London still feels it is worthwhile as part of its trade relations, destination familiarisation, etc. Some £100,000 has been invested in the scheme.

STEPS is the Spanish Tourist Office's own two-day trade fair in the UK and is totally organised by the London office. The cost is reportedly very high, and the event time-consuming, but it is nonetheless thought to be really worthwhile by the UK trade. Spanish sellers pay HQ a fee to participate but the 300 or so UK agents who participate (2003 figure) do so at no cost to themselves. For the first time this year, the public is being invited to attend STEPS — from late afternoon through the evening on the second day — at what is being touted as a special Spain Marks evening.

STEPS and the Spain Specialist Programme are two of the main reasons why the Spanish Tourist Office in the UK is regularly nominated for — and often wins — the *Travel Weekly* Globe Award for the best tourist office in the UK. The office is considered to have one of the highest profiles of any foreign tourist office in the UK — not surprisingly, perhaps, given the importance of the UK market for the destination.

Market Segmentation

Sun & beach holidays clearly dominate in terms of purpose of trip, although the UK — unlike many of Spain's other key sources — has been diversifying. The fastest-growing segment is city breaks — stimulated by the wide availability of low-fare airline seats. And the independent share of UK travel — i.e. those organising their trips without using the travel trade at all — is also growing strongly.

The key segments being promoted by the tourist office in the UK market are:

- city breaks — especially to Madrid, Barcelona, Valencia, Seville, Bilbao, Cordoba and Granada;
- learning Spanish;
- art/culture — museums, monuments, sights and world heritage;
- sport — mainly golf, sailing, (but also skiing, horse-riding);
- fiestas;
- nature — open spaces, national parks and active tourism;
- wellness/spas;
- rural tourism — staying on farms, B&B, etc.; and
- pilgrimages — travelling along historic routes.

Enquiries

Data for 2002 (rounded) shows that the Spanish Tourist Office in London received a total of more than 2.2 million consumer enquiries during the year — through different channels:

Phone calls (2 lines)	51,000
Visits to the office	9,000
Fax/letter	26,400
Emails	25,300
Internet hits at www.tourspain.co.uk	2,100,400

Since the office has to move anyway, management is considering abandoning the 'walk-in' enquiry desk. But such matters reportedly take a long time to decide on.

Partnership Marketing

Although there is no consistent partnership marketing, the private sector does buy exhibition space for trade shows such as World Travel Market under the Turespaña umbrella, and it provides support for other promotional events. As an example, there is an agreement with Iberia and some Spanish hotel groups to host family/press etc.

Image/Brand Development

In the UK alone, over £2 million was spent in 2003 on image/brand development — mostly on printed media advertising, using the Spain Marks campaign. This is the largest expenditure item in the UK office's budget.

Managing Positive Publicity/PR

London has noted a growing interest in Spain's golf courses by British golfers, so it took a stand at the British Open and at the Irish Open. This was considered better use of funds than attending many trade shows — the Spanish Tourist Office in London thinks there are too many in the UK and it is better just to focus on the major ones — e.g. WTM, Convex.

Handling Negative Perceptions of the Country/Product

Nothing is done without the approval of HQ. The advantage is that HQ can decide to put more funding into correcting a poor image following a negative event/negative publicity. It tried to help Galicia, for example — the area worst hit by the oil slick — by facilitating platforms for the region to meet with the press and trade, and to explain what actions had been taken. It also used its overseas offices to set up press interviews, etc.

In the case of the unpopular Balearics eco-tax introduced in May 2002 and abolished in October 2003, HQ did nothing public, even though Turespaña disapproved of the tax. This was partly because the tax was only paid by those staying in licensed hotels — tourists in villas, yachts, unlicensed apartments, etc., did not pay. When the tax was lifted, however, the London office held a press lunch to let the media know, and other relevant offices did similar things.

Lessons from Spain

An 'old-school' NTO ...

Although there is talk about big changes pending re the structure and role of Turespaña and the organisation of tourism generally in Spain, nothing is expected to happen until after the May 2004 elections, when a new Secretary General of Tourism, and possibly even a new Secretary of State for Trade & Tourism, will be appointed. (As already indicated, following the defeat of former Prime Minister Aznar's party by the Socialists, the nature of these changes is now very uncertain. But few expect a quick reduction in bureaucracy.) Meanwhile, Turespaña represents one of the 'old school' national tourism organisations and fully funded by government.

... and other Weaknesses Inherent in such Bureaucracies

Interviews carried out with Turespaña management, as well as with senior level representatives from the autonomous regions, municipal tourist offices and the private sector, all suggest that the tourism support system is overly bureaucratic and very costly to run. Few other NTOs can afford to operate so many offices abroad — all of which are full-service offices with no shared costs — and think of opening new offices without looking for ways to cut costs.

Until now, there has been no serious effort to reduce costs, or to find ways of becoming more efficient or cost-effective.

While, for the NTO itself, the size of the budget and other resources available (e.g. manpower) are very welcome, it recognises that Spain will one day likely suffer the trend occurring all over the developed world — i.e. the disengagement of government from tourism promotion and the need to find private sector partners to share costs.

Turespaña management itself says that it needs to be much more involved with the industry and that this would improve its level of market intelligence. In addition, it recognises that the operation is overly centralised. This presumably makes the whole operation rather cumbersome and slower to respond to market opportunities.

But Turespaña Has some Key Strengths, Notably Its Brand Image ...

Nevertheless, Turespaña is rated highly in terms of its advertising effectiveness. Its different — all very highly successful — campaigns over the years have enhanced the country's tourism image, even if its Everything under the Sun campaign of the early-1990s strengthened its image as a sun & beach destination at the expense of its other attractions.

... and Experienced Expatriate Staff

On the positive side, the highly experienced team running the offices abroad is also seen as a major strength of Turespaña's operation. The majority of foreign office directors have more than 20 years of experience in the business, and are extremely familiar with their markets. This gives them a lot of credibility with the local travel trade and goes a long way to explaining why its offices abroad win awards for 'best foreign tourist office' and such like.

Strong Regional Focus on Tourism

Although duplication of efforts on the part of Turespaña and the autonomous regions has been a problem over the years, the fact that the regions local/municipal tourism authorities are strong and highly focused on tourism is a major strength. Most importantly, it helps to ensure buy-in by all stakeholders — consumers and local communities, as well as the public sector and industry — which, in turn, helps to stimulate tourism development.

Consejo Promotor del Turismo/Tourism Promotion Council

This kind of council would be a good example for other NTOs to consider — as long as it is taken seriously by all participants, meets on a regular basis and develops concrete action plans rather than just strategies.

Product Clubs

Turespaña tried to introduce these in the mid-1990s, following the success of the French version. But the local travel trade rejected the concept. There is now reportedly talk of trying to revive the concept and, this time, the trade and other sectors of the industry are all positive about the idea.

Chapter 13

Benchmark Lessons

Following the analysis of the eight countries and their NTAs/NTOs, several key areas emerge as important when benchmarking their performance. A summary of the techniques and approaches adopted and key lessons learned is provided in this chapter.

Structure

It has been apparent throughout this research that, in order to continue to compete in the international marketplace, the NTOs need to continually evolve. Structural and procedural changes are evident in most of the case studies and at times make comparisons difficult. In the case of Ireland, for example, the structure of the NTO is recent and perhaps too early to identify as a best practice exemplar. In addition, the Netherlands' NTO structure at HQ level at least will change dramatically over the next few months, and South Africa is potentially suffering from too much restructuring and too many reviews. Nonetheless, some valuable lessons can still be drawn from the information obtained.

Of the NTO structures considered, Australia perhaps provides the best overall model by virtue of its total tourism support system and NTO effectiveness. For example, the NTO's interaction with the State and Territory Tourism Organisations (STOs) is worthy of detailed consideration. In addition, the minister responsible for tourism is a cabinet level post. A consultative relationship with the private sector is key to success, together with effective inter-ministerial committees and a strong private sector lobbying group. The Australian NTO is also undergoing significant change, in part to try to address the country's disappointing tourism performance since the summer Olympics in 2000, but also as a result of a change in CEO and industry questions regarding the role of the NTO. The changes that are underway in Australia are positive and, among other, aims seek to reduce overlap between the various functions including research. In addition, the decision to differentiate the roles of the NTO (to focus on country brand) and the STOs (to focus on marketing destination and products) is considered likely to enhance the already good partnership between the NTO and the states and territories. They are likely to confirm the NTO as one of the most successful.

The Canadian NTO structure, although now regarded as successful, has evolved through a series of mistakes since its creation, and was criticised for being too reactive. The structure of the Irish NTO has, as noted above, changed fairly recently. The earlier, relatively simple, structure — generally regarded as successful — has now been complicated by the desire to achieve pan-Ireland tourism marketing. Separate agencies for the Republic and for Northern Ireland continue to operate and undertake domestic tourism marketing, although the island of Ireland's NTO, Tourism Ireland Limited, acts as their agent abroad.

Although the structure for the support of tourism in France can be considered overly bureaucratic, the NTO is one of the most successful, particularly given that its role is to deal only with marketing and promotions. Despite the many layered tourism support system, there is excellent buy-in from the provincial tourism authorities to NTO campaigns. This is also the case in Spain, where the various local/municipal authorities of the autonomous regions demonstrate an equally strong focus on tourism. But the NTO structure in Spain is also bureaucratic and over-centralised, with a high number of staff and overseas offices together with strong financial support from central government. To date, little effort appears to have been made to reduce operational costs, although this has now been recognised and changes are being considered. The NTO recognises that it needs to become more involved with industry and the potential benefits of this are considered in the next section.

Key Lessons on Structure

- Simplicity of structure is desirable;
- A clear distinction should be made between the roles of the NTO and the others involved in the tourism support structure;
- There should be clear links between the NTO and any regional or local tourist boards but the NTO has to be the lead marketing agency;
- Consultation is vital to minimise overlap of roles;
- Consultation with industry is key to success and should be undertaken wherever possible particularly when new strategies, brand development and marketing campaigns are being considered;
- Following consultations, the strategy should then be communicated by the NTO at national level to the regions to ensure buy-in to a national brand and destination building campaign;
- Communication of research findings and consumer analysis free of charge helps build industry buy-in and creates a more informed and pro-active industry.

E-media/Customer Relationship Management (CRM)

The development of a central portal/national website for the tourism sector is ubiquitous in most NTOs. In the majority of cases, the burden of the significant development costs falls on the NTO/government and involvement of private sector partners in sharing the cost and return is unusual. It is worth noting that it is anticipated that the Canadian NTO will outsource its website in the future with a potential cost saving of some £85,000 per annum.

Australia, Canada, France and Spain, at least, have all stressed that e-media and customer relationship management (CRM) are key areas for development. The importance of managing the customer base has been recognised not only for the opportunity to achieve new sales and repeat visits, but also to increase buy-in from the private sector. By providing relevant information on visitor source markets from research conducted by the NTO, the private sector will more readily recognise the connection between the efforts of the NTO and the potential to increase visitor arrivals. Communicating research findings together with additional information that is useful to tourism SMEs through the NTO website can assist the private sector to develop. In the Netherlands, the strong brand directs customers to its highly acclaimed website, the Holland Platform, where they can also book online. The site is supported by tourism as well as non-tourism businesses, all looking to increase exposure and business.

For some NTOs, the website and CRM underpin strategy. Australia's NTO website, www.australia.com, for example, is at the heart of its marketing activities and drives the whole marketing programme, reducing costs and increasing effectiveness. The site had 10,000 pages in 2003 and 60 language/country combinations. A particular success is the Ozplanner tool — an interactive trip planning facility for prospective visitors. The website is also used to communicate NTO activities and partnership opportunities to industry. As mentioned earlier, the industry also has access to extensive research through the website.

Effective management of the NTOs' existing and potential customers is seen as essential by many NTOs, and the website can be a key tool to enhance effectiveness in this area. Canada has specifically recognised this area as one for key investment for the foreseeable future and is set to re-launch its already comprehensive website in 2004 using enhanced technology and with improved content.

Key Lessons on E-media/CRM

- E-media has been a major development cost for NTOs worldwide.
- Real innovation and best practice emerge from the private sector (and notably the travel industry) rather than from competitor NTOs.
- CRM is now a central element of many NTO sites and Australia's approach merits greater attention.

Partnerships

Here lies, perhaps, one of the major challenges facing any NTO to attract industry buy-in and investment in terms of time, resources and finance. It is clear that in most of the NTOs examined, there is a large expectation that the state will take the lead in a range of areas, notably in terms of international, and to some extent domestic, marketing of countries and destinations. The solution to building private sector buy-in is demonstrated in only a minority of countries — although the share is growing fast. Involvement and commitment of industry in terms of funding and financial leverage is more apparent than real at many competitor NTOs. One of the most effective approaches to increasing buy-in is through marketing committees, which canvas industry to participate in marketing/advertising/promotional campaigns that correspond to the real needs of the industry.

It is notable that in the so-called tourism success stories of countries such as the Republic of Ireland, state expenditure, staffing costs, staff numbers and general operating costs are among the highest examined, with very low levels (4%) of industrial leverage identified. Canada represents a model for consideration but involvement with industry in this country has matured over a number of years and has been built around a number of milestones which help set the context for maturation of a relationship where the private sector can be seen as a real and active partner. Nonetheless, despite CTC's success in attracting private sector funding for many campaigns in Canada, the marketing budget is still considered inadequate to ensure that competitiveness is not reduced.

In Spain, the strong focus on tourism by the autonomous regions helps encourage buy-in by all stakeholders including consumers, local communities, industry and the public sector. In addition, the role of the Tourism Promotion Council ensures that the public and private sector have a say in decisions involving the Spanish tourism product.

The NBTC's staff who are based in offices abroad play an important role in securing contributions to marketing and promotional campaigns from a wide range of industry and non-industry partners. These marketing campaigns simply would not be possible without contributions from industry. In New Zealand, government funding is 100% although the government's goal is to obtain private sector support in the medium to longer term as public sector funding at the current level cannot be sustained.

The development of product clubs in both France and Canada was designed to unite and drive forward clusters of like-minded individuals and related businesses in a co-operative venture in terms of product and service quality improvement, cluster marketing and development and upgrade. The concept assists the industry in responding to the needs of the ever-changing international tourism market and tourists' desire for new experiences. It provides an area context that goes beyond regional or administrative boundaries and focuses on saleable developments. Some public sector leverage is appropriate in order to catalyse developments.

Having conceived the concept in 1987, the product clubs' approach of the French NTO is well respected and considered fair despite some minor concerns that small businesses may not be able to participate due to club entry costs. However, in Canada the concept became a victim of its own success — there were as many as 44 product clubs in February 2004. Nevertheless, the CTC says it is committed to the product club programme, launched in 1996. Encouraging small businesses to develop new products by building partnerships not only helps improve Canada's competitiveness but also provides the means for these businesses to participate in CTC programmes, the CTC maintains.

The Canadian product club is a product development partnership, established and led by tourism industry stakeholders including SMEs. The group pools its resources to develop new market-ready products. Successful candidates enter into a contractual rangement whereby the CTC agrees to match the partnership's funds for a period up to three years, after which time the club is expected to 'graduate' as a sustainable partnership.

By 2004, several changes had been introduced to streamline the process and to encourage the development of products that better meet current market demand and trends. For example, as a first step in the evaluation process, partnerships must submit an executive summary. If accepted at this stage, proponents will then be asked to submit five-year business plans. In this way, the process can quickly identify those proposals that do not qualify, thereby minimising the time, effort and cost to interested groups.

Enhancing the Level of Buy-in from the Travel Trade

Improving the level of buy-in by tour operators and travel agents — and indeed by non-tourism businesses — generally receives limited attention in benchmark comparators. The travel trade can however be a highly valuable consultative ally if it has been courted and a relationship has developed. It receives very early indicators of market movement and advance bookings and provides a strong data source for domestic marketing. In Canada, the NTO assembles a wide range of specialist tour operators from internet-based companies to traditional volume tour operators in order to glean key trends data in major generating markets. Feedback is through committees, which are formally set up with an industry chair and documented minutes, and which provide tangible guidance to relevant marketing committees.

In addition, Canada through its 'Canada Counsellors' training programme and Australia via the 'Aussie Specialist Programme' aim to improve travel agents' knowledge of their countries and products to achieve greater sales. Similar programmes are operated by South Africa and Spain. Clearly, this tactic to increase travel trade buy-in only works if the programme is appropriately designed. If there is a high dropout rate – as in the case of Spain's training programme for the UK – the overall impact could be negative.

Several of the NTOs demonstrate how innovative schemes can draw in non-tourism businesses to mutual benefit. Maison de la France has made creative use of non-tourism businesses — high fashion goods and perfumes, in particular — to promote the brand France, while SAT encouraged London cabbies to promote South Africa and used the Chelsea Flower Show, rather than a travel exhibition, for a visibility campaign. Other creative partnerships include the NBTC's relationship with Caffé Nero and promoters of the film *Girl with a Pearl Earring*, and Canada's marketing campaign with FNAC Photo (France) and Caldo-Caldo (Italy).

In a number of destinations, profile and motivation have been successfully catalysed through imaginative partnerships between the travel trade and NTOs. The airport stopover free city tour has been successfully used by a range of Southeast Asian NTOs in the past (e.g. in Singapore and Hong Kong) and more recently by Iceland. The aim here is to build knowledge, interest and desire about a destination through delivery of a free-taster or aperitif. There are other ways to build destination awareness at the point of entry, especially near queuing areas in airport terminal buildings, which offer the opportunity to provide destination data, images and visual information (both Singapore and Dublin have successfully adopted this technique).

Using Canada again as an example, three types of partnership marketing have been used: the NTO takes the lead in marketing with the partner contributing funds; the partner manages the campaign and the NTO contributes a share; or a contribution in kind is received from third parties (£9.8 million in 2002).

Key Lessons in Partnership Development

- The formation of close links with strong private sector bodies are essential. By consulting with, and encouraging opinions from, such bodies, the NTO is more likely to achieve recognition and respect and achieve buy-in to the implementation of new policies;
- The examples highlighted show how tourism and non-tourism private sector businesses can become, and remain, vital partners and catalysts in visitation and repeat utilisation. The potential for securing a stronger working partnership for the benefit of inbound tourism could be developed further;

- Working relationships should be created with industry in order to build credibility for the NTO and to assist in achieving buy-in to the tourism product, maximising the potential benefits for all parties;
- Contributions should be sought from industry partners wherever possible, whether for part funding of a marketing campaign or sharing overseas office space;
- In the medium to long term, the NTO can seek to reduce funding involvement by increasing the number of partners and extending their funding involvement in marketing campaigns.

Building Credibility with Industry

The private sector of the travel and tourism industry has become increasingly sophisticated in its use of market research and data on consumer trends. It is no surprise that the sector has little patience with NTOs that produce late, limited and in some cases unrepresentative, research and market information.

This is an important element in building credibility and demonstrating worth and value. Every effort must be made to involve industry in production and presentation requirements as well as providing them with timely and cutting edge data. Distribution of summary data on topical rather than chronological/historical data is recommended. CTC provides a useful example of an NTO that has learned about research output the hard way. The successful release of the first Canadian TSA almost caused uproar in the Canadian tourism industry when the age of the data was revealed. (It was several years out of date although, to be fair, sufficient data was not available to be able to carry out a reliable, meaningful analysis using later data.)

To stem rising criticism, CTC went on to produce tourism indicators that would provide current and forecast data for the industry. However, once again, CTC failed to appreciate the need to produce user-friendly statistics and instead produced the full indicators in published form with little or no analysis or commentary. Although the full listing of indicators are among the best in the world, the figures are highly detailed, lengthy and not simple to apply to an industry context. Thus CTC learned crucially about how, when and to whom data and research should be released in order to build credibility for themselves, and for their research findings.

Of the other NTOs considered, the research undertaken and provided by New Zealand's and Australia's NTOs is current, extensive and easy to use. This is also the case with South African Tourism and Maison de la France, although most data relating to France's tourism comes directly from the NTA, the Direction du Tourisme. The NZ and Australia data is also linked to the Research Council and other government statistics sites. The ATC provides a substantial amount of research via its website, helping build relationships with industry. It feels that it has a responsibility to develop and continually enhance the research output for the regions and this leads to a mutually beneficial relationship in which the NTO receives enhanced credibility and co-operation. A vast range of consumer surveys related to various market segments are available on the Australia site together with government strategy review papers. The Australian Bureau of Tourism Research has an annual budget of £1.8 million and it is estimated that the total spend on tourism-related research in Australia is £7.7 million annually. As part of the redevelopment of the NTO in Australia, the new body, Tourism Australia, will receive more funding for research to focus on improved targeted marketing, particularly research into global customer segmentation.

The development of quality data to enhance industry-oriented research and development is considered essential. In Canada, the CTC research division now enjoys considerable respect in the industry for responding to industry demand for user-friendly market-oriented statistics that are continually used to provide a context and backdrop for the private sector to plan future campaigns. Recent features in the publication, 'Outlook', focus on the development of outbound marketing strategies in new areas rather than the usual provision of bar graphs and past performance data. Research is seen to be about forecasting and constructive assistance as well as being about historical tracking. The speed of research outputs is also impressive when compared with that of most other countries. CTC's monthly trade magazine is now only produced electronically, saving costs and simplifying communication.

Maison de la France has also recognised the benefit of focused research and works closely with the Direction du Tourisme (which deals with major surveys and is jointly responsible for the TSA). Research has helped focus and diversify its market sectors and geographic areas. The South African NTO has focused on scientific research to assist development of its marketing and segmentation strategies. The development of a TSA for South Africa is a key future aim to improve forecasting and to provide valuable trends data for all stakeholders in the tourism industry. Similarly Australia, having already developed a TSA, is focused on utilising solid research as a basis for the development of its marketing and development strategy. The close relationship between research and marketing strategy and actions will be enhanced further when both are combined under Tourism Australia.

Rapidity of data production may be considered a key rating criteria. NTO research that provides outputs that are regular and up-to-date are considered of greatest value and generate positive PR for the NTO. Some analysis and simple forward appraisal/forecasting is also recommended; Canada recognises that it needs to move towards more predictive modelling with the ongoing development of scenario planning, forecasting and tourism indicators.

Key Lessons in Building Credibility with Industry

- Build a strong research culture and stress the importance of the analysis and interpretation;
- The use of the NTO website is critical in developing a user-friendly research data interface with industry and consumers;
- Wide-ranging data should be provided with access to other government sites where appropriate;
- The data provided should be timely;
- The data provided should be easy to use with a straightforward commentary;
- Details of marketing campaigns (and results) should be included;
- Strengthening data through the creation and maintenance of a TSA and developing alliances with academic institutions is desirable;
- The development of forecasts and scenario planning is encouraged.

Office Rationalisation and Emerging Markets

The high cost of operating overseas offices has been a key factor in the decision to close some existing offices in recent years, as already discussed. South Africa has closed offices that are not showing a good return on investment. CTC has also reduced its number of offices and, although all offices have been located in Canadian embassies, it is exploring cheaper alternatives. All office-share arrangements with the embassies were to cease by the end of March 2004. The ATC has closed offices in several countries including Japan (Osaka, but still has an office in Tokyo), Denmark, Sweden, Philippines, Indonesia and Latin America, reducing its overseas presence to 20 main target markets.

Offices in emerging markets are, however, being considered by many NTOs with a focus on new markets in Asia and Eastern Europe. Canada, for example, is opening a new office in Beijing and is experimenting with a new structure in India where private sector partners/stakeholders are pooling resources to open an office that will operate on a commercial basis. France had already attempted a similar strategy in Taiwan by funding the operations of a Taipei office through selected private sector members and partners of the NTO. Spain is also focusing on new markets despite having the largest international presence of all other NTOs in the study. Offices have opened in Poland and China in the past few years and it is anticipated that a further East European office will open in the near future.

Key Lessons in Office Rationalisation and Emerging Markets

- An NTO should monitor operational costs and attempt to assess the benefits of representative offices and close offices where not viable;
- Explore alternative options such as sharing offices with other public and private sector organisations;
- Emerging markets should continue to be explored;s
- Benefit could be obtained from working together in partnership with other NTOs in the same region to share the costs of exploration and establishing a presence. (The Scandinavian Tourist Office in Beijing is an excellent example of a successful partnership between NTOs of different countries.) The cost of the proposed presence and the risks involved in establishing a new office would consequently be reduced for each partner.

Building the NTO Team and NTO Internal Communications

Crucial to the successful operation of any NTO is the belief and buy-in the organisation enjoys from its own employees. This is best achieved in larger organisations through imaginative use of technology and frequent briefings and meetings. A critical and cost-effective tool here is the internal intranet, which helps keep employees connected with current campaigns and which tasks management is undertaking.

To build a learning and development culture, this primary information source can be supplemented by familiarisation visits, staff conferences, opinion surveys and a programme of multi-skilling staff and allowing them to transfer internally within the organisation. The aim here in large organisations is building buy-in, belief and commitment. The programme where it is working effectively will also seek to involve external agencies in order to provide expert briefings for staff on tactical and medium-term issues. This helps to build external communications, key alliances and external profile.

The team operating the offices abroad for the Spanish NTO are highly experienced, with the majority of the directors having in excess of 20 years experience and a number of awards. Staff running the Netherlands' offices abroad also appear to be highly respected since they are specialised in different sectors of the markets in which they operate, having often been recruited from industry.

A key lesson here is that the NTO should recognise the benefits that experienced and/or qualified staff based in the offices situated abroad can bring. Most important are practical knowledge/experience in the travel industry; a strong network of industry contacts built up over many years in one destination; a fresh, creative approach that could come from having worked in other sectors; and like-minded team players with lots of energy working closely with industry in their home country to ensure they address industry needs.

Building Brand and NTO Marketing Commitment

A strong, consistent and enduring brand is crucial to the country's tourism success (Morgan et al., 2004). The brand has to be well managed and policed in terms of use and appearance, etc. A strong brand can achieve buy-in greater than the originating NTO and tourism sector.

Highly successful national branding often incorporates a lifestyle, or life-choice expression that is synonymous with the appeal of the nation. Typical descriptors include:

- Natural beauty;
- Heritage;
- Purity;
- Escape;
- Relax;
- Friendly.

These are popular and enduring themes among successful competitors. All are suitable for more sophisticated higher-spend markets. For example, the Canadian brand highlights a strong environmental commitment, thereby recognising the importance of nature for tourism and highlighting the potential vulnerability of these to tourism development.

In those countries where there is strong buy-in to the brand and unified support for the marketing efforts of the NTO (e.g. New Zealand with its '100% Pure NZ' brand), this is often a result of a combination of factors.

- The development of a strong image and brand appeal that is genuine, original and enduring;
- The identification of tourism marketing and, where appropriate, related functions (quality assurance, product development, etc.) with a single unified agency;
- The acceptance of tourism as a key sector of the economy that merits support, buy-in and belief.

For the NTO in Australia, the brand underpins all marketing strategy. The innovative Brand Australia was created in 1995 and is now being refreshed to ensure that there is more effective communication of the brand to target markets. A new 'Premium Plus' brand will further enhances Australia's brand position. The brand image and related advertising campaigns by Spain, such as 'Everything Under the Sun' or the current 'Spain Marks' and by Australia, 'Same Planet — Different World' are also particularly successful.

Where brands have changed and shifted, lacking appeal and buy-in, it is often in cases where a number of agencies have responsibility for tourism functions, where the regional or local voice remains strong and where the position of tourism in the economy is not highly rated. Obviously, the merits of a marketing campaign and brand development can be judged in their own right, but when the factors detailed above are not in place, then commitment will be low.

The key lesson for NTOs is to focus on consistent branding as a key factor in achieving global recognition. The brand should continually be reviewed, updated and enhanced.

Promoting and Marketing Mixed Products

The combination of unusual and contrasting visitor experience has characterised some of the most recent approaches of New Zealand's NTO and has served to move attention away from New Zealand's relatively limited urban offer. The mixing of activities (ranging from safe adventure to high-adrenaline sports) combined with natural heritage has created an increased appeal in a long-stay, aspirational destination which fits with an enduring strap frequently used by staff in promoting the destination — 'See more, do more, come back'.

Diversification of appeal away from overdependence on one major product offer, or customer base, would seem to be a characteristic of more successful NTO marketing campaigns. Overt reliance on one customer source can leave a country highly vulnerable to 'shocks' in that source country. Consequently, a contrasting portfolio of products and services and a broadening of national market appeal would offer an appropriate development option for NTOs.

Key Lessons in Promoting and Marketing Mixed Products

- Product and activity marketing must be dynamic;
- Tourism promotion should suggest itinerary/outline combinations;
- Multiple product promotions offer greater variety and appeal, and can serve to stimulate consumer demand.

Using the Media to NTO Advantage

Carefully managed use of the media can produce wide-ranging results for NTOs. Media coverage of the launch of Canada's TSA, for instance, provided a badly needed wake-up call to the industry, as well as to different levels of government, as to the importance of tourism to the national economy. The careful management of the media over this period helped to stimulate co-operation between different sectors and highlighted the need for public–private partnership in areas such as marketing, promotions and advertising in source markets.

Positive television and film coverage is also very important. Increasing broadcast media coverage through tag-on campaigns, or achieving positive PR, is a powerful and highly cost-effective tool. Whether this is via Hollywood narrative, IMAX production or cult film setting, the coverage can be advantageous for the destination. New Zealand, in particular, has been extremely successful with the benefits obtained from the *Lord of the Rings* trilogy. The UK has of course achieved global coverage through television coverage (BBC World) and VisitBritain has developed tourism potential on the back of film successes such as Harry Potter.

Key Lessons in Using the Media to NTO Advantage

- New Zealand has benefited significantly from film locations, as have Ireland and Scotland in previous years;
- Where the use of location incentives is outside the control of the NTO, efforts should be made to build key alliances with film makers via sponsorship and awards.

Business and MICE Tourism

This valuable market has received increasing attention from NTOs. However, growing global competition may make it difficult for established destinations to enhance, or even maintain, share. For example, Asia's share of the international conference sector has grown considerably in recent years eroding Europe's share (EIBTM, 2004). In Australia, this sector will become a key priority with targeted investment. Australia's first global brand awareness programme was launched in 2001 but, due to increasing global competition, its world ranking fell and a separate business tourism unit was subsequently created within the ATC's marketing development group. Its promotional activities include a business tourism online newsletter and 'Dreamtime', an annual event for the international incentive travel sector. In addition, Team Australia (a collaboration between the NTO and the Australian Association and Convention Bureau) is actively involved in sales missions overseas. Branding in this sector is again an important factor for success for NTOs so they can differentiate their destinations from other business destinations.

In Canada, business and MICE tourism accounts for 19% of all international receipts, with the NTO's MICE programme focusing on relationship building and advertising to strengthen existing business and create new opportunities. City destination marketing offices compete fiercely to attract MICE custom with focused campaigns marketed around:

- city meeting facilities;
- city tour information;
- city leisure potential;
- city icons.

Key Lessons in Business and MICE Tourism

- City products drive business tourism and the consequent high-spending business tourist;
- Strong city marketing (as demonstrated by the Sydney Visitor & Convention Bureau is extremely aggressive, as is Vancouver) is more effective than national marketing to this sector;
- Partnership marketing with chambers of commerce, retail networks and other city institutions/organisations can enhance the impact;
- The NTO's role is critical in helping to co-ordinate bidding efforts for international MICE events by ensuring that their cities do not waste their energy and resources competing against each other;
- NTOs can also support bids for international events by maintaining an effective, overarching brand for their country, and by making sure that a range of pre- and post-event options are highly visible.

Benchmarking Now and in the Future

The evolution of such sectoral- and organisation-specific benchmarking is well illustrated in the case studies of this book and in the comparative analysis of this chapter. Inevitably, NTAs and NTOs must look beyond their competitors, and take lessons from businesses, which are directly targeting disposable income. Future benchmarking and advanced competitor comparison should seek to cross sectors, identifying sectors such as leisure, retail and electronic/virtual providers. Interesting lessons about reframing marketing, purchasing and consumption are being evidenced not in the offices of NTOs, but rather on the websites of low-cost airlines.

The examples highlighted in this report demonstrate clearly that, while strict comparisons are not always meaningful, there are a number of areas in which NTO benchmarking can be useful and informative. Interesting lessons are to be learnt on issues as diverse as overseas representation, or productivity per employee, to return on marketing investment. But NTOs must look beyond their direct competitors in their own regions to identify a diverse range of best practice.Importantly, there is no reason why benchmarking should be restricted to tourism. Other industries and economic sectors — many of which are far more cutting edge — all have important messages to convey to the travel and tourism industry.

NTOs will only survive and grow if they embrace the lessons of these other exemplars and focus all their attention on what their customers and potential customers really want from a tourism product or service.

References

Balm, G.J. (1992). *Benchmarking: A practitioner's guide for becoming and staying best of the best*. Schaumburg, IL: Quality and Productive Management Assoication Press.

Barsky, J.D. (1996). Building programme for world class service. *The Cornell Hotel and Restaurant Quarterly, 37* (1), 17–27.

Baum, T. (1994). The development and implementation of national tourism policies. *Tourism Management, 15*(3), 185–192.

Baum, T. (1999). Themes and issues in comparative destination research: The use of lesson-drawing in comparative tourism research in the North Atlantic. *Tourism Management, 20,* 627–633.

Bemowski, K. (1991). The benchmarking bandwagon. *Quality Progress, 24*(1), 19–24.

Bemowski, K. (1994). Benchmarking turns a corner. *Purchasing, 117*(7), 74–76.

Bordas, E. (1994). Competitiveness of tourist destinations in long distance markets. *The Tourist Review, 3,* 3–9.

Bramwell, B., & Lane, B. (2000). *Tourism collaboration and partnerships: Politics, practice and sustainability*. Clevedon: Channel View Publications.

Breiter, D., & Kline, S.F. (1995). Benchmarking quality management in hotels. *FIU Hospitality, 13*(2), 45–52.

CBI and DTI (1994). *Competitiveness: How the best UK companies are winning*. London.

Cook, S. (1995). *Practical benchmarking — a manager's guide to creating competitive advantage*. London: Kogan Page.

Coopers and Lybrand (1995). *A survey of benchmarking in the UK*. London.

Deegan, J., & Dineen, D. (1997). *Tourism policy and performance: The Irish experience*. London: International Thomson Business Press.

Dore, L., & Crouch, G.I. (2002). Promoting destinations: An exploratory study of publicity programmes used by national tourism organisations. *Journal of Vacation Marketing, 9*(2), 137–151.

Dosrch, J.J., & Yasin, M.M. (1998). A framework for benchmarking in the public sector. *International Journal of Public Sector Management, 11*(23), 91–115.

Dwyer, L., & Kim, C. (2003). Destination competitiveness: Determinants and indicators. *Current Issues in Tourism, 6*(5), 369–413.

Edgell, D.L. (1999). *Tourism policy: The next millennium*. Champaign, IL: Sagamore Publishing.

EIBTM. (2004). *Industry trends and market share report*. Reed Travel Exhibitions.

Fayos-Solá, E. (1996). Tourism policy: A midsummer night's dream? *Tourism Management, 17*(6), 405–412.

Fuchs, M., & Weiermair, K. (2004). Destination benchmarking: An indicator-system's potential for exploring guest satisfaction. *Journal of Travel Research, 42,* 212–225.

Hall, C.M. (1994). *Tourism and politics: Policy place and power*. Chichester: Wiley.

Hall, C.M., & Jenkins J.M. (1995). *Tourism and public policy*. London: Routledge.

Harrison, D. (Ed.). (1992). *Tourism and less developed countries*. Chichester: Wiley.

Henderson, J. C. (2004). Paradigm shifts: National tourism organisations and education and health-care tourism. The case of Singapore. *Tourism and Hospitality Research, 5*(2), 170–180.

Jeffries, D. (2001). *Governments and tourism*. Oxford: Butterworth-Heinemann.

Johnson, P., & Thomas, B. (Eds). (1992). *Perspectives on tourism policy*. London: Mansell Publishing Limited.

King, J. (1993). Benchmarking on empty. *Computerworld, 27*(51), 73–78.

Kozak, M., & Rimmington, M. (1997). Benchmarking: Towards a role in destination management. *Proceedings of international tourism research conference*, 8–12 September, Bornholm, Denmark.

Kozak, M., & Rimmington, M. (1998). Developing a benchmarking model for tourist destinations. In: *Proceedings of the 3rd annual graduate student and graduate research conference in hospitality and tourism*, 8–10 January, Houston, TX, USA.

Lavery, P. (1996). Funding of national tourism organisations. *Travel and Tourism Analyst, 6*, 80–95.

Mazanec, J.A. (1997). *International city tourism*. London: Connell.

Morgan, N., & Pritchard, A. (2004). Meeting the destination branding challenge. In: N. Morgan, A. Pritchard & R. Pride (Eds), *Destination branding: Creating the unique destination proposition* (2nd ed.). Oxford: Elsevier, Butterworth-Heinemann.

Morgan, N., Pritchard, A., & Pride, R. (Eds). (2004). *Destination branding: Creating the unique destination proposition* (2nd ed.). Oxford: Elsevier, Butterworth-Heinemann.

Morrison, A.M., Braunlich, C.G., Kamaruddin, N., & Cai, L.A. (1995). National tourist offices in North America: An analysis. *Tourism Management, 16*(8), 605–617.

Ooi, C.-S. (2002). Contrasting strategies: Tourism in Denmark and Singapore. *Annals of Tourism Research, 29*(3), 689–706.

Pizam, A. (1999). The state of travel and tourism human resources in Latin America. *Tourism Management, 20*, 575–586.

Prideaux, B., & Cooper, C. (2002). Marketing and destination growth: A symbolic relationship or simple coincidence? *Journal of Vacation Marketing, 9*(1), 35–51.

Ryan, C., & Zahra, A. (2004). The political challenge: The case of New Zealand's tourism organisations. In: E. Morgan, A. Pritchard & R. Pride (Eds), *Destination branding: Creating the unique destination proposition* (2nd ed.). Oxford: Elsevier, Butterworth-Heinemann.

Shetty, Y.K. (1993). Aiming high: Competitive benchmarking for superior performance. *Long Range Planning, 24*(1), 34–44.

Smith, S.L.J. (1999). Toward a national tourism research agenda for Canada. *Tourism Management, 20*, 297–304.

Spendolini, M.J. (1992a). *The benchmarking book*. New York, NY: Amacom.

Spendolini, M.J. (1992b). The benchmarking process. *Compensations and Benefits Review, 24*(5), 21–29.

The Travel Business Partnership. (2004). City Profiles, Issue no. 18, April 2004: The Changing Role of National Tourism Organisations.

Wales Tourist Board. (2002–2003). *Wales tourism business monitor*. Cardiff: WTB (range of editions).

Wöber, K.W. (2002). *Benchmarking in tourism and hospitality industries*. Wallingford, Oxon: CABI.

WTO. (1994). *National and regional tourism planning: Methodologies and case studies*. London: Thomson Learning.

WTO. (1996a). *Budgets of National Tourism Administrations*. Madrid: WTO (Author: Cockerell, N.).

WTO. (1996b). *Towards new forms of public and private sector partnerships. The changing role, structure and activities of National Tourism Administrations and National Tourism Organisations*. Madrid : NTO (Author: Cockerell, N.).

WTO. (2000). *Public–private sector cooperation: Enhancing tourism competitiveness*. Madrid: WTO (Author: Cockerell, N.).

WTO, & ETC. (2003). *Evaluating NTO marketing activities*. Madrid: WTO.

Additional References and Sources Applicable to the Individual Country Case Studies

Australia

- Commonwealth Department of Industry, Tourism & Resources (DITR): www.industry.gov.au;
- White Paper for Tourism, November 2003;
- DITR Annual Reports, 2002–2003;
- The Australian Tourism Satellite Account, 2002–2003;
- Australia Tourism Commission (ATC), now renamed Tourism Australia: www.tourismaustralia.com;
- ATC Corporate Plan 2003–2008;
- ATC's consumer website: www.australia.com;
- Bureau of Tourism Research — now within Tourism Research Australia: www.tourismaustralia.com;
- Tourism Forecasting Council — now within Tourism Research Australia: www.tourismaustralia.com;
- Australian Bureau of Statistics: www.abs.gov.au;
- Domestic tourism: www.seeaustralia.com.au;
- Australia Tourism Data Warehouse: www.atdw.com.au;
- MICE sector: www.meetings.australia.com;
- Australian Tourism Export Council (ATEC): www.atec.net.au;
- Austrade: austrade.gov.au;
- Ausindustry: ausindustry.gov.au;
- Indigenous Business Australia: www.iba.gov.au;
- Tourism Task Force Australia (TTF): www.ttf.org.au;
- Essential Australia Travel Guides, 2004;
- ATC 20030/4 United King Market Profile (issued 12 June 2003).

Canada

- Canadian Tourism Commission: www.canadatourism.com;
- Canadian Tourism Commission, Canadian tourism facts and figures 2000–2002;
- Canadian Tourism Commission, Annual report 2002: The big picture;
- Canadian Tourism Commission, Tourism: Canada's tourism monthly/Canada's tourism business magazine — various issues 2003 and 2004;
- Canadian Tourism Commission 2003: 'Who we are and what we do';
- Canadian Hotel Association;
- Industry Canada: http://www.ic.gc.ac/;
- Tourism Vancouver.

France

- Maison de la France: www.franceguide.com;
- Direction du Tourisme: www.tourisme.gouv.fr;
- Enquête aux Frontières;
- Le Conseil National du Tourisme: www.tourisme.gouv.fr;
- L' Observatoire National du Tourisme (ONT): www.ont-tourisme.com;
- Ministère de L' Equipement, des Transports, du Logement, du Tourisme et de la Mer: www.equipement.gouv.fr;
- L'Association Française de l'Ingérieurie Touristique ('lAFIT):www.afit-tourisme.fr;
- Tourism Satellite Account 20030/4, Central Statistics Office;
- Annual General Reports, Maison de la France 2001, 2002 and 2003.

Ireland

- Tourism Ireland: www.tourismireland.com;
- Faílte Ireland: www.ireland.travel.ie;
- Faílte Ireland (2003), Tourism Facts 2002;
- Northern Ireland Tourism Board (NITB);
- Department of Arts, Sports & Tourism (Republic of Ireland): www.arts-sports-tourism.gov.ie;
- Department of Arts, Sports & Tourism, 'Mission Statement 2003–2005';
- Department of Enterprise, Trade & Investment (Northern Ireland);
- Irish Tourist Industry Confederation: ITIC Tourism News;
- New Horizons for Irish Tourism: An Agenda for Action: www.tourismreview.ie.

Netherlands

- Netherlands Board of Tourism & Conventions (NBTC): www.holland.com (formerly Toerisme Recrfeatie Nederland);
- (NB: www.holland.com gives access to consumer, regional, city, industry and MICE information);
- Dutch Ministry of Economic Affairs: www.ez.nl;
- Association of Provincial & Local Tourist Offices (ANVV).

New Zealand

- The Ministry of Tourism: www.tourism.govt.nz;
- The Ministry of Tourism: New Zealand tourism strategy 2010;
- The Ministry of Tourism: Towards 2010. Implementing the New Zealand tourism strategy;
- Tourism Statistics: www.stats.govt.nz;
- Tourism Research Council New Zealand: www.trcnz.govt.nz;
- Tourism New Zealand annual report 2002–2003.

South Africa

- www.SouthAfrica.net;
- South African tourism annual reports 2002 and 2003;
- Strategic plan 1 April 2003–31 March 2008;
- Tourism growth strategy, May 2002 and April 2004;
- Domestic tourism report 2002/2003;
- Global competitiveness phase 1 results;
- Department of Environmental Affairs and Tourism (DEAT): www.environment.gov.za;
- www.indaba-southafrica.co.za;
- Tourism Business Council of South Africa: tbcsa.org.za;
- Various state tourist bodies.

Spain

- State Secretariat for Trade and Tourism: tourspain.es;
- Turespaña: www.spain.info;
- Turespaña annual marketing plan;
- Plan Integral del Turismo Espanol — PICTE 2000–2006;
- Turespaña UK: www.tourspain.co.uk;
- Institute of Tourism Studies (IET).

Author Index

Balm, G.J., 2
Barsky, J.D., 2
Baum, T., 5
Bemowski, K., 1
Bordas, E., 2
Bramwell, B., 7
Braunlich, C.G., 6
Breiter, D., 2

Cai, L.A., 6
CBI and DTI, 2
Cook, S., 1–2
Cooper, C., 6–7
Coopers and Lybrand, 2
Crouch, G.I., 8

Deegan, J., 125
Dineen, D., 125
Dore, L., 8
Dorsch, J.J, 1
Dwyer, L., 1

Edgell, D.L., 5
EIBTM., 237

Fayos-Solá, E., 7
Fuchs, M., 2

Hall, C.M., 5–7
Harrison, D., 5
Henderson, J. C., 24

Jeffries, D., 5, 7
Jenkins J.M., 5
Johnson, P., 5

Kamaruddin, N., 6
Kim, C., 1

King, J., 1
Kline, S.F., 2
Kozak, M., 2

Lane, B., 7
Lavery, P., 7

Mazanec, J.A., 7
Morgan, N., 9, 235
Morrison, A.M., 6

Ooi, C.-S., 1

Pizam, A., 1
Pride, R., 235
Prideaux, B., 6–7
Pritchard, A., 9, 235

Rimmington, M., 2
Ryan, C., 8–9

Shetty, Y.K., 1
Smith, S.L.J., 24
Spendolini, M.J., 1

The Travel Business Partnership., 7
Thomas, B., 5

Wales Tourist Board., 2
Weiermair, K., 2
Wöber, K.W., 1
WTO and ETC., 32
WTO., 1–2, 5–9, 21, 24

Yasin, M.M., 1

Zahra, A., 8–9

Subject Index

Approved Destination Status (ADS), 42, 47, 150, 163, 197
Australia, 6, 8, 9, 14, 15, 17, 21, 23, 25–27, 31, 32, 37–65, 73, 87, 123, 163, 165, 170, 172–175, 182, 188, 197, 202, 203, 227–229, 231–233, 235–237

Benchmarking
  Approaches, 1–3
  Definition, 1
  Future, 150, 238
  Lessons
    Australia, 227–229, 231–233, 235–237
    Brand, 227–229, 231, 235–238
    Business and MICE Tourism, 237–238
    Canada, 227–231, 233, 234, 237
    Customer Relationship Management, 228, 229
    E-media, 228, 229
    Emerging markets, 234
    France, 228, 230, 231, 234
    Ireland, 227, 229, 237
    Marketing, 227–233, 235–238
    Netherlands (The), 227, 229, 235
    New Zealand, 230, 235, 237
    Offices, 234
    Partnerships, 229–232
    South Africa, 227, 231, 233, 234
    Structure, 227–228
    Spain, 228, 230, 231, 234, 236
Brand
  Country brand, 8, 56, 65, 227
  Lessons, 9, 63, 92, 118, 136, 160, 181, 204, 224

Budgets (Resources and Funding)
  Australia, 6, 21, 25, 31, 46, 54, 232
  Canada, 17, 21, 31, 71, 88, 220, 230
  France, 6, 21, 22, 71, 103, 108, 109, 218
  Ireland, 19, 22, 128, 131, 218
  Netherlands (The), 17, 20, 143, 146, 198, 216
  New Zealand, 170, 171, 177, 182
  Public Sector, 6, 19, 33, 78, 216
  South Africa, 6, 185, 195
  Spain, 6, 25, 216, 217, 223, 225
Business Tourism, 14, 15, 23, 46, 49, 53, 55, 58, 60, 69, 71, 98, 99, 119, 124, 139, 158, 165, 237, 238

Canada, 8, 14, 17, 19, 21, 25, 31, 33, 57, 59, 63, 67–95, 97, 111, 113, 115, 123, 134, 170, 182, 197, 202, 215, 218, 220, 228–231, 233, 234, 237
Customer Relationship Management (CRM), 60, 61, 94, 95, 113, 114, 135, 151, 152, 200, 221, 228, 229

Definitions
  NTO, xxii
  NTA, xxii
Domestic Tourism
  Australia, 40, 45, 46, 48, 49, 56
  Canada, 67, 68, 79
  France, 97, 114
  Ireland, 124, 125, 127
  Netherlands (The), 143, 147, 148, 159
  New Zealand, 161, 165, 170
  South Africa, 188, 190, 196
  Spain, 21, 217

E-Media, 228, 229
Emerging Markets, 2, 26, 27, 30, 112, 115,
        131, 147, 150, 151, 218, 234
European Travel Commission (ETC), 32,
        112, 151
European Union (EU), 19, 24, 103, 124,
        127, 129, 136, 137, 213, 216
Events, 14, 23, 43, 51, 98, 117, 133, 142,
        149, 152–153, 166, 170, 176, 185,
        195, 196, 218, 222, 238

France, 6, 8, 14, 17, 21, 25, 26, 30, 34, 35,
        39, 41, 54, 57, 59, 61, 71, 73, 77,
        84, 90, 97–121, 139, 150, 156,
        169, 176, 188, 195, 197–199, 209,
        215, 217, 218, 228, 230

General Sales Agent (GSA), 29
Government
    Involvement in tourism, 5, 33, 34,
        145
    Unifying force, 8, 33
Greece, 7

International tourism
    Australia, 37, 40, 41, 51, 55, 60, 61
    Canada, 71
    France, 97, 101
    Ireland, 121, 134
    Netherlands (The), 143, 149, 153
    New Zealand, 161
    South Africa, 185, 187, 189, 191, 199,
        201
    Spain, 207
Ireland, 14, 26, 57, 61, 107, 121–137,
        156–158, 169, 195, 218, 222

Key Facts
    Australia, 38
    Canada, 68
    France, 98
    Ireland, 122
    Netherlands (The), 140
    New Zealand, 162

South Africa, 186
Spain, 207

Marketing
    Advertising, 6, 53, 222, 229
    E-Marketing, 24, 31, 60, 61, 65, 84, 87,
        95, 102, 113, 114, 151, 152, 156,
        200, 220, 221
    Consumer, 56, 59, 62, 156
    Plans, 114, 115, 213, 215, 217
    Segmentation, 58, 64, 197, 204, 218,
        223
    Trade, 201
Media, 9, 21, 24, 32, 48, 54, 56, 60, 63,
        72, 112, 113, 116, 118, 147, 150,
        151, 153, 169, 170, 172, 173, 176,
        177, 196, 200, 215, 220, 222, 223,
        228, 229, 236, 237
MICE, 14, 23, 46, 58, 71, 72, 98, 116,
        124, 142, 146, 149, 157, 160, 165,
        183, 188, 198, 199, 203, 205, 208,
        218, 222, 237, 238

National Tourism Administration
    As co-ordinator and catalyst, 7
    Australia, 232
    Canada
    Definition, xxii
    France, 232
    Ireland, 126
    Netherlands (The), 143
    New Zealand, 232
    South Africa
    Spain, 212, 221
National Tourism Organisations
    Australia
        Australian Tourist Commission, 41,
            49, 65
        Tourism Australia, 46, 49
    Budgets, 132
    Canada
        Canadian Tourism Commission, 67,
            76, 83, 86, 89, 95
    Definition, xxii

France
Maison de la France, 101, 103, 105, 106, 108, 111, 117
Ireland
Tourism Ireland, 132, 133, 136
Bord Failte, 135, 136
Legal Status, 17–35
Netherlands (The)
Netherlands Board of Tourism and Conventions, 143, 151, 158
New Zealand
Tourism New Zealand, 166, 168, 182
Ownership, 17
Performance, 2, 32
Representative Offices, 25
Resources and Funding, 35
Role and Activities, 20, 35
South Africa
South African Tourism, 189
Spain
Turespana, 211, 214–216, 224
Staff, 2, 30
Structure, 17, 35, 227, 228
Netherlands (The), 7, 8, 14, 16, 25, 30, 57, 61, 85, 90, 99, 107, 139–160, 169, 188, 195, 197, 198, 215
New Zealand, 8, 14, 15, 21, 25, 26, 30, 37, 51–53, 57, 73, 77, 130, 161–183
Niche markets, 48–50, 86, 118, 133, 221

Offices and Staff, 25, 146–147
Organisation for Economic Co-operation and Development (OECD), 63, 97

Planning Cycle, 52, 79–80
Political Climate, 6, 33, 139
Partnerships
Canada, 83, 84, 88, 92, 94
France, 102, 103, 112, 119, 120
Netherlands (The), 156, 157, 159, 160
Public–Private Sector Partnerships, 7, 237
Public Relations, 32, 62, 72, 85, 88, 112, 116, 117, 171, 173, 215

Research
Australia, 46
Canada, 76–79, 90
Definition, 139
France, 103, 104, 113, 114, 120
Ireland, 129, 131
Netherlands (The), 139, 149, 153
New Zealand, 166, 167, 170, 171
South Africa, 188, 200
Spain, 220
Resources and Funding, 35, 54, 78, 108, 131, 147, 170–171, 195, 216

South Africa, 6–8, 14, 21, 25, 26, 54, 57, 73, 107, 130, 169, 185–205, 218
Spain, 7, 14, 16, 17, 21, 73, 97, 107, 115, 123, 130, 150, 207–225, 228
Staff and Offices
Australia, 52
Canada, 77
Definition, 25
France, 106
Ireland, 129
Netherlands (The), 146
New Zealand, 169
South Africa, 194
Spain, 215
Statistics
Absolute Statistical Comparison, xxi–xxii
International Tourism Receipts, 15, 16
Number of Arrivals, 13
Number of International Nights, 13
Structure of NTOs, 17–35, 227, 228

Tourism Satellite Account (TSA), 35, 40, 63, 64, 76, 79, 97, 120, 129, 142, 182, 189, 200, 204, 208, 214, 219, 232, 233, 236
Tourism Support System, 41, 49, 63, 137, 143, 211, 224, 227, 228
Tourism Performance
Australia, 37
Canada, 67
France, 97

Ireland, 121
Netherlands (The), 139
New Zealand, 161
South Africa, 185
Spain, 207
Trends in, 11–16

USA, 25, 37, 51, 54, 57, 59, 60, 73, 97,
    101, 107, 115, 118, 121, 130, 139,
    150, 165, 173–175, 182, 197–199,
    218, 220

Visitor Attractions, 76, 129, 135, 172, 173,
    175

World Tourism Organization, 1, 2, 5–9, 14,
    15, 21, 24, 32, 67, 85, 97, 119,
    129, 188